S0-BRF-203

THE DUPING OF THE AMERICAN VOTER

Robert Spero

THE DUPING OF THE AMERICAN VOTER

Dishonesty and Deception in Presidential Television Advertising

Lippincott & Crowell, Publishers

New York

 For information address Lippincott & Crowell, Publishers, 521 Fifth Avenue, New York, N.Y. 10017. Published simultaneously in Canada by Fitzhenry & Whiteside Limited, Toronto.

FIRST EDITION

Designed by C. Linda Dingler

U.S. Library of Congress Cataloging in Publication Data

Spero, Robert.

The duping of the American voter: dishonesty and deception in presidential TV advertising.

Bibliography: p.

Includes index.

1. Presidents—United States—Election.
2. Advertising, Political—United States.
3. Electioneering—United States. 4. United States—Politics and government—1945–
I. Title.

JK524.S68 324.973'092 79-28547

ISBN 0-690-01884-3

---

80 81 82 83 84 10 9 8 7 6 5 4 3 2 1

For
Jan Spero
and for our children
Josh, Jeremy, Jessica

Contents

Q. True or false:
“Madison Avenue sells politicians like soap.”

A. False.
Unfortunately.

FIRST NOTES ON THE LAST ELECTIONS

This book is about the way presidents have been elected in America since the appearance of the political television commercial, for twenty-eight years now the chief political campaign weapon.

By its examples, the book's thesis can be extended to the way political campaigns are waged for all publicly elected offices in this country—Senate, House of Representatives, governor, mayor, state legislature, city council, county executive, even school board—if the campaign for that office has fallen under the spell of the television commercial and therefore requires, in the most literal sense, the use of the commercial as an election fix.

The examples show how presidential candidates steal votes under the guise of campaign truth and how they lay down smoke screens to mask what have consistently turned out to be their true intentions upon assuming office. This is not done with mirrors; it is done with advertising.

The political television commercial has also come to tell us much about the character and motives of the unelected men and women who help make presidents, whom presidents choose to help them govern—or rule, as the case may be. As such, the political commercial has come to be as much a metaphor as a major cause for the condition we now find ourselves in, whether we are commoners or philosophers. Political rot has been with us always; the difference today is that it seeps unnoticed into our living rooms and into our heads in what appear to be benign microimages.

We may yet realize that television can be controlled—and that if it is, politicians can be, too. We may also see that control is not the bleak and insurmountable task we imagined it to be.

THE DUPING OF THE AMERICAN VOTER

1

THE ARROGANCE AND THE DANGER OF POLITICAL ADVERTISING

Deception and distortion in the campaigns of Carter and Ford

A leadership responsible only to an uninformed or partially informed electorate can bring nothing but disaster to our world.

EDWARD R. MURROW

If there is a dividing line between liberty and license, it is where freedom of speech is no longer respected as a procedure of the truth and becomes the unrestricted right to exploit the ignorance, and to incite the passions, of the people. Then freedom is such a hullabaloo of sophistry, propaganda, special pleading, lobbying, and salesmanship that it is difficult to remember why freedom of speech is worth the pain and the trouble of defending it. . . . It is sophistry to pretend that in a free country a man has some sort of inalienable or constitutional right to deceive his fellow men. There is no more right to deceive than there is a right to swindle, to cheat, or to pick pockets.

WALTER LIPPMANN,
The Public Philosophy

Jimmy Carter misrepresented facts about himself in order to be president.

Gerald Ford misrepresented facts about the state of the nation in order to remain president.

Both candidates looked into television cameras and said things that misled the public. They made deceptive statements on news programs, at shopping centers, in magazine articles, at convention halls, at stump dinners, in high school gyms, and during what were billed as serious national debates.

Yet nothing served Carter and Ford so well as the television commercial. Nothing created and nursed their lies so effectively and made them so palatable. Nothing could be controlled so carefully and made to appear so benign. Nothing but the television commercial could be programmed so far in advance to reach so many people at one time—again and again and again—without disclaimer or interference.

Political candidates and their political media specialists dislike thinking of their thirty-second television commercials as product commercials. To them the product commercial is a huckster's device, a tool unfit for the grand strategies of statesmen, kings, and presidents. Let analysts write as much as they like about the "selling" of the presidency; politicians cannot afford to admit the reality of it. After all these years, they still refuse to picture themselves as being jobbed about the country like a bar of soap. *Their* purposes and *their* messages, after all, are high-minded, serious, and selfless; it would be as wrong as it would be undignified to compare the affairs of the White House, the state house, or the Capitol with what goes on at a supermarket checkout counter.

These are elegant protests from some very plain Americans who owe most, if not all, of their critically important elected positions to the effects of images from a 45-foot strip of film—a film moving at 24 frames per second and transmitted through space at 186,282 miles per second before entering the viewer's brain through the eyes by means of television X rays powered by a 25,000-volt cathode ray tube inside the television set: the thirty-second commercial. A *sales* commercial, no matter how it is received.

The persistent refusal of politicians to be linked with a common product commercial, while understandable socially, is the most dangerous deception of all. For the approach of politicians to advertising, the process by which their commercials are created, the stiff-arm tactics their media buyers use at television networks and independent stations to force their commercials into only the highest-rated program periods, the millions of dollars spent to do this, the television environment in which the commercials are shown, and the perception of those commercials by the public are the same methods and results that characterize the product commercial. In fact the political commercial is identical to the product commercial in every way but one:

Political commercials are in no way regulated for truth in advertising, nor can they presently be regulated.

This single difference that separates the political from the product commercial is the vital distinction for politicians who of necessity must disguise from the voter their backgrounds, beliefs, and programs in order to be elected. It should be recognized as such by a people concerned, confused, dismayed, and angry about the way their would-be leaders are elected to office, hold on to office, and misuse the power they are given.

This vital distinction is the reason why political advertising—now the principal means of communication and persuasion between candidate and voter—is without peer as the most deceptive, misleading, unfair, and untruthful of all advertising, especially on television, the most powerful of our advertising media. Today the sky is the limit in political advertising with regard to what can be said, what can be promised, what accusations can be made, what lies can be told. Short of libel or slander—charges that are almost never pursued legally during or following an election—the only restriction on political advertising is that it be identified as such.* Thus a politician can and will make charges in a television commercial that he or she would think twice about making before a live audience. Angry, disbelieving crowds—so far—do not challenge political commercials.

This vital distinction allows a politician to get away with making unsubstantiated claims in a television commercial, while a television reporter, if he or she should be so industrious, must be so cautious in describing the veracity of those same claims that the claims themselves will almost certainly never be properly questioned and investigated or the facts brought to the public's attention.

Without this vital distinction, few if any of the 1976 Carter and Ford commercials, beginning with Carter's crucial television efforts in the primary campaigns, would have been allowed on television in the form in which they were produced. They could not have met the standards that network television imposes on the most trivial product commercial. The manner in which the presidential campaign was waged might then have been seriously altered and the outcome of the election reversed; the political parties might well have selected different candidates, especially in the case of Jimmy Carter.

Each year dozens of high-level and low-level politicians across the land, including some in the Congress and occasionally one in the White House, are admonished, censured, indicted, recalled, dismissed, fined,

*One rarely pursued exception is the Federal Communications Commission's "personal attack" rule, which stipulates that if a television station broadcasts an attack on a person's character, integrity, honesty, or other such personal qualities, the station is required to offer the person attacked a specific time on the station to respond, within a specified time, whether or not that person is a politician. The rule does not apply when the attack is a fleeting remark within a more general context or when it concerns foreign figures.

and sometimes packed off to prison for unethical behavior and illegal acts in elected office. It is interesting to observe how enraged constituents howl their contempt as the culprits cower and flee; for the same constituents earlier sat dumbly before their television sets, never batting an eye, as candidate after candidate used unethical and perhaps illegal advertising to obtain the same public offices in the first place.

If a corporation attempted similarly unethical television advertising—and managed to get it on the air—the result would be embarrassing public and intra-industry warnings at least. More likely there would be costly litigation growing out of suits brought by the government, competitors, and consumer groups; heavy fines running into the tens and hundreds of thousands of dollars; further embarrassment as reports of the legal action appeared in the trade press and local and national media; expensive and embarrassing counter-advertising in which the offending corporation, as required by the government, notably by the Federal Trade Commission, would prominently disclose its fraudulence to the public; a badly tarnished image, sometimes difficult to clean; a great loss of business; a precipitious decline in the price of the corporation's stock and a reduction in its dividends; and, though rare, prison sentences for the officers involved at both the corporation and its advertising agency, for both are potentially culpable. All these are punishments that apply when product advertising is found to be misleading, deceptive, unfair, or false.

But, in fact, out of tens of thousands of television commercials created each year for leading corporations, comparatively few get on the air that are misleading, deceptive, unfair, or false by present standards. Further, commercials that have met broadcast standards and have appeared on television can be forced off should standards change or competitive or consumer complaints prove valid.

Corporations and their advertising advisers have not become simon-pure in their evolvement from street hucksters. Historically, bending the truth has been inseparable from selling. What has prevented the truth from being bent out of all proportion by corporations and their advertising agents is the phenomenal growth of advertising regulation over the past decade.

Let the Seller Beware

Product advertising, unlike political advertising, is today a highly regulated business. Hundreds of rules, codes of ethics, and standards of conduct are imposed on a corporation selling that prototypical bar of soap by government regulatory bodies and by the advertising industry's self-regulating apparatus to prevent the corporation from making false and deceptive advertising claims—in all media, but primarily on television.

Because of television's ability to reach from 30 million to 80 million people at once, and its unprecedented power to change their minds when it does reach them, it is now mandatory for advertising agencies and their corporate sponsors to submit product and even public service commercials to television networks and stations for clearance. No commercial is allowed on the air without approval. The standards used to judge truth in product advertising are now so high and so rigid that tens of thousands of the new commercials submitted each year in manuscript form to major networks are initially rejected. (Herminio Traviesas, former NBC vice president, reports that nearly *half* of the 48,000 commercials submitted to that network are turned down because they violate or fail otherwise to satisfy one or more of the 127 stipulations contained in NBC's "Broadcast Standards for Television.")

Typical violations encountered in material submitted for approval are:

1. No satisfactory evidence of the integrity of the advertiser.
2. Product or service unavailable.
3. Lack of evidence to support claims and authenticate demonstrations.
4. Taste of presentation unacceptable.
5. Competitors not fairly and properly identified.
6. Competitors discredited, disparaged, or unfairly attacked.
7. Commercial claims invalid because market conditions on which the original claim was based no longer prevail.
8. Testimonials do not honestly reflect in spirit and content the sentiments of the individual represented.
9. Claims and statements made in a testimonial, including subjective evaluations of testifiers, are not supportable by facts or are not free of misleading implications.
10. Claims or representations have the capacity to deceive, mislead, or misrepresent.
11. Claims unfairly attack competitors, competing products, or other industries, professions, or institutions.
12. Unqualified references to the safety of a product, if package, label, or insert contains a caution or if the normal use of the product presents a possible hazard.
13. The use of "bait and switch" tactics which feature goods or services not intended for sale but designed to lure the public into purchasing higher-priced substitutes.
14. Misuse of distress signals.

15. Scare approach and presentation with the capacity to induce fear.
16. Interpersonal acts of violence and antisocial behavior or other dramatic devices inconsistent with prevailing standards of taste and propriety.
17. Damaging stereotyping.
18. Unsupported or exaggerated promises of employment or earnings.

There are two reasons why the television networks are so cautious about the kinds of product commercials they will allow on the air. The first has to do with the attempt to present viewers with tasteful commercials (the degree of their success here is perhaps arguable). The second reason cuts closer to the networks' bone; it is the fear of tangling with one of the following nine federal agencies that regulate product advertising.

- The Federal Trade Commission (FTC), the most important and most aggressive of the agencies, prohibits unfair and deceptive acts in commerce, including false advertising. Its investigations often range far beyond the truth of commercials to the effect of commercials on viewers.
- The Federal Communications Commission (FCC) requires radio and television stations to operate in the public interest and to take all reasonable measures to eliminate false, misleading, and deceptive advertising. Since the broadcasting stations are licensed by the FCC, it is clearly not in their interest to broadcast false and deceptive commercials.
- The Food and Drug Administration (FDA) requires truthful disclosure of ingredients and prohibits false labeling and packaging of foods, drugs, cosmetics, and devices.
- The Alcohol, Drug Abuse, and Mental Health Administration prohibits any statement from wineries, breweries, and importers that may mislead the consumer with respect to age, manufacturing process, guarantees, or scientific data.
- The United States Postal Service prohibits advertising that would use the mails to defraud or to obtain money or property under misrepresentation.
- The Securities and Exchange Commission (SEC) prescribes the form of advertising that may be used for new securities offerings and specifies disclosures for promotional material distributed by brokers, dealers, and investment advisers.
- The Civil Aeronautics Board (CAB) can investigate and remedy deceptive descriptions of air fares and service.
- The Federal Deposit Insurance Corporation (FDIC) and the

Federal Home Loan Bank Board influence and establish advertising practices of banks and savings and loan institutions.
- The Federal Reserve Board regulates consumer credit advertising under the Truth in Lending Act.

In addition to these agencies, forty-eight states and the District of Columbia have advertising laws that are similar to those of the FTC. And many cities have their own consumer affairs departments, which often have stricter rules than either the state or the federal government.

Networks reject only half the commercials submitted to them because attorneys who specialize in advertising regulation study carefully the nuances of the words and visuals of every commercial proposed for broadcast. Major advertising agencies now have separate legal departments, and no commercial may leave the premises without their official stamp. When the agency's client receives the manuscript of the commercial, its own lawyers review it for deceptive and misleading statements and impressions. The commercial is frequently reviewed by the agency's outside law firm, usually one that specializes in advertising law. And the client also frequently submits the commercial to an outside law firm for approval. It is often more difficult to get a commercial out of the hands of the lawyers than on the air.

The advertising industry's own regulatory apparatus has not been exhausted once a commercial is cleared for broadcast. The National Advertising Review Board (NARB) and its parent body, the National Advertising Division (NAD) of the Council of Better Business Bureaus, were set up in 1971 by the industry in the belief that self-regulation is preferable to government regulation and challenges from the consumer movement. Complaints of false and deceptive advertising are received by the NAD from consumers, consumer groups, an NAD monitoring group (usually made up of people from the advertising and business communities), and from the NARB board or general membership. If investigations of the claims are found to be valid, the results are published in the trade and public press. A bad press and the public embarrassment which follows are usually weapons enough to cause the offending advertisers to modify or withdraw their advertising.

Let the Voter Beware

Much of the product advertising approved for television may be innocuous, dopey, irritating, childish even for children, and beside the point in the lives of most adults, but very little of it today will be false or deceptive by the time it has filtered through the layers of regulation for home consumption.

Not so for political candidates, especially candidates for president. They are required to meet no broadcast standards of behavior and ethics. They are policed by no government agency. Their political media specialists are beholden to no self-governing regulations. Political advertising is considered "protected speech" under the First Amendment. Similarly, the Communications Act of 1934 prohibits a television station from censoring material broadcast by "any person who is a legally qualified candidate for any public office" if that person wishes to "use a broadcast station" to advertise his or her views and if the station "affords equal opportunities to all other such candidates for that office."

The magnificence of the First Amendment lies in its implicit call for a free market of ideas in which speech of all kinds should not only be allowed but encouraged. The concept that an unfettered public ought to discover for itself which politicians are inept and dangerous, and which political ideas and programs are faulty and false, in order to exercise its right of rejection is the only thing that prevents a democracy from becoming dictatorial.

However, as politicians make use of it in the form of the political commercial, the First Amendment has never been so corrupted. It has been made a smoke screen behind which the unscrupulous candidate can confidently shout "fire" in the crowded nation—without fear of penalty, and with high office the all-too-frequent reward. And while the First Amendment hardly requires people to speak when they wish to remain silent, candidates, and particularly incumbents, use its protection in political advertising *not* to warn the public of the imminent danger of unpopular fires, even though the incumbent is usually the only person in a position to smell the smoldering evidence.

Furthermore, since the passage of the Campaign Financing Act, taxpayers may now rub salt into their own wounds as they helplessly watch the government extract funds from the federal treasury to pay for these deceptive campaign practices—$10 million in matching funds per candidate during the prenomination period, $20 million thereafter. Many major corporations spend far less in a comparable period on advertising. For example, according to the Television Bureau of Advertising, the Carter for President Committee spent $3,474,500 on network television alone in 1976, which ranked them 144 out of 454 advertisers. This is more money than was spent by such companies as American Airlines, Du Pont, B. F. Goodrich, Sealy, Sony, and Wrigley. The

President Ford Committee ranked 170 in the list of network television advertisers. The candidates spent the remainder of their television advertising money for spot commercials.

In an age of severe nuclear, economic, racial, religious, environmental, legal, and social stress and breakdown, unrestricted political advertising has further exacerbated the public temper by implying, like the scheming nineteenth-century merchant, *caveat emptor—let the buyer beware.* Not even a two-bit bar of soap is allowed to do that anymore.

The Candidate as a Product—"Not Legally Approved"

Most people took the Carter and Ford commercials at face value without questioning their intent or their honesty. Only after Carter was safely inside the White House and the first returns began coming in on the "real" Jimmy Carter did the political analysts and the academicians become contemptuous of the television advertising of both Carter and Ford—where, they discovered suddenly, the most substantial part of the campaign had been fought. The political analysts also decided, just as suddenly, that there had been an undue emphasis on style over content in the commercials. "The candidates were smart enough to concentrate on style since they had nothing to say," a typical analyst observed, thinking to trace the origin of the country's ripening disappointment with Carter.

The most influential political analysts have been trained in and write in the print medium. They reject the influence and power of the television medium. They do not wish and cannot bring themselves to acknowledge or give credit to a medium they consider intellectually inferior. Thus the print analysts "literally" cannot "see" what is going on in a commercial, whether for a product or a politician, and thus they underestimate its effect on the public. That is why the criticism of political advertising always misses the point and always comes too late—that is, after the election. It has been that way since the first political television commercial twenty-eight years ago.

This is the point: What appear in political (and product) commercials to be nothing more than little balloons of style are not just style. They are content—content that in 1976, as in previous campaigns, the voters were promised was truthful.

The commercials of Carter and Ford were brilliantly lined with images, symbols, and words chosen with great care by their political media specialists to project more than hazy impressions of the candidates and their programs. There were "facts" stated or implied in the commercials: fleeting, superficial, oversimplified, slanted, cynical, deceptive, and false, but passing as facts nonetheless.

It is not true that Carter and Ford resorted to so-called commercials of style because they had nothing to say. They said a great deal, albeit in a few words, and almost all of it was misleading, deceptive, or false in some way. But the problem, the unfairness to the voter and the danger to the electoral system, was not limited to the commercials themselves. It included the political analysts who did not challenge the truth of the commercials when they appeared on television, who did not force the candidates to reveal everything about their backgrounds and ideas from the first day of the primary races, who did not themselves reveal the truth when the candidates would not or could not. When the political writers did report on the campaign commercials, which was not much and not often, they reported on the "style" they saw, thereby supporting by inference (and in writing) the truth of the political myths being spun on the television medium the writers scorned. With the political analysts sitting on their backsides, the political camps of Carter and Ford were free to use their deceptively simple-looking commercials as smoke screens to hide from the uninformed viewers the true backgrounds, beliefs, and intentions of the men who would be president and the true condition of the country at the time of the campaign.

The two commercials for Carter and Ford that are analyzed in the following pages were keystones of their campaign themes and promises and, unfortunately, are superb examples of political deception and falsehood. Throughout the campaign they ran at frequent intervals on all three major television networks and on many independent stations, during prime evening hours when the viewing audience numbers 80 million or more. Since television sets are turned on for an average of more than four hours a day, most viewers were sufficiently exposed to the commercials for them to have made an indelible impression.* Yet if these commercials had been subjected to the tests that govern product advertising on television, both would have failed—Carter's on nine counts, Ford's on ten. Of the violations on pages 5 and 6, they were guilty of numbers 1, 2, 3, 4, 7, 8, 9, 10, 12, 13, and 18. Their major violations: making claims and statements unsupported by facts or free of misleading implications and making claims or representations having

*It may not have been possible for viewers to be conscious of the effects on them of the Carter and Ford commercials (or any political or product commercials). Some scientists and psychologists now believe that as the artificial light-produced images from a television set enter the viewer's eyes, brain, and body, a neurophysiological effect is produced that resembles a form of hypnosis. The brain, in a sense, ingests—and retains—images.

MY OWN CAMPAIGN

CARTER: I started my own campaign twenty-one months ago. I didn't have any political organization.

Not much money. Nobody knew who I was.

We began to go from one living room to another. One labor hall to another . . .

beauty parlors, restaurants. . . .

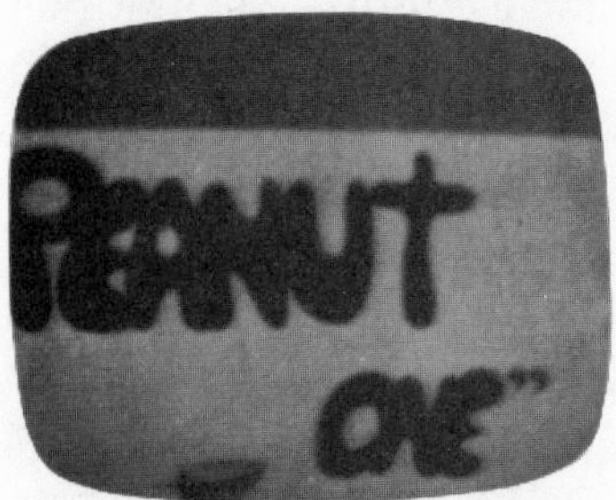

Talking to people. And listening.

To special interest groups I owe nothing. To the people I owe everything.

the capacity to deceive, mislead, or misrepresent. This made their integrity as advertisers questionable and therefore the taste of their presentations unacceptable. Had they revised their commercials to meet product advertising standards, there would have been very little left of the originals.

My Own Campaign
Sixty-second Carter commercial, 1976
Nine network code violations

"Nobody knew who I was"

Jimmy Carter was able to convert his alleged political anonymity into a bona fide campaign credential, perhaps his most important one. Yet he was not anonymous to influential members of the Eastern political and financial establishment, nor was he anonymous to Democratic leaders in the hinterlands.

Three years before the 1976 campaign "officially" began, the peanut farmer whom nobody knew was handpicked by Zbigniew Brzezinski, then a powerful political scientist at Columbia University with an international reputation as a cold war hardliner, to be a member of the newly formed Trilateral Commission.

The brainchild of Brzezinski and his patron, Chase Manhattan Bank Chairman David Rockefeller, the Trilateral Commission was a carefully chosen group of prominent business executives, academicians, labor leaders, and politicians from the United States, Western Europe, and Japan.* According to the *New York Times,* the commission was created "to reflect thinking in the nations of its members and to influence decision makers throughout the democratic industrialized world," and to promote "the habit of working together on political, economic, and security issues in the three regions"—perhaps along the lines Rockefeller and Brzezinski thought most productive for Chase Manhattan and the coterie of men who, with little interruption or challenge, had designed, influenced, and implemented U.S. military and economic policies since World War II.† To name the corporate bases of just some

*Some would say that Rockefeller was Brzezinski's supplicant at a time when Chase was attempting to maintain its position as a commanding global power in the face of falling profits.

†Richard J. Barnet has noted that most of the "top 400 Presidential appointments [in national security management] since 1945 could be located [in the international law firms and investment banking houses] in ten city blocks in five of America's largest cities." (Stavins et al., *Washington Plans an Aggressive War,* p. 202.)

of the Trilateral's members is to list the international industrial-financial-media elite: Bank of America; Brown Brothers, Harriman; Caterpillar Tractor; CBS; Chicago Sun-Times; Coca-Cola; Continental Illinois National Bank & Trust; Exxon; Hewlett-Packard; Los Angeles Times; Sears, Roebuck; New York Times; Time, Inc.; Texas Instruments; Wall Street Journal; Wachovia Bank & Trust. And, from foreign-based corporations: Barclays Bank; Bank of Tokyo; Datsun; Fiat; Hitachi; Seiko; Shell; Sony; Toyota.

The seventy-four Americans (out of a total membership of some 250) chosen for the Trilateral Commission during its formation in late 1972 and early 1973 were well known in the international political-economic community. When asked why an ex-governor of Georgia who was virtually unknown outside the Deep South had been invited to join that august group, Brzezinski said they had been impressed that Carter had opened up trade offices for Georgia in Brussels and Tokyo. "That seemed to fit perfectly into the concept of the Trilateral." And Carter apparently had caught David Rockefeller's eye as early as November 1971, when the banker invited him to New York for lunch.*

The Trilateral Commission ran on a fast track. The opening of a few trade offices, even if Carter *had* done the nitty-gritty work, seemed a thin qualification for membership. Why, then, choose the obscure Carter? Did Brzezinski—whose international appetites appeared to be much greater than those of a mere director of policy studies for the commission—and Rockefeller see in Carter, who even then was running for president, an opportunity for the commission to sponsor an ambitious but pliant unknown for the White House, a man whom they might influence, who would appear to the world as an "outsider" free of the taint of corruption and disassociated from the previous decades of United States interventionist policies overseas?

Remember what was happening in 1973, at the time of the Trilateral Commission's formation. The public tide was beginning to run against Richard Nixon and his men. Some Watergate convictions had been returned, other indictments had been made. Haldeman, Ehrlichman, Kleindienst, and Dean had resigned. A high Army general, Alexander Haig, had been made White House chief of staff. Archibald Cox

*It is not known what Rockefeller discussed with the Georgia "farmer," but it would have been a surprising omission if they had not exchanged pleasantries about mutual friend J. Paul Austin, chairman of the board of Coca-Cola, a contributor to Carter's 1970 gubernatorial campaign, and a man very much interested in Carter's future. Naturally, Austin would become a member of the Trilateral Commission. (See Chapter 8 for more about Carter's relationship with Coca-Cola.)

had been named special prosecutor for Watergate. The Senate Watergate inquiry had begun on television. It was a propitious time for those who were concerned with maintaining and regaining power. Carter's admission into the elite club, Gerald Rafshoon would say during the 1976 presidential campaign, was "one of the most fortunate accidents of the early campaign and critical to his building support where it counted." Political media specialist Rafshoon's choice of the word "accident" could be considered arch; the Trilateral Commission and candidate Carter appear to have obtained what each wanted from the other.

Writing in the *New York Times Magazine* five months after Carter's inauguration, Leslie Gelb, quoting a source who had watched Carter and Brzezinski at the Trilateral Commission, said Brzezinski "spent time with Carter, talked to him, sent him his books and articles, educated him."

Repaying the debt, Carter, on naming Brzezinski his national security adviser in a press conference, said he was "one who has been the key adviser for me as I've been an eager student in the last two or three years in learning about international affairs and the proper relationship between the maintenance of peace and an adequate defense for our country."

To make certain that there would be a "proper" relationship between the maintenance of peace and defense, seventeen members of the Trilateral Commission agreed to accept key posts in Jimmy Carter's new government of Washington outsiders. Beginning with Vice President Walter Mondale, ten men were assigned national security roles. Three of them had been instrumental in creating and enforcing the nation's Vietnam policy: Brzezinski, who had been on the policy-planning staff of the State Department (1966–1968), where, according to political writer Peter Meyer, he was considered "one of the more outspoken Vietnam war hawks"; Cyrus Vance, the secretary of state, who had served as general counsel in the Defense Department (1961–1962), secretary of the Army (1962–1963), deputy secretary of defense (1964–1967), and special assistant to Lyndon Johnson; and Harold Brown, the secretary of defense, previously secretary of the Air Force under Robert McNamara, where, according to Meyer, he "once suggested the bombing of the civilian population of North Vietnam while directing Lyndon Johnson's bombing of the rest of the country."

The other seven national security appointees were Lucy Wilson Benson, under secretary of state for security assistance; Robert R. Bowie, deputy to the director of central intelligence for national intelligence; Richard N. Cooper, under secretary of state for economic affairs; Warren Christopher, deputy secretary of state; Richard Holbrooke, assistant secretary of state for East Asian and Pacific affairs; Gerard C. Smith, ambassador at large for nonproliferation matters; and Paul Warnke, director, Arms Control and Disarmament Agency.

Two members of the Trilateral Commission went to the Treasury Department: W. Michael Blumenthal as secretary and Anthony M. Solomon as under secretary for monetary affairs.*

Four members of the commission became ambassadors: Richard Gardner, to Italy; Elliot L. Richardson, at large; Leonard Woodcock, former president of the United Automobile Workers, to China; and Andrew Young, to the United Nations.

It was rich company for the loner from Plains whom Jimmy Carter's campaign commercials so seriously portrayed and so successfully exploited.

If the Trilateral Commission gave Carter his credentials with the international movers and shakers, the position he obtained as head of the Democratic National Committee's Congressional Campaign Drive for the 1974 elections opened up and cemented essential contacts with hundreds of state and local Democratic party leaders and consultants throughout the country.

Before Carter's term as governor of Georgia expired he offered his services to Robert Strauss, the Democratic National Committee chairman. Strauss, deeply involved in rebuilding the party after the McGovern licking, never dreamed "Carter would use the committee post as a springboard to jump into the 1976 presidential race." Perhaps Strauss thought the token position would be a good way to keep a loyal Democrat happy and busy while gaining for the party the services of Carter's infectious smile at a time when Washington was in the dumps. It did not matter much what Strauss thought; with his usual pragmatism, Carter sensed that the job could be what he made of it.

As a first step, Carter detached Hamilton Jordan from his governor's staff in Atlanta and sent him to Washington to be his executive director, his "eyes and ears at the national committee." Systematically and skillfully, Carter began to establish himself in Democratic party circles outside Washington, meeting with state party leaders at regional

*When Carter fired Blumenthal as part of the White House shake-up of July 1979, another member of the Trilateral Commission quickly filled the gap. Hedley Donovan, former editor in chief of Time, Inc., was named by Carter to be his senior adviser.

seminars and offering himself as an instrument of national party assistance. "If it hadn't been for that," Jody Powell said later, "nobody would have known Jimmy."

Nor, Powell might have added, would Carter have had the chance to gather "an elaborately detailed portrait of voters which revealed how hungry people were for symbols they could believe in" after a decade of tragedy and despair. Later the Carter campaign strategists would throw those symbols in the voters' faces. For the symbols became the key to the advertising that would manipulate so well the people Carter claimed to love so much. But long before Carter would announce in his television advertising that "to the people I owe everything," the self-proclaimed small-town populist had first made certain that the people to whom he owed everything were the right people to know.

Besides the falsehood of anonymity, Carter's presidential campaign strategists brilliantly spun three more myths that became the heart of their man's campaign on and off television.

"I started my own campaign twenty-one months ago"
"I didn't have any political organization"

Carter did not have a network of field workers in the early stages of his campaign (it is a rare nonincumbent who does), yet he certainly had a very sound and very active political organization that began to work for his election *four years or more* before he officially announced his candidacy.

The people who advised him, as a campaign tactic, to boast about his lack of political organization *were* his organization. It was a simple deception that went unchallenged by political writers when it appeared in the form of a television commercial, even though the Carter organization were no strangers to the national media before the primaries began and had been well known by the Georgia press for years before that:

- ***Charles Kirbo, the political mentor,*** first sniffed Carter's political potential in 1962 when he helped him to win a contested seat in the Georgia State Senate. A leading partner in King & Spalding, Atlanta's most prominent law firm, Kirbo provided Carter with entree to the firm's most important clients, Coca-Cola and the Trust Company of Georgia, the industrial-financial aristocracy of the South. (Became trustee of Carter's peanut business and unofficial political adviser.)
- ***Hamilton Jordan, the political strategist,*** had been with Carter

since his first (unsuccessful) gubernatorial campaign in 1966, when he was youth coordinator. (Became Carter's White House chief of staff.)

- *Joseph Powell, the political press secretary and general aide,* had been at Carter's side on his political travels through Georgia since 1970. (Became presidential press secretary.)
- *Gerald Rafshoon, the political media specialist,* had devised Carter's media strategy and created his advertising and "media events" since the 1970 gubernatorial campaign. (Became special assistant for communications.)
- *Peter Bourne, the doctor-turned-political-philosopher,* had written in 1972 what was probably the first memorandum to Carter outlining why he should make a serious run for the White House in 1976. (Became a presidential adviser; later resigned because of alleged involvement in potential drug-use violation.)
- *Patrick Caddell, the political poll taker,* began advising Carter in 1972. He showed Carter how to position his presidential campaign in order to capitalize on the mood of the country after Watergate and, some say, on the "born again" religious phenomenon. (Became the president's official poll taker.)
- *Stuart Eizenstat, the political policy director,* had drifted in and out of the Carter political organization since the 1968 gubernatorial campaign, when he briefed Carter on issues and helped him frame politically useful positions. (Became presidential assistant for domestic affairs.)
- *Landon Butler, the political lawyer,* had worked for Carter in the governor's mansion and was an important member of the presidential strategy meetings Jordan would hold beginning in 1973 to discuss how Carter would win in 1976. (Became a White House assistant.)
- *Robert Lipshutz, the political fund raiser,* a wealthy Atlanta attorney, had raised important campaign money and served as treasurer of Carter's 1970 gubernatorial and presidential campaigns. (Became the White House counsel; later resigned to become co-trustee with Kirbo of Carter's trust fund.)
- *Thomas Bertram Lance, the political confidant and possible presidential campaign banking connection,* was one of Carter's closest friends and advisers before the 1970 gubernatorial campaign. (Became director of the Office of Management and Budget; later resigned under fire because of suspicious personal financial dealings; indicted by a federal grand jury.)
- *Rosalynn Carter, the political wife,* probably was and is Carter's number one political adviser. He often spoke of her as a substitute candidate, "a perfect extension of me." (Came to

sit on key White House meetings and to undertake diplomatic missions for her husband despite her nonappointive capacity.)

- *The Trilateral Commission, the political-economic establishment connection,* particularly Brzezinski, who, after tutoring Carter, wrote the candidate's foreign policy speeches during the nomination phase of the campaign.

The Atlanta campaign staff of the governor who had "no political organization" carefully laid plans to make him president of the United States.

The ink on the headlines proclaiming Richard Nixon's landslide victory in 1972 was hardly dry before Hamilton Jordan handed Jimmy Carter a carefully drawn-up memorandum of seventy pages which outlined the steps Carter must take to win the Democratic nomination for president in 1976. In 1973, the governor would be "projected as the heaviest of the governors in accomplishments." In 1974, Carter would be shown "as a leader in the Democratic party and someone involved in bringing it back." In 1975, he would be a "heavyweight thinker, leader in the party who had some ideas for running the country." The 1976 plan was simple: "Carter—a Presidential candidate."

Carter would follow Jordan's blueprint with an engineer's precision and diligence. Two months later he did everything but announce his presidential intentions in a speech before the National Press Club in Washington, a traditional forum for proclaiming such intentions.

Back in Atlanta for the rest of 1973 and early 1974, the "inner circle"—Jordan, Bourne, Rafshoon, Butler, Powell, Kirbo, and Lipshutz—met constantly with Carter to "discuss his progress and political developments."

"During the time remaining in Carter's [gubernatorial] term," political reporter Jules Witcover wrote after the 1976 election, "maximum use was made of the governorship as both a forum and a magnet for drawing in the influential, the prestigious, the informed. . . . Prominent national politicians, business and labor leaders, journalists, college professors with particular expertise who went there [to Atlanta] found themselves invited to the [governor's] mansion for discussions with Carter . . . to get him better known and to extend his familiarity with and knowledge of a broad range of subjects as befitted a presidential candidate."

What were all these influential, prestigious, and informed people suddenly doing in the mansion of this not-very-well-known governor? What was the attraction? Was the governor simply offering them some old-fashioned Southern hospitality? Did their presence not raise questions among the press—even among the press who were invited? Hungrier reporters might have inquired—or at least remembered when the campaign "officially" began and the candidate began weaving images of the "unknown" newcomer without links to Washington and the Eastern and international establishments.

Adopt a "learning posture," Jordan had advised Carter in a second memorandum in 1974. "You don't pretend to . . . know everything and . . . a major aspect of your campaign will be to travel the country . . . and learn." In seeking the presidency, Jordan noted, "Most men . . . are so consumed by their ambition that they will do anything to be elected. You have to attempt to separate yourself from this stereotype of the ambitious candidate who lacks commitment to anything, and establish yourself as a man of integrity."

That year Carter began traveling across the country, ostensibly for the Democratic party's congressional campaign but also to lay the groundwork for his own ambitions.

In 1975 Carter began to travel officially in his own behalf, covering two hundred cities and towns in forty states. Punishing as it was, his travel may be seen as another campaign ploy. His savior, Carter would later acknowledge, would be television. "For all the frenetic comings and goings of his twenty-two [official] months on the stump, most Americans had their only look at Jimmy Carter, and Jerry Ford, on their TV screens."

In 1976, using the "facts" from the previous years' work as material for this key television commercial, Carter would appear as the unknown without "any political organization," who started his "own campaign twenty-one months ago," modestly misstating the actual start by at least two years. For the Carter campaign organization, the unregulated political commercial was alchemy of the highest order. Each time a new viewer saw the commercial, Carter's image of the unknown country boy, instead of drying up, was extended. No one challenged it. The commercial stayed on the air. In the weeks before the election it was still being used effectively.

"I didn't have 'much money' "

After the 1976 election, a few political writers began to question the relationship between Bert Lance's complex loan activities and the money used to keep Carter's campaign going, in 1975 and particularly in April and May 1976, when the Supreme Court held up matching federal funds for the candidates involved in the presidential primaries.

Writing in *New York* magazine in October 1977, Doug Ireland wondered whether all of the $4 million that Bert Lance loaned Jimmy Carter in fact went into Carter's peanut business. "Where did Carter get the money to plane around the country from early 1974 until he won the Iowa caucuses at the tail end of 1975?"

Toward the end of 1977 a federal grand jury was impaneled in Atlanta to investigate Lance, who had by then quit as director of the Office of Management and Budget because of alleged criminal violations of the law.

In April 1978 the Securities and Exchange Commission and the comptroller of the currency filed a ninety-page complaint against Lance, accusing him of "fraud and deceit" and "unsafe and unsound banking practices" while a banker in Georgia.

In the *New York Times* of March 19, 1979, William Safire pointed out that the Carter family business had been given what was perhaps an unusual expansion of credit in 1975 and 1976, when cash flow (for the campaign) became important. "We know that through unlawful means, loan repayment checks were kited and held so as to give the Carter business a big cash 'float,' " Safire wrote.

The following day Attorney General Griffin Bell appointed New York attorney Paul Curran as special counsel to investigate the possibility that loans from Lance's bank to Carter's peanut business ended up in Carter's campaign.

On April 29, 1979, the *New York Times* reported that the Federal Election Commission audit of Jimmy Carter's 1976 election campaign showed that the Gerald Rafshoon Advertising Agency (the Carter campaign agency) "extended as much as $645,000 in credit" to the Carter campaign, "including $211,000 for television time that had to be purchased with cash at a time when the agency itself was having financial difficulties." The *Times* report said it was "not clear how the Rafshoon agency was able to underwrite television production costs for the campaign."

On May 23 Lance and three business associates were indicted on 33 criminal counts along the lines of the SEC and comptroller of the currency complaints.

On October 16, after a six-month investigation that took sworn testimony from President Carter, the Curran report showed that while Carter's peanut business received a $1.1 million unbonded loan from Lance's bank during the 1976 spring primaries, "no evidence whatsoever was discovered that any monies were diverted from the [Carter] warehouse into the campaign."

Gerald Rafshoon's advertising agency, which earlier had been cleared (though not unanimously) by the Federal Election Commission of allegedly providing illegal financial assistance to the Carter campaign during the general election, was also cleared by Curran of charges of using money from unknown sources to extend credit to Carter's primary campaign. What Rafshoon did, according to *New York Times* columnist William Safire, was to delay "taking his profit of 15 percent from media commissions and extended that credit to the campaign."

This was Rafshoon's privilege if he could afford to operate a business this way; it is not how the consumer advertising world normally works. Even if deferring media commissions were not considered bad business, advertising agencies, from the largest on down, could rarely afford to do it because they are themselves frequently faced with serious monthly cash flow problems. As Safire commented, "Message to candidates: hire only agencies that regularly carry their clients."

Many questions would seem to have been answered by the Curran report, yet one remains: If Jimmy Carter had "not much money," as he claimed in his advertising, how was he able to campaign for so long with such ease?

One obvious explanation, and one which political writers seem to forget, was that Carter's peanut business was not always in rocky financial shape. Gerald Rafshoon's images may have portrayed Carter as a plain farmer, implying a man of modest means, but money had not been a problem for Carter for some time and he had said so.

"I've got a good business and I've got a lot of employees and I make good money," Carter told the Kennedy School in Atlanta in 1971.

"I am a farmer. I grow certified seed on my farm. I have a very prosperous business, one I can afford to leave for the next nine and a half years—for the campaign and two terms in the White House. . . . I am a businessman. I am almost a professional planner," he boasted to a luncheon audience in Baltimore in 1975, in an effort to establish his serious campaign intentions.

Indeed, by the seventies the Carter peanut business (as differentiated from a "farm") was a "multi-million-dollar" operation encompassing "over 3,000 acres of farm and timber land across three Georgia counties," grossing "$2.5 million a year" and supplying "peanuts worldwide." Some farmer!

"In retail politics," wrote Jules Witcover after the campaign, "the candidate himself must bear a heavy burden. . . . Freed of the obligation of public office and self-sufficient financially in a pre-election year without legal impositions on spending, [Carter] was able, through 1975, to campaign with uncommon diligence."

In the Pennsylvania primary, Witcover said, "Carter took steps to assure that he had adequate funds for a strong media effort. . . . He arranged to borrow heavily, including $100,000 against his personal assets—a tactic now permitted by the Supreme Court's ruling, which lifted restrictions on how much of a candidate's financial resources he could put into his own campaign. Neither [Henry] Jackson nor [Morris] Udall had similar personal wealth, so they were stymied on this front, although Udall borrowed what he could."

Yet during the campaign no one questioned the discrepancy between Carter's obvious supply of money and Rafshoon's commercial images claiming a lack of it. The urban press, the television crews, and the journalists went down to Plains, looked at the Carter warehouse, looked over the Carter farm equipment, took pictures of the candidate wading in huge peanut piles, trudged with him through an acre or two of the 3,000, and then went home to write about the modest farmer from Plains. Rafshoon's television myths soon became certified journalistic fact. So brainwashed (or irresponsible) did the media become that when Carter's peanut holdings were put into a trust after the election —hardly a necessary legal device for the average farmer from Plains, Georgia—it was reported as a straight piece of news without comment or question. But all along, even Carter's number one supporter had known the truth:

"I know Jimmy writes about how poor we were, but really, we were never poor," Miss Lillian said fondly about her son. "We were just like all country people. We didn't feel poor and we always had a car. We had the first radio in Plains. We had the first TV set."

"To special interest groups I owe nothing"

At least four powerful special interest groups were necessary to Carter's success in 1976. When this commercial first ran at the time of the primaries, it appeared that only one of them—the Trilateral Commission—was interested in a Carter victory, and this alone could cast doubt upon the accuracy of that statement. But when the general election campaign against Ford entered its final, decisive stages, the commercial continued to be broadcast, opening Carter's claim to additional questions. For by then he had courted and won the support of leaders of three of the most significant major special interest groups in the country:

- *Blacks.* Influential Congressman Andrew Young (the Trilateral Commission member whom Carter later appointed ambassador to the United Nations) came out for Carter early and, despite passing annoyance over Carter's "ethnic purity" remark, led the way for him in the black communities. Blacks became the key to Carter's majorities in a number of Southern states.
- *Labor.* Three labor members of the Trilateral Commission came out early for Carter: I. W. Abel, president of the United Steelworkers of America; Lane Kirkland, then secretary-treasurer of the AFL-CIO; and Leonard Woodcock, president of the United Automobile Workers. Labor supported Carter in vast numbers. Sinologists may have wondered about Woodcock's ambassadorial credentials, in view of his career as a UAW organizer and official.
- *Jews.* American Jews were wary at first of Carter's "born again" revelations (on religious grounds) and concerned about what his position on Israel would be (on ethnic grounds). He came out strongly for Israel, taking what amounted to an anti-Arab stance. Carter told fellow Georgian Morris B. Abram that he knew few Jews outside of Georgia (no doubt meaning Jewish "leaders") and asked if Abram would help him get acquainted with others. Abram, with national credentials because of his former presidencies of Brandeis University in Massachusetts and the prestigious American Jewish Committee, obliged. Why so much interest in the Jews? Obviously, campaign contributions were welcome. But more important was the fact that Jews historically turn out to vote in extremely high numbers, probably achieving a higher percentage of voters than any other ethnic group in America. In New York and California the margin of the Jewish vote can often give a candidate those states' electoral votes in a close race.

It goes without saying that presidential candidates always seek the support of large special-interest blocs. The issue here is not that Carter sought and received such support but that from early in the primaries almost to Election Day he implied through this commercial a complete independence from them.

"I started my own campaign" "I didn't have any political organization" "Not much money" "Nobody knew who I was" "To special interest groups I owe nothing".

Deceptive, misleading, and unfair claims. If Jimmy Carter had made commercials for peanuts with statements like these, no television station would have accepted his advertising. But in 1976 slightly more than half the television viewers watching Carter's unregulated political advertising took what he said on faith.

Faith has its place, but it is no longer a good enough way to elect the nation's leadership.

Living in Peace
Sixty-second Ford commercial, 1976
Ten network code violations

This key Gerald Ford campaign commercial seemed harmless enough, yet it was as deceptive, misleading, and unfair as Carter's commercial, and it was far more dangerous on three counts: (1) it played on two of the public's most vital concerns, peace and jobs; (2) it used as authority for its statements the enormous power of the office of the president on behalf of a man who had not been elected to the position and who could not have mastered the complex and devious ways of the country's national security apparatus in the brief time he had held office; and (3) its brand of doublethink was a rhetorical smoke screen that masked the actual condition of the country.

The term *doublethink* (defined in *Webster's* as "The keeping of two contradictory ideas in one's mind at the same time and the conscious belief in both of them") is not used lightly. George Orwell, who invented it in his novel *1984,* may have been more influential in 1976 than either the public or Gerald Ford's political media specialists knew. Compare this passage from Orwell's frightful look into the future with Ford's commercial:

> Nobody heard what Big Brother was saying [on the telescreen]. It was merely a few words of encouragement, the sort of words that are uttered in the din of battle, not distinguishable individually but restoring confidence by the fact of being spoken. Then the face of Big Brother faded away again, and instead the three slogans of the Party stood out in bold capitals:
>
> WAR IS PEACE
> FREEDOM IS SLAVERY
> IGNORANCE IS STRENGTH.

Orwell has by now become a cliché, probably because the world has lived close to the grain of *1984* for so long that it resists reminders of its truth. Too bad; if the voters whom the Ford com-

CHORUS: There's a change that's come over America. . . . We're living here in peace again.

We're going back to work again.

It's better than it used to be. I'm feeling good about America.
FORD: Today America enjoys the most precious gift of all. We are at peace.

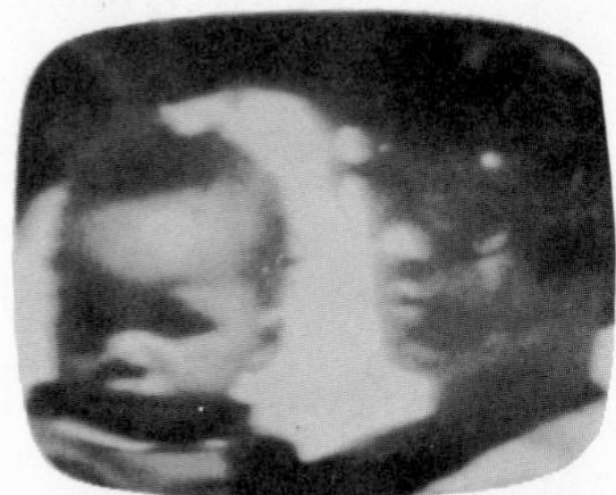

ANNOUNCER: We're at peace with the world. And at peace with ourselves. . . .

We know we can depend on him to work to keep us strong at home.

We know we can depend on him to work to ease tension among the other nations of the world. . . .

Peace with freedom. Is there anything more important than that?

mercial converted had remembered their *1984,* they might have realized they were being manipulated by their government (a counterpart—for the moment, at least—to Orwell's Ministry of Truth) in a manner not so different from that of Big Brother. Thus, on the Ford telescreen:

- The illusion of PEACE was a benign form of WAR.
- The absence of physical SLAVERY was far from being FREEDOM for tens of millions of Americans.
- The perception of STRENGTH was IGNORANCE.

Taking apart Ford's commercial, as the press should have done in 1976, reveals what its Rotarian approach did not tell the voters.

"We're living here in peace again"

People can decide what peace means to them personally. But if you accept on faith the politician's definition that peace is the absence of actual fighting, you owe it to your children, if not to yourself, to recognize this fact: Since before World War II, more than forty years ago, the military operations and militaristic instincts of the government of the United States (regardless of the individual administration) have dominated the lives of Americans to an astounding degree. In terms of comfort (the reason why half the population no longer wants to hear about military domination) as well as despair (the reason why the other half feels unable to do anything about it), the military, their political frontmen in Congress and in the White House, and their industrial "subsidiaries" are the architects of American society and the principal orderers of the nation's priorities, whether or not a single shot is being fired. So when Gerald Ford's chorus was singing its lullaby of peace over pictures of blissful, smiling children and adults, it should have been mandatory that the television screen show at least some of these disclaimers:

- On October 1, 1976, Ford's Department of Defense submitted a budget of $100.1 billion, a record for any one year and an *increase* of $9.9 billion from the previous year for the nation "living in peace again."
- Included in the military budget were requests from the Army, Navy, and Air Force for five kinds of jet fighter planes, a radar plane, six kinds of missiles (including two for submarines), two kinds of helicopters, two kinds of tanks, and a guided missile frigate.

- With the addition of Ford's Pentagon "peace budget," considerably over *one trillion dollars* had been spent on the military since the end of World War II.
- The federal government spent from fifty to seventy cents of every budget dollar for military operations past, current, and future. (Budget analysts often disagree on how to account for *known* military and civil activities of the Defense Department—extraordinarily high regardless of interpretation. The total budget usually does not include social security or unemployment insurance payments.)
- When Ford proclaimed that the country was at peace again, he implied a winding down of America's vast military efforts after Vietnam. Here is how the American taxpayer benefited by being at "peace": The savings anticipated from ending the Vietnam War—$30 billion a year—did not automatically revert to the civilian sector. In fact, as Charles Schultze, former director of the Bureau of the Budget (and now Carter's chairman of the Council of Economic Advisers) had pointed out as far back as 1968, most of the projected "Vietnam dividend" had been committed to *new* military programs even before it became available.

The American military has such a staggering amount of money to play with that it could almost casually toss away incomprehensible amounts—such as "$23 billion on missile systems that either were never deployed or were abandoned." How can *any* American government look the public in the eye and claim that it lacks the funds to help the poor, to clean up the environment, and to keep its libraries open? Here Ford had committed violation number 12: Unqualified references to the safety of a product (Ford and his claims of peace), if normal use presents a hazard (the manner in which the national security apparatus uses the public's money).

"We know we can depend on him to work to ease tension among the other nations of the world"

Ford's idea of easing tension was to maintain American troops in posts throughout the world. Much was made by the Republicans about the removal of half a million Americans from Vietnam; nothing was said about the 465,000 who remained elsewhere. Almost half of this number were stationed in West Germany, and another 45,000 were stationed in Japan, presumably to defend the ever-soaring economies of our wealthy former foes.

As a further gesture toward peace, on March 26, 1976, the Ford administration signed a pact with Turkey for military bases in exchange for $1 billion of military aid, and a pact with Greece for military bases in exchange for $700 million of military aid. Then, on October 19, eighteen days after the Pentagon had submitted its military budget, the United States (along with Great Britain and France) *vetoed* a United Nations Security Council resolution to ban arms to South Africa.

The United States retained its position as the number one supplier of arms to the world.

Foreign military aid brought a great deal of comfort and an even larger amount of cash to those blue-chip corporations euphemistically referred to as defense contractors but whose main business can only logically be described as the preparation for war. Many of the most famous names in American business were largely dependent on the Pentagon for their survival. In 1976, for example, the Council on Economic Priorities calculated that Defense Department contracts accounted for 47 percent of Lockheed's sales, 42 percent of General Dynamics' sales, 69 percent of McDonnell Douglas's sales, 65 percent of Grumman's sales, and 85 percent of Congoleum Corporation sales. In the case of Northrop Corporation, Pentagon contracts "surpassed 100 percent of the company's sales." Indeed, so intertwined is the relationship of military and industrial America that many defense contractors are only organizations of managerial and technical capabilities. Ling-Temco-Vought Aerospace Corporation, for example, owned just 1 percent of its office, plant, and laboratory space; it rented the other 99 percent from the U.S. government.

Perhaps as many as one out of every ten employed workers in America worked in defense industries or directly for the military. The Atomic Energy Commission, the National Aeronautics and Space Administration, and other defense-related activities were not included in this estimate.

Millions of these workers, their industrial plants, the generals and their Pentagon subordinates, and their supporters and hired hands on Capitol Hill and in the White House itself conspired to equip the United States with over 11,000 nuclear weapons targeted on the Soviet Union. Each of the United States' nuclear submarines could destroy 160 cities. A conservative estimate of the number of nuclear weapons needed to destroy the Russians is put at 100; a more radical estimate, which allows for the ability of the Soviet air defenses to destroy some of our nuclear weapons, is put at 800. Even that number, arms control expert Richard J. Barnet has pointed out, provides the United States with "far more killing power than could conceivably be needed for deterrence." But the ultimate stupidity and deceit of the ordering, manufacture, and placement of these nuclear weapons—whether they number 11,000 or 100—is that they do not and never will *protect* America in the event they are used. No less a hawk than former secretary of defense Clark Clifford has pointed out that neither the United States nor the Soviet Union "could expect to emerge from an all-out nuclear exchange without very great damage—regardless of which side had the most weapons or struck first."

It is one thing for a government to arm prudently against potential enemy attack of the greatest magnitude. It is something quite different to hide its military dreams, its imperial intentions, and, in Richard Barnet's words, an economy based on death, behind slogans of national security; it is morally deceptive and financially misleading to the citizens who pay the bills.

The price the citizen pays for a government's unchecked political deception may be the end of citizenship. Indeed, the citizen may have been moved closer to this end through commercials such as this than he or she has yet to recognize or understand.

"There's a change that's come over America"

"We're going back to work again," the Ford chorus sings over a disingenuous picture of a young black at work on a lathe.* In the United States in 1976, the "change that's great to see" included the following:

- Black unemployment remained nearly 13 percent.
- Unemployment for the general population was stuck at 8 percent. (This equaled 7.8 million people.)
- Black youth unemployment was 40 percent.

*In reality, a black would have had difficulty getting a union job such as the one portrayed. Why did Ford show so many blacks in his commercial when his chief advertising writer, Malcolm MacDougall, had said, "We had given up on the black vote even before Mr. Butz's [racial] remarks"? Explanation No. 1: the guilt felt by liberal Republicans on Ford's campaign staff. Explanation No. 2 (the more likely one): Including blacks in the commercial gave the *appearance* of liberalism. Ford hoped to convey this not to blacks, whose votes he had indeed ruled out, but to the fence-sitting Eastern and Northern white liberal Democrats who could not decide about Carter's brand of Southern-sounding Populism. In any event, it was another television code violation: Unsupported or exaggerated promises of employment or earnings.

- Total youth unemployment was 19 percent.
- Civil rights and other issues of concern to blacks were glossed over.
- The economy was being described as "sad," "stagnating," "sliding."
- The tax structure was tortured and inequitable.
- Deficit spending was excessive.
- Cities were breaking down after decades of neglect and bad management, the flight of the middle class, the flight of industry, unfair welfare loads, outmoded equipment, the inability to raise taxes from an ever-declining economic base and, in some cases, the failure to raise money by the sale of municipal bonds. (The case of New York City was by no means unique; it was simply the most obvious and most publicized.)
- The cost of health was skyrocketing.
- Education faced acute economic problems; school systems in New York, Chicago, Detroit, and many smaller cities were running out of money.
- After eight years of Republican talk about law and order, the major concerns of Americans were crime, violence, and corruption and lawbreaking on the part of people in government.
- The number of poor increased by 2.5 million, a number that included people not ordinarily found in poverty statistics: whites, families with a male head, and others not classified as elderly.
- As many as 10 million Americans were suffering from hunger.
- There were perhaps 30 million Americans who would be classified as underdeveloped if they lived in a foreign country.
- Infant mortality rates in the United States were among the highest in the world.
- Twenty-three million Americans—one out of five—between the ages of 18 and 65 did not know how to read or write well enough to function adequately in U.S. society, according to the U.S. Office of Education.

As the cases of human misery mounted during the 1976 campaign, the man whose commercial claimed he would "keep America happy and secure" vetoed a $56.6 million appropriation for education, employment, health, and welfare programs because the bill lacked "fiscal responsibility." The sum of $56.6 million was approximately equivalent to the cost of three F-14 jet fighter planes.

If you were above the functional literacy level, you might have turned away from television for a moment and read some of these shocking facts, which are available in easily obtainable books. If you lived in an American city, the facts might have hit you over the head. If you watched television closely, or if you could hear the radio above the din of a traffic jam, the fleeting telegrams of misery that today pass for broadcast news might have made some impression on you, and you might have railed against political smoke screens such as the one thrown up by Ford in this commercial. But few did, and Gerald Ford, bearer of good tidings, the man who had looked at America and found nothing distressing that he wished to discuss with you before the election, nearly won. A change of ten thousand votes in Ohio and Hawaii would have beaten Jimmy Carter. Ten thousand votes; a poor crowd for a major league baseball game.

Most political analysts believe that if the campaign had lasted one more week, Ford, using commercials such as this one, would have won.

No political analyst questioned the implications of such commercials.

2

THE FIRST MISLEADING PRESIDENTIAL CAMPAIGN COMMERCIAL

Ike as a TV trailblazer

You're sabotaging Democracy. You're trying to take a complex presidential personality, trim it down to a few slogans, reduce it to fifteen seconds, and use your rat-ta-tat-tat technique.

HARLAN CLEVELAND, editor of
The Reporter, to
Rosser Reeves,
creator of General Eisenhower's
campaign advertising, in 1952

Even the makers of political commercials still find it extraordinary how a simple few seconds of film not only can change enough votes to influence history but may cause history to be made. Yet in 1948, when television often worked with the smoothness of a windup toy, only one person had thought to turn the television commercial into a political weapon—a weapon he would later demonstrate. His name was Rosser Reeves, great-grandson of a Confederate cavalry general, licensed pilot, yachtsman, musician, international chess player, and master of the relentless advertising hard sell for the Ted Bates Agency.

The politician whom Reeves sought to persuade of the value of the television commercial was the governor of New York, Thomas E. Dewey, then Republican candidate for president. One can imagine the incredulous expression of the very proper Dewey as he listened to the advertising executive's wheezy, Southern-drawled explanation of how the wonders of advertising penetration could take him from Albany to the White House. It had no doubt been pointed out to Dewey that Rosser Reeves was the young man who had helped to bond the slogan "Cleans your breath while it cleans your teeth" to the brains and mouths of half the republic, to the enormous pleasure and profit of the Colgate Palmolive Peet Company.

Tom Dewey did not buy the idea of lowering himself to the commercial environment of a toothpaste ad. That was simply too inelegant an idea for a man who envisioned for himself an important place in American history. Certainly a man of Dewey's prominence did not need to be commercialized to beat the hick Truman. Rosser Reeves would have to wait another four years to become the godfather of the first political commercial for a presidential candidate.

In the meantime, it was estimated that Dewey could have won the necessary electoral votes in the close 1948 election if he had been able to change the minds of just 14,000 people in seven key counties in and around Chicago, a city which was a major originating point for network television programs that year and which thus possessed a great many of the few million television sets then in use—more than enough to make the difference for Dewey. Tom Dewey had committed a grave blunder; Dwight D. Eisenhower would not be allowed to repeat it in 1952.

It is tempting to catalogue Eisenhower's political advertising as a museum relic because it was the first to use television. Yet it bears a remarkable and perhaps a not very surprising resemblance to Jimmy Carter's presidential commercials, and in its way it was just as deceptive and unfair.

That the grandfatherly Eisenhower was openly deceptive and unfair even before he occupied the White House may come as a nasty shock to those who remember him as the most admired living American in 1952. His landslide victory over Adlai Stevenson that year was simply the reaffirmation of a remarkable outpouring of hero worship from a nation that was still deeply grateful for (or for what they knew of) his services to them in World War II. If Eisenhower had never gone near a television camera, his margin of victory would still have been ample; such were the unique conditions of his candidacy.

Eisenhower's campaign managers, however, fearful of the uncommon political literacy of Adlai Stevenson, and perhaps of his penchant for telling the truth, behaved as though defeat was a distinct possibility. The Republicans' apprehension opened the door to a brand new television product, the politician. Since then television advertising has been the *sine qua non* for all serious politicians, beginning with presidential candidates.

Each year since 1952 the cost of television advertising has risen, driving up the already exorbitant price of becoming a "public servant" and thereby tightening the grip of the wealthy on the nation. Moreover, now that the majority of campaign monies is spent on television advertising, discussion of the complex issues of life and death which society has created for itself (and which part of it now wishes to solve) has been encapsulated into simplistic slogans in order to fit neatly within the tiny space of a television commercial.

Inevitably, the raw power of the television commercial to radiate across politically imposed boundaries at first eroded and then all but ruined the party system, depriving the public of the personal attention that only the political party was able to provide. Men and women elected from obscurity, with little or no party principle or allegiance, could remain aloof from the electorate for years at a time with the assertion that they were "independent."

Because the political commercial, like its product counterpart, had to reach the most people for the least cost to be a practical investment, it was pitched to the lowest common denominator. The political message thus became almost instantly homogenized. This further undermined the usefulness of the party system by evening out many of the remaining differences between political ideologies. Voters were then left with the "choice" of two parties standing for virtually the same things.

In the afterglow of Eisenhower's stunning victory, television was praised as a magnificent new force for democracy and applauded for its potential power. No one imagined that one day we might end up on the verge of sloganizing ourselves out of existence.

Little has changed in political advertising since 1952. The bulk of the Eisenhower advertising was concentrated in spot commercials that were scheduled for the middle of the most popular television programs, such as *I Love Lucy,* on the correct theory that viewers would be "tricked" into watching the political messages because of their reluctance to switch the dial from their favorite entertainment. The commercials were shown mainly in the East and the Midwest, where it was believed Eisenhower might be weakest. Almost all the commercials were scheduled to run during the final three weeks of the campaign. The Republican strategy was to obtain maximum penetration with its advertising at minimum risk of boring viewers whose minds, they believed, were incapable of holding much more in the way of ideas and information than was normally given them in commercials for mouthwash and hemorrhoid preparations. By releasing Eisenhower's commercials just before the election, the Republicans knew it would be much too late for Stevenson to appear on television with an effective rebuttal. "It was enormous pressure," said Reeves.

Reeves's commercials were the height of simplicity. His idea was to get people from every state to ask Eisenhower a question. Eisenhower's answers would show that he had complete comprehension of the problems posed and a determination to do something about them —without committing himself to "strait-jacketing" answers that might hamper his presidency. The approach, said Ben Duffy, president of Batten, Barton, Durstine & Osborn advertising and a major force in the campaign, was one of "merchandising Eisenhower's frankness, honesty and integrity."

The Republican campaign managers, knowing they were buying thousands of spots for their commercials, wanted Eisenhower to cover dozens of themes. Reeves, however, had built a career on isolating a single, dramatic claim for a product and hitting away at it with barely a change for sometimes as long as ten years. He persuaded Eisenhower's people of the foolishness of fragmenting their message, and they finally compromised on three issues. This decision led to the first use of research to determine scientifically a political campaign strategy. Reeves, the cynic, remembers his innovation with relish.

> There [are] no if's, and's, or but's to what [politicians] believe. They want to know what the public *wants* and then they *change* their beliefs much as you would change the color on a package of corn flakes if your research department said [the public] didn't like the color that's on it. These people simply want to get elected. They don't have any personal beliefs. The Kennedys didn't. I don't think Eisenhower did. I don't think any of them do. And if they did, their personal beliefs are crowded under to say what is going to get them the maximum number of votes. . . . Eisenhower, once he got into politics . . . wouldn't say "boo" without reading the poll.
>
> My spots came out of the poll. I went out to Princeton and sat Gallup [who had never done political campaign polling] down and said, "I've got to have three claims that will get the most votes." That's the way politics is today. David Ogilvy [the advertising genius, once Reeves's brother-in-law] said the day will come when candidates are elected by polls rather than polling booths. Boy, is that true today.

Gallup learned that the country was concerned most about the war in Korea, corruption in Washington, and inflation and taxes. Reeves wrote fifty commercials, each based on one of those themes, and they were filmed in a single day. When Reeves saw how easily the filming was going despite Eisenhower's protests (during the filming Eisenhower is supposed to have said, "To think that an old soldier should come to this"), he dashed off another twenty-eight commercials, passing each script on to the chain of command under Eisenhower for approval when he finished it. That was all the approval the commercials received before going on television.

Five weeks later, as planned, Reeves opened up on Stevenson with a vengeance. His cunning media blitz never let up until the election. More than $1.5 million was spent by the Republicans for commercial time in a three-week period—a huge sum in 1952 (and equivalent to about $9 million at today's prices). That amount of money and the way in which it was spent represented another political campaign milestone.

Faced with Reeves's "secret weapon," Stevenson was virtually helpless. Already struggling against the Eisenhower name and brand of charisma, battered by innuendoes from Eisenhower's running mate, Richard Nixon, who called him an "appeaser" and a "dupe" of Alger Hiss, stigmatized as the first divorced presidential candidate, and distrusted in many quarters for his intellect, Stevenson responded with a discussion of what he believed was required of the country if it was to accept the challenge of the second half of the century. While Republicans were blitzing the public with fifteen-second Eisenhower commercials, Stevenson reiterated eloquently the themes of his acceptance speech ("Let's talk sense to the American people") in a series of half-hour television programs.

Eisenhower's commercials have been characterized as simplistic, innocuous, and even demagogic, but *deceptive* and *unfair* are terms that have never been applied to them, possibly because in death, as in life, it has been assumed that everybody should like Ike. Measured by a network television code for product advertising today, however, this typical Eisenhower commercial is guilty of nine violations:

1. No satisfactory evidence of the integrity of the advertiser. When Rosser Reeves put the words "The Democrats have made mistakes but aren't their intentions good?" into the mouth of an anonymous woman, he deliberately created an issue that did not exist and then pretended to solve it with Eisenhower's famous reply.
3. Lack of evidence to support claims.
4. Taste of presentation unacceptable.
6. Competitors discredited, disparaged, or unfairly attacked.
9. Claims and statements made in a testimonial are not supportable by facts or are not free of misleading implications.
10. Representations have the capacity to deceive, mislead, or mis-

WOMAN: The Democrats have made mistakes, but aren't their intentions good?

EISENHOWER: Well, if the driver of your school bus runs into a truck, hits a lamppost, drives into a ditch, you don't say his intentions are good. You get a new bus driver.

represent. What specifically were the Democrats' mistakes? What were their intentions? Of course Eisenhower doesn't say; instead he substitutes a not-so-silly yarn about a reckless school bus driver, unsubtly pinning the image on Truman—and by implication on Stevenson—without noting what he would do that would be different or better.

12. Unqualified references to the safety of a product. In this case, the Democrats. The school bus driver analogy, as Rosser Reeves knew very well, was not plucked from the blue. For much of America, the school bus driver bears more responsibility for the safety of children than perhaps any other individual, including members of the child's family. The school bus is a sensitive issue. However hokey or simpleminded Eisenhower's yarn was, to use it in such an unqualified manner was unfair.
15. Misuse of distress signals. If Eisenhower had a deep concern about the Democrats' mistakes—Korea, inflation, corruption—he might have spelled out his ideas in lengths longer than a quarter of a minute—unless, of course, as Reeves pointed out, the general had no personal beliefs in the first place.
17. Scare approach and presentation with the capacity to induce fear.

In 1952 Rosser Reeves created a political environment and a campaign method which radically altered the concept of political campaigning and the definition of American democracy. The oversimplification of serious issues is as old as politics. The commercialization of serious issues into misleading trivialities, heated up and driven at the speed of light by television, was a dubious innovation that has become more serious and more dangerous with each election.* Today Reeves, crusty and razor sharp in his seventieth year, recognizes this about others who advertise political candidates, though he does not seem to apply it to the past.

What Reeves believes he did in 1952 "was merely packaging in very, very brief form what Eisenhower stood for. Almost naïve. Terribly honest compared to today . . . .

"If you were running for office and you stood for balancing the budget . . . and I wrote a spot in which you said, 'Let me in there, and if it's possible we will balance the budget, even if we have to get a Constitutional Convention to do so,' then that's *honesty.* But if you go to [an agency] and . . . say, 'Write me some spots to poison the water for our competition,' . . . that's a little *crooked,* isn't it?

When Reeves reflects on using polls to determine how a politician should alter his or her beliefs, he seems to forget that it is a campaign tactic he promoted as much as anyone.

"It's a distortion and twisting of democracy that's incredible. People are not saying what they think is good for the country. Camille Desmoulins in the French Revolution had a wonderful quote: 'The mob is in the streets. Tell me where they are going so I can be their leader.' You haven't got a democracy when you have that situation. It is true of an enormous percentage [of Congressmen]. It's true of every politician I've ever worked for . . . Truman and Eisenhower . . . Javits and Rockefeller . . . and Lindsay [John Lindsay, former mayor of New York City]. Every single one was exactly the same."

Thus began the era of televised political manipulation.

*Although Eisenhower was heavily dependent on television and advertising in his 1956 rematch with Stevenson—in which his landslide was even greater than in 1952—his election is the only one in the history of presidential television advertising where the victorious candidate appears not to have needed or used advertising to camouflage his background or policies. However, advertising certainly helped Eisenhower project the image of a president too busy with state affairs to involve himself with ordinary stump campaigning (and its enervating effects, surely appreciated by a man who had suffered a heart attack in September 1955 and an ileitis attack five months before the election).

Since Rosser Reeves had retired from the political wars, Eisenhower's advertising was handled exclusively by Batten, Barton, Durstine & Osborn. The ill-starred Stevenson-Kefauver campaign hired the New York advertising agency of Norman, Craig & Kummel.

3

THE 1960 CAMPAIGN

A commercial footnote

Kennedy realized that his most urgent campaign task was to become better known for something other than his religion. . . . The answer was television.

Theodore Sorensen

. . . nobody could get through to Dick.

A Nixon television adviser

In a close presidential election, the credibility of the political analyst depends on how swiftly he or she can sagely reveal the single event, incident, or decision that turned the tide for the victor or did in the loser.

Yet such was the ripening glamour of television in 1960, with the emergence of John Kennedy as its first political star, that all astute analysts instantly agreed that the event responsible for Kennedy's hair-line victory over Richard Nixon was his performance in the television debates, particularly the first one.

In an election in which the margin of victory was less than 120,000 votes out of more than 68 million cast, and in a time when a less cynical nation could be touched by small acts of apparent decency (and be easily duped by bold lies as well), some factors in the campaign other than the television debates might have been of more serious consequence:

- *The call to Mrs. King.* If Kennedy had not been urged repeatedly to telephone Mrs. Martin Luther King to express his concern over the jailing of her husband, he might have failed to win Illinois (where his plurality was only 8,858 votes), a state with a heavy black constituency that had been roused by King's civil rights dreams.
- *The missile gap.* If Kennedy had not dreamed up the issue of the country's missile inferiority to Russia and its general lack of military preparedness, he might have failed to win Missouri

(where his plurality was only 9,980 votes), a leading state in the manufacture of engines for missiles and rockets.

- *The Houston speech.* If Kennedy had not converted his Catholicism into political capital before a convention of Protestant ministers, he might have failed to win Minnesota (where his plurality was only 22,018 votes), a state with a heavy concentration of Lutherans and one that had gone Republican in nineteen of the previous twenty-five presidential elections.
- *Nixon's appearances.* If Nixon had not been hospitalized for two vital weeks at the beginning of the campaign and then insisted on driving himself, his staff, and the press accompanying him into a state of exhaustion by attempting to visit all fifty states (and if he had used makeup to cover his sickly appearance during the first debate), he might have won the necessary votes in the states named above and overcome the 66,841 votes that gave Kennedy victory in Michigan, a state that had voted Republican in twenty-one of the previous thirty-one presidential elections, including the 1940 election, when Roosevelt ran for a third term.

Any one of these events or decisions could have been given the credit for Kennedy's narrow victory, had there been no television. But in the midst of the Kennedy glitter no analyst would put his or her job on the line by picking anything other than television as the new and undisputed political kingmaker. Yet the coalescence around the television debates as *the* decisive factor seems questionable.

No one saw the need to master television earlier in the campaign than Kennedy himself. Theodore Sorensen, the candidate's speechwriter and counsel, notes how in a swing through West Virginia Kennedy had observed the "tiny ramshackle shacks with no plumbing and no newspapers or magazines, but with large television aerials. He had seen surveys showing twice as many Americans citing television as their primary source of campaign information as those citing press and periodicals."

The Kennedy organization never knowingly missed a television opportunity. Kennedy appearances were scheduled early enough in the day to get free coverage on local and network evening news shows. Statewide television hookups were used for Kennedy's major state addresses. Kennedy made a number of nationwide television speeches and a series of short films for television presenting his views on specific issues. And he used commercials.

Yet for all Kennedy's obvious ease with television and the matchless campaign advantages it provided him, television may have contributed less to his victory than did Richard Nixon's curious decision to stay out of the medium that he had once used so effectively.

For it was Nixon's emotional "Checkers" speech on national television in 1952 that ensured his political prominence even as it saved his political hide. Had Nixon used his time, strength, and ample Republican campaign funds in a similar way on massive doses of political commercials in key areas of the country in 1960, he could well have overcome Kennedy's thin margin. The political lessons of Rosser Reeves and his Madison Avenue colleagues would have been more than a match for the Kennedy charm.

But, as Theodore White has reported, Nixon in those days feared the tag of "Madison Avenue." Even when his television advisers, volunteers from some of New York's best advertising agencies, deliberately took office space one block *off* Madison Avenue, Nixon avoided them and the plans they had devised to use television as it had never been used before. "From July 25th—the night of Nixon's acceptance speech in Chicago—until October 25th," White writes, "three months went by in which Nixon not once appeared in a national television broadcast under his own control of circumstances."

Nixon's decision not to pull out all the stops by using the highly skilled political commercials that would have been created for him by his advertising advisers, perhaps more than any other decision or event on either side, was the most decisive in the campaign. When viewed in the light of Kennedy's commercials, Nixon's decision is all the more fascinating, for Kennedy's political advertising, in addition to its surprising amateurishness, could easily have been attacked for its dirty politics.* When measured against the network advertising code, the two Kennedy commercials shown here contained serious violations.

Ike's Press Conference
Sixty-second Kennedy commercial
Four network code violations

These were the violations in *Ike's Press Conference:*

*One commercial showed a silly cartoon image of Kennedy while a singing group chanted, "Kennedy, Kennedy, Kennedy." It is difficult to see how this helped Kennedy's chances. Yet the fact was that he was on television with *something,* however vapid, and Nixon was not. Guild, Bascom and Bonfigli, a small agency, was retained by the national committee to handle Kennedy's advertising, but some commercials seemed to bear the imprint of Kennedy's "Irish Mafia," led by Lawrence O'Brien and Kenneth O'Donnell.

IKE'S PRESS CONFERENCE

ANNOUNCER: Every Republican politician wants you to believe that Richard Nixon is, quote, experienced. . . .

but listen to the man who should know best, the president of the United States. A reporter recently asked President Eisenhower this question about Mr. Nixon's experience.

REPORTER: I just wondered if you could give us an example of a major idea of his that you had adopted in that role, as the . . . as the decider and final . . .

EISENHOWER: If you give me a week, I might think of one. I don't remember. (LAUGHTER) . . .

ANNOUNCER: President Eisenhower could not remember, but the voters will remember. For real leadership in the sixties, help elect

Senator John F. Kennedy president.

ANNOUNCER: This historic moment is brought to you by Citizens for Kennedy.

SENATOR KENNEDY: As I said at the beginning, the question before us all . . .

is can freedom in the next generation conquer or are the Communists going to be successful?

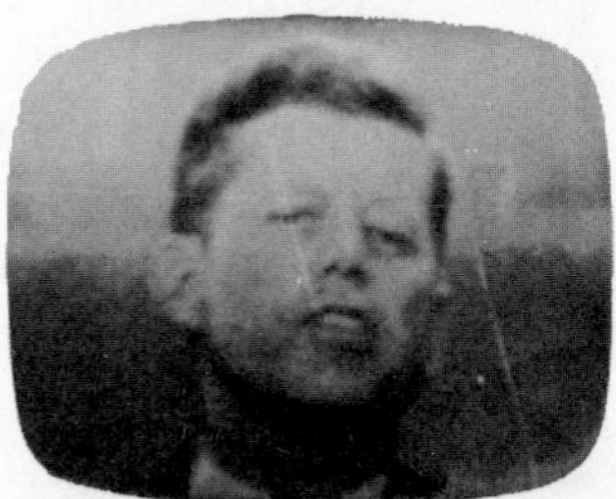

That's the great issue, and if we meet our responsibilities, I think freedom will conquer. . . .

If we fail to develop sufficient military and economic and social strengths here in this country, then I think that the tide could begin to run against us, and I don't want historians . . . to say these were the years when the tide ran out for the United States. I want them to say these . . .

were the years when the United States started to move again . . . I think we're ready to move. . . .

1. The integrity of the advertiser (Kennedy) was at issue for using such footage, obviously without Eisenhower's permission.
4. The presentation was therefore in bad taste.
6. Nixon was blatantly and deliberately disparaged and unfairly attacked.
8. The use of the office of president for a Democratic commercial was obviously not approved by Eisenhower.

Kennedy made a number of commercials that were based on excerpts from the debates and from his campaign speeches. One commercial contains footage from the first Kennedy-Nixon television debate. The first frame contains three separate advertising code violations. It cannot be seen readily in the pictures that appear here, but on the average-size television set Nixon appeared weak and sickly in comparison to the vigorous-looking Kennedy, an obvious reason why the Democrats chose to keep repeating the commercial throughout the campaign, even after subsequent debates, when Nixon looked and spoke better. Thus the Kennedy commercial helped to neutralize the later Nixon performances.

However, the question is, Who gave the Democrats permission to use the debate footage? Certainly not Nixon; probably not the American Broadcasting Company, which televised the first debate; and probably not moderator Howard K. Smith. Leaving out the network television code, Kennedy's commercial may have been libelous. Measuring the commercial by the television code, it would have been unacceptable because part of its presentation was in bad taste, unfairly disparaged Nixon, showed him in an unfair manner, and did not include his rebuttal.

There are major violations in the main body of the commercial that illustrate the campaign Kennedy waged and provide a preview of how he would view the presidency. Kennedy's repeated urging concerning the need for "freedom" to "conquer" (the Communist threat), the "responsibility" of the country to do so, the need to "develop sufficient military . . . strength," the need to start to "move again" and to be "ready to move" were code words for Kennedy's missile gap/military unpreparedness fairy tale, and thus they made the commercial deceptive and misleading. The language also represented a misuse of distress signals and a scare approach with the capacity to induce fear—two more violations.

Had there been a television code for political commercials in the close 1960 election, the violations in Kennedy's commercials could well have boomeranged against his general campaign. Not only would his commercials have been nullified, the resultant bad publicity, which would have been leaked to the press, would probably have caused Kennedy to alter his strategy just when he had taken the offensive, and at the same time provided Nixon with fresh impetus to get his beleaguered campaign off the ground.

4

THE MASKING OF A QUAGMIRE

How Lyndon Johnson deceived the little girl and her daisy

I am not going to lose Vietnam.

President Lyndon Baines Johnson,
November 24, 1964, two days after
the Kennedy assassination

On the evening of September 7, 1964, at 9:55 Eastern Daylight Time, any slim hope that Barry Goldwater may have harbored of making a respectable showing in the presidential election ended when an NBC television technician pushed a button at the network's operations center in New York and sent out to some 50 million viewers of *Monday Night at the Movies* what was shortly to become the most famous and most controversial commercial ever created for either a politician or a product: a little girl dissolving into a cloud of atomic dust as the president of the United States described the consequences of not loving each other.

Barry Goldwater was never seen in Lyndon Johnson's commercial, nor was he mentioned. But there was not the slightest doubt that the commercial had taken dead aim on what were said to be the Republican nominee's views on using the nuclear bomb against the country's enemies. The president's advertising scored a direct hit.

The next morning Senator Everett Dirksen, the powerful Republican from Illinois, sent a blistering protest to the National Association of Broadcasters, charging that the Johnson commercial was "in violation of your widely heralded code of ethics."

On the floor of the Senate, Thruston Morton, a Republican from Kentucky, ranted about "President Johnson's efforts over national tele-

THE LITTLE GIRL AND THE DAISY

(BIRD SINGING) GIRL COUNTING AS SHE PULLS PETALS OFF DAISY: One, two, three, four, five, six, seven, eight . . .

MAN: Ten, nine, eight, seven,

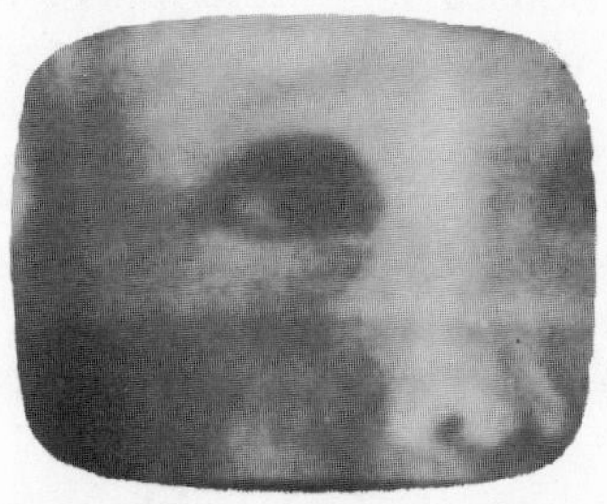

six, five, four, three, two, one, zero.

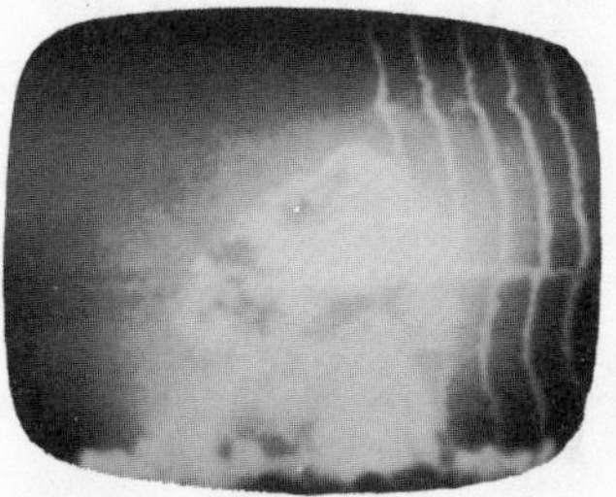

(ATOMIC EXPLOSION) LYNDON JOHNSON: These are the stakes, to make a world in which all of God's children can live,

or to go into the darkness. We must either love each other or we must die.

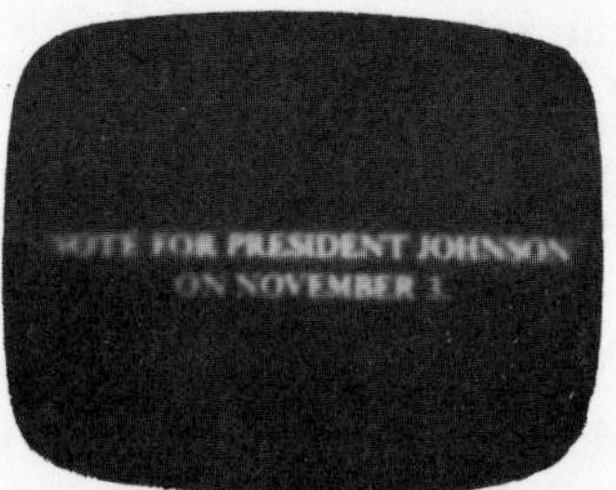

ANNOUNCER: Vote for President Johnson on November 3. The stakes are too high for you to stay home.

vision . . . to win the election by scaring the wits out of the children in order to pressure their parents" and promptly inserted the text of both the commercial and his anger into the *Congressional Record* for posterity.

The *New York Times* and *Advertising Age,* the trade paper, devoted columns to the commercial. The BBC showed it on its noncommercial network to give the English an idea of how the Americans were conducting their presidential campaign. Thousands of indignant Americans jammed the NBC switchboard to protest, wrote letters, and sent so many telegrams to Democratic National Committee headquarters in Washington that the room which housed its Western Union receiver was three feet deep in messages when the morning man opened up for work.

The protests were far from being entirely partisan. The Fair Campaign Practices Committee reported that hundreds of complaints came from registered Democrats. And on *Meet the Press,* Hubert Humphrey, who was Johnson's vice presidential running mate, called the commercial "unfortunate."

The little girl and her daisy were never seen again in public. The Democratic National Committee, fearing a backlash of sentiment against the president from both parties, withdrew the commercial before it had the chance to damage Johnson as much as it had his Republican opponent.

But her memory did not fade. The little girl was merely the opening salvo of a carefully orchestrated assault on Barry Goldwater, prepared by a White House working hand in hand with one of the most respected and certainly the most innovative advertising agency of the day, Doyle Dane Bernbach.

Doyle Dane Bernbach had started a creative revolution in New York a decade before with its advertising for two clients, Ohrbach's department store and Levy's rye bread. ("You don't have to be Jewish to love Levy's Real Jewish Rye," the headline read over a photograph of an Indian.) By 1964 the agency had achieved an international reputation for product advertising for such clients as Volkswagen ("Think small"), Avis Rental Cars ("We try harder, we're only number 2"), Polaroid, El Al Airlines, and Jamaica tourism. The Johnson campaign was its first venture into politics. William Bernbach himself took charge of the prestigious account—and would pride himself on the job he did. With Lyndon Johnson as client, Doyle Dane Bernbach turned its superb creative talents from advertising that ingeniously pictured the pleasant side of its clients to a campaign of vicious political attack that, in Theodore White's words, made the agency "happy as a dog in a meat market."

Barry Goldwater's television commercials were forgotten as quickly as they appeared, but sixteen years later Lyndon Johnson's advertising is still seen by some as a textbook campaign on how to elect a president. People who can remember little else about the Johnson-Goldwater campaign swear that they saw the little girl and her daisy going up in a fireball that evening in 1964. People who were toddlers then can accurately describe the action and repeat the sequence of numbers. And some people still compete for what they consider the honor of having created it,* still become aggressive when they are deprived of the credit, still do not understand sixteen years later that they were duped by the president of the United States and his most trusted advisers into using their talents to deceive the public about the dirty little war in Vietnam.

Lyndon Johnson had a choice to make when John Kennedy's assassination made him president in November 1963: either to shut off the small, covert involvement in Indochina or to widen it in an attempt to keep the Communists out of South Vietnam and to maintain America's hold on the edge of its empire. He chose a wider war.

Doyle Dane Bernbach's directive from the White House in the summer of 1964 was to heat up the electorate and get out the vote in order to create a landslide for the president. The White House believed that the landslide was required to put down the right-wing nuclear nuts once and for all, for the safety of the country, it was said, and to allow Johnson to emerge from the shadow of Jack Kennedy so that he might govern in his own right. What the agency did not realize was that it would actually be spinning a mass-media cover for the false and deceptive movements of a government that, according to its own documents, was willing and even eager to gamble on war in Vietnam from the day it came to power.

The cover, in a very real sense, was deceptively simple: Pretend to offer the public, its Congress, and the world the hand of peace while making certain that the warmonger label was fastened tightly to Goldwater. To pull it off, Johnson and his national security managers activated the most penetrating communications device ever created—the

*Both Doyle Dane Bernbach and Tony Schwartz, an expert in audio response theory and practice and a political media specialist, have claimed credit for the creation of *The Little Girl and the Daisy* since the night it went on the air.

structured, tightly controlled television commercial—and arranged with Doyle Dane Bernbach to use it brilliantly. Goldwater walked into the trap just as innocently as the advertising agency that set out to get him.

The year 1964 is a watershed in the history of political advertising—and therefore in the perceptions of the electorate of what it is actually voting for. It was the first time that an American government used advertising not for the purpose of attaining power or remaining in power—a foregone conclusion from the moment Barry Goldwater was nominated—but in order to cover up the true nature of its actions.

More than a decade after Lyndon Johnson was driven from the White House when an enraged public finally learned the truth and the price of those actions, intelligent people who hold high corporate offices have decided to conclude that the escalation of the war was not really Johnson's fault but was the result of an ill-fated inheritance left to him by Kennedy, who had received it from Eisenhower. "The generals deceived Johnson." "He had little choice." "He was pushed into the war." "He was never objectively informed about the situation." "Little by little, he found himself doing things that he didn't want to do." "He had a wall of military men around him." Intelligent people, William Bernbach among them, still make these claims.

It is a sentimental view, unsupported by fact, yet it is a familiar response of Americans to leaders who deceive them. In Lyndon Johnson's case, he knew precisely what the situation was in Vietnam before he became president, and he knew precisely what he was doing after he became president, as studies of the war have shown.

In fact, in 1965, two years before Defense Secretary Robert McNamara commissioned the secret history of United States involvement in Indochina that became known as the Pentagon papers, Bill Moyers, Johnson's principal assistant, seemed to go out of his way to demonstrate Johnson's independence from his advisers, particularly the generals. In an interview with Columbia University historian Henry Graff, Moyers said the president was not "the prisoner of any man" and was not "the prisoner of statutory responsibility"—which Graff took to mean "the chain of command."

Moyers told Graff that the president talked to many people in and out of government about Vietnam, "including especially Dean Acheson [secretary of state under Truman] and Abe Fortas [a powerful Washington attorney and close friend of Johnson's, whom he appointed to the Supreme Court in 1965] . . . President Johnson, said Moyers, 'relies less on military advice than any President since Wilson.' (I understood 'military advice' [Graff wrote] to mean 'advice from the military.')"

The events of 1964, and the crucial decisions which led to that fateful year, fit uncomfortably into the elementary history books that American children are raised on. The men who were gathered around the president are now gauzy images, and the memories of the war they so meticulously planned are often indecipherable and hard to place in proper order.

So it is not merely instructive, it is necessary to place the men, the events that were their making, and the political advertising which served as their cover, in the context of that time in order to see how cleverly the three were interwoven and how they combined to dupe the nation.

VIETNAM: THE HORROR AND THE SMOKE SCREEN* 1945–1965

After Japan was defeated in World War II the French attempted to recover their colony in Vietnam, but they were challenged by Ho Chi Minh's Communists, who sought independence for their country. The Pentagon papers show that Ho wrote to President Truman for help. There is no record of a reply. Instead, Truman reversed American policy of noninvolvement in Vietnam, recognized the French puppet Bao Dai, and provided military assistance to the French colonial forces. To no avail; they were defeated by Ho, and in 1954 they signed the Geneva accords. Vietnam was temporarily partitioned into two zones —the Communist North and the West-supported South—until nationwide elections could determine who would unify the country. A two-year grace period was designed to allow the South to prove it could rebuff Ho by popular vote. Ho agreed because he believed his reward

*The Vietnam chronology has been reconstructed primarily with the help of two sources. The first, *The Pentagon Papers* as published by the New York Times (Bantam Books, 1971), contains many of the secret government memorandums, cables, and instructions connected with three decades of U.S. decision-making in Indochina; excerpts from a narrative analysis of these documents written by thirty-six unnamed government officials; and reports and summaries of the material written by *New York Times* writers. The second source, *Washington Plans an Aggressive War* (Vintage Books, 1971), is divided into three sections. This chronology has depended generally on the first section, a historical essay by author Ralph Stavins based (according to the book's preface) on "more than 300 interviews . . . of top presidential advisers to Presidents Kennedy and Johnson, generals and admirals, middle-level bureaucrats who occupied strategic positions in the national security bureaucracy," and civilian and military officials "who carried out policy" in Vietnam; "informants with documents . . . including informal minutes of meetings . . . [and] portions of the . . . Pentagon papers."

for ousting the French—reunification under his leadership—was being postponed, not denied.

The accords, which the United States promised not to disturb, prohibited foreign troops and bases on Vietnamese soil. But days after the signing the Eisenhower government called them a "disaster" and took action to halt further Communist expansion by providing economic and military aid to the new South Vietnamese government headed by Ngo Dinh Diem, substituting U.S. advisers for the French, and sending in CIA agents to conduct "paramilitary operations."

Feeling his power, Diem ignored the reunification election date in 1956, a provocation of the Communists that led to the second Indochina war. Two years after the canceled election, despite CIA reports that Ho was the clear symbol of nationalism in much of the South as well as in the North and could unify Vietnam without a fight, Washington blindly believed that Diem could somehow overcome the Communist objectives. Three years after the canceled election, Ho Chi Minh decided to reunify the country by whatever measures he considered appropriate.

By 1960 Washington was alarmed that less than 5,000 Viet Cong (guerrilla supporters of the Communists) would overthrow Diem, who, it suddenly discovered, was weak and despised by the peasants. The Eisenhower government created the "domino" theory, which argued that the North's dominance over the South would end U.S. political and economic interests not only in Vietnam but in all of Southeast Asia, much of the Orient, and possibly as far as the mid-Pacific. America would have to withdraw from the center stage of global politics.

At this point John F. Kennedy became president. Although the United States considered itself committed to South Vietnam, the Pentagon papers show that Kennedy transformed Eisenhower's "limited-risk gamble" into a "broad commitment" to stop the Communists. Kennedy and his advisers considered defeat unthinkable, believing the introduction of Americans into the region would give the South Vietnamese the "elan and style needed to win." This the Kennedy administration proceeded to do in secret.

April 1961

Kennedy takes his first steps into the Vietnam quagmire, asking Deputy Secretary of Defense Roswell Gilpatric to draw up plans to beat the Communists.

May 1961

The Gilpatric task force submits "A Program of Action to Prevent Communist Domination of South Vietnam" to Kennedy. It calls for possible use of American troops, a bilateral treaty between the United States and Diem's government, and a program of covert action. Kennedy approves.

Later in the month Lyndon Johnson is initiated into the ways of Vietnam when Kennedy sends his vice president to Southeast Asia as a gesture of support for Diem.

During his meeting with Diem, Johnson calls him the "Winston Churchill of the Orient" and urges him to request American ground troops. Diem declines except in the event of open warfare, pointing out that the presence of U.S. troops would be a breach of the Geneva accords. Diem suggests that the *appearance* of legality could be preserved if troops came into Vietnam under a smoke screen, as the U.S. Military Assistance and Advisory Group.

Johnson returns to Washington, appearing committed to greatly expanded United States intervention in Vietnam. He writes Kennedy:

> The battle against Communism must be joined in Southeast Asia with strength and determination to achieve success there—or the United States, inevitably, must surrender the Pacific and take up our defenses on our own shores. . . .
>
> The struggle is far from lost in Southeast Asia and it is by no means inevitable that it must be lost. . . .
>
> There is no alternative to United States leadership in Southeast Asia. . . . This decision must be made in a full realization of the very heavy and continuing costs involved in terms of money, of effort and of United States prestige. *It must be made with the knowledge that at some point we may be faced with the further decision of whether we commit major United States forces to the area or cut our losses and withdraw should our efforts fail. . . . I recommend we proceed with a clear-cut and strong program of action.* [Emphasis added.]

October 1961

Kennedy orders General Maxwell Taylor and Special White House Assistant Walt Rostow to Vietnam to explore the desirability of sending U.S. troops there.

Taylor and Rostow stop in Hawaii to confer with Admiral Harry Felt, U.S. commander in the Pacific. Rostow asks what plans have been made in the event of open war with the North Vietnamese. One question centers on nuclear weapons, which will occupy a major role in the election campaign for president of the United States three years hence. Says Felt: "Plans were drawn on the assumption that tactical nuclear weapons will be used if required and that we can anticipate requests being made for their use if action expands into a 'Phase 4' situation" —by which Felt means an invasion of the South by the North Vietnamese and Chinese.

When Johnson succeeds Kennedy, the new president will not be surprised by plans such as these.

November 1961

General Taylor proposes sending 6,000 to 8,000 U.S. troops to South Vietnam. The excuse will be a flood on the Mekong River delta; to the outside world, the troops will be coping with it on behalf of the South Vietnamese people.

Throughout the fall Kennedy's advisers and members of the Joint Chiefs of Staff send him memos outlining their strategies for Vietnam and the number of American troops and amount of matériel it will take to implement them. Kennedy's policy, as Ralph Stavins later pointed out, "was to accelerate the war while denying that he was doing it. His policy was to prosecute a private war. . . . He disregarded the counsel of his advisers only to the extent that they preferred a public war."

1962

In the White House and at the Pentagon, this year is referred to as the optimistic period. Some of the reasons:

- Washington continues to feed U.S. troops into Vietnam. Over the next twenty-two months Kennedy sends more than 16,000 troops to Southeast Asia. They will serve, the U.S. public is told, only as "advisers" to the South Vietnamese Army.
- U.S. special forces execute numerous covert operations in North Vietnam.
- Kennedy authorizes the first use of heavy firepower by sending newly armed helicopters to Vietnam.
- The U.S. Navy sends minesweepers and DeSoto destroyers on patrols along the North Vietnamese coast.

- The U.S. Air Force sends planes on surveillance and reconnaissance missions over North Vietnam.
- The 303 Committee is formed to manage U.S. covert activities in Vietnam. It is composed of Kennedy's senior national security advisers and deputies from the Defense and State departments.
- Operation Ranchhand, a plan to destroy crops in North Vietnam and expose its supply routes by defoliating the jungles along highways and trails, is given presidential approval.

Although Lyndon Johnson and his advertising agency will be very interested in the issue of defoliation during his presidential campaign two years later, neither he nor those who manage the program show any concern about the hunger, sterility, and forced migration it will cause the peasants in the North. (As a member of the National Security Council, Johnson will certainly have been in on such discussions or know their details.)

1963

The Viet Cong demonstrates its superiority over the South Vietnamese Army despite the "advice" the South receives from the United States. Washington believes the Viet Cong cannot be defeated as long as the United States is handcuffed by the constraints of covert military operations.

August 1963

Diem has become a problem for the administration. In June the world was stunned by a photograph of a Buddhist monk committing suicide by fire in Saigon. The Buddhists are opposed to Diem, a Catholic, and Diem is urged by the United States to be conciliatory to their demands for equality. Six weeks later his army ravages the main Buddhist pagodas in Saigon and other cities. Monks are shot, holy statues are destroyed. The U.S. National Security Council begins meeting on a daily basis to attempt to dispose of the Diem question.

A part of the August 31 meeting is particularly interesting for what it reveals about Lyndon Johnson's views on American involvement. To summarize that part:

Dean Rusk, secretary of state, urges that Diem be retained.

Paul Kattenburg, chairman of the State Department's Vietnam

Working Group, argues for immediate withdrawal of American forces from Vietnam—done honorably.

Rusk, appalled by Kattenburg's remarks, counters that "we will not pull out of Vietnam until the war is won and that we will not run a coup [on Diem]."

Both Defense Secretary Robert McNamara and Vice President Johnson agree with Rusk. Johnson adds that "it would be a *disaster to pull out,*" that "we should stop playing cops and robbers and get back to talking straight to the GVN [Government of Vietnam]," that "we should once again go about *winning the war.*" (Emphasis added.) He recommends that "someone talk tough to them—perhaps General Taylor."

November 2, 1963

Diem is overthrown in a coup and shot to death. According to the Pentagon papers study, (1) Kennedy knows about plans for the coup and has approved them every step of the way; (2) United States "complicity in [Diem's] overthrow" heightens "our responsibilities and our commitment" in Vietnam. With Diem gone, the United States has reached a pivotal point in its involvement in Vietnam. Instead of backing the cabal of South Vietnam Army generals, the United States can think carefully about its commitment. It can choose to disengage—to cut it off clean.

After the coup the United States discovers that the Viet Cong are much stronger than had previously been thought and that the South Vietnamese Army is much weaker. Instead of doing less in Vietnam, the United States decides to do more.

November 22, 1963

President Kennedy is assassinated. Lyndon Johnson is sworn in as the 36th president.

Although now the problem in Vietnam is much more complicated and the commitment vastly deeper, Johnson has the same fundamental choice with regard to U.S. policy that Kennedy had when he became president: to withdraw or to widen the war.

Whatever his doubts and fears, however uncertain he may be in the aftermath of America's shock and sorrow over Kennedy's death, Johnson nevertheless moves instantly and clandestinely to implement Kennedy's Vietnam policies. Now they are Johnson's policies.

November 24, 1963

Henry Cabot Lodge, U.S. ambassador to Vietnam, meets with President Johnson. Lodge reports that things are very bad in Vietnam; if Vietnam is to be saved, Johnson will have to face some very difficult decisions in the near future.

"I am not going to lose Vietnam," Johnson says. "I am not going to be the president who saw Southeast Asia go the way China went."

Lodge wonders about Johnson's political support.

Johnson replies, "I don't think Congress wants us to let the Communists take over Vietnam."

Later Johnson goes to the State Department and ends a talk (and any doubts about his intentions) to its assembled personnel with these carefully chosen words: "And before you go to bed at night I want you to do one thing for me: ask yourself this one question. . . ." He pauses for effect, then says slowly and emphatically: *"What have I done for Vietnam today?"*

November 26, 1963

Lyndon Johnson issues National Security Memorandum (NSM) 273, a confidential document that has the effect of continuing and widening Kennedy's covert war as well as laying the foundation for an overt war.

February 1, 1964

Plan 34a, a program of secret military operations in North Vietnam growing out of President Johnson's November 26 NSM 273, begins. Phase One, scheduled from February to May, is to consist of intelligence operations and a limited number of destructive acts against the North. Phases Two and Three are to step up the pace of Phase One and increase destruction of targets vital to North Vietnam's economy. During this period, talk of pulling back from the covert war is nearly nonexistent. For example, General Taylor, chairman of the Joint Chiefs of Staff, writes Secretary McNamara that the November 26 memorandum "makes clear the resolve of the President to ensure victory over the externally directed and supported communist insurgency in South Vietnam."

March 16, 1964

McNamara, returned from Vietnam, reports that "the situation has unquestionably been growing worse" and recommends "new and significant pressures upon North Vietnam." These include "hot pursuit" of the guerrillas into Cambodia and "retaliatory bombing strikes" into the North by the South Vietnamese Air Force *and* by an American air commando squadron operating in South Vietnam with planes carrying South Vietnamese markings.

March 17, 1964

Johnson approves McNamara's recommendations and directs that the planning "proceed energetically."

March 19, 1964

Johnson retains Doyle Dane Bernbach as his advertising agency for the 1964 presidential election campaign. (The agency originally had been selected by Kennedy in 1963.) Johnson directs Doyle Dane "to plan and coordinate with him through Bill Moyers at the White House."

March 20, 1964

Johnson cables Ambassador Lodge that he is intent on "knocking down the idea of neutralization [in Vietnam] wherever it rears its ugly head."

April 1964

Doyle Dane Bernbach, with the overwhelming advantage of a shoo-in candidate, a long lead time, ample money, and direction from Moyers and other Johnson aides at the White House, begins to work on the president's advertising strategy. When it is clear that Goldwater will be the Republican candidate, Moyers's clear directive to the agency is: "Attack, jolt Goldwater, put him on the defensive from the beginning."

An advertising strategy of "nuclear responsibility" (peace) is developed for Johnson. It is, more accurately, a strategy of discrediting Goldwater for "nuclear irresponsibility" (war). Doyle Dane Bernbach does not appear to realize that the effect of its strategy will be, in David Halberstam's words, to have "camouflaged the question of Vietnam, removing it from debate, from the public eye and from the journalistic eye." It strains logic and credibility to believe the same is true about close aides and friends of the president.

Johnson confidants Clark Clifford, Abe Fortas, and James Rowe are involved to some degree in Doyle Dane Bernbach's decisions. The agency goes over its television strategy with Moyers, Richard Goodwin, and Lloyd Wright, who assisted Moyers at the Democratic National Committee. The three usually applaud the agency's ideas. But it is Moyers, "the chief idea channel of the campaign" and "the chief companion of the conscience of the President," who seems to have the most influence with Johnson with respect to the role and direction of the advertising. When (according to one report) Doyle Dane later showed Johnson the first versions of its "nuclear responsibility" television commercials, the president asked a few questions, then commented, "You know what you're doing," and left the room. The Doyle Dane people apparently think the president is lukewarm about their presentation, but Moyers and Johnson aide Jack Valenti assure them that the meeting has gone well.

April 19 and 20, 1964

Rusk, William Bundy (assistant secretary of state for Far Eastern affairs and older brother of McGeorge Bundy), and General Wheeler meet in Saigon to review scenarios with Ambassador Lodge for escalating U.S. military involvement against North Vietnam.

May 23, 1964

William Bundy prepares a thirty-day scenario for graduated military pressure against North Vietnam, culminating in all-out bombing of the North. The scenario includes a draft for a joint congressional resolution that will authorize whatever is "necessary" in regard to Vietnam.

June 15, 1964

Political and military preparations for increased U.S. involvement in Vietnam are now complete. The national security apparatus awaits Johnson's order to expand the war. William Bundy has urged a congressional resolution to affirm U.S. resolve and provide the president with a tool for flexible action.

Johnson, focusing on the Democratic convention in August and the fall presidential election campaign, puts Vietnam on hold. He wants a landslide. He knows he will not get it unless he goes into the campaign with clean hands. Wider U.S. actions will be suspended until after the elections. A code word is created to refer to the new timing: "December."

July 15, 1964

Barry Goldwater is nominated as the Republican candidate for president.

July 16, 1964

In his acceptance speech Goldwater declares, "Extremism in the defense of liberty is no vice." Most of the media and the majority of Americans laugh at the "hip-shooting" senator.

July 19, 1964

Washington finds it difficult to control political and military events in Vietnam. South Vietnamese General Nguyen Khanh, who had seized control of the government early in the year, begins to whip up war fervor in the South, breaking a promise to Lodge and Rusk to consult with the United States before making public his intention to declare war on North Vietnam.

Late July 1964

After what the Joint Chiefs of Staff call a "slow beginning," the clandestine Plan 34a raids against North Vietnam accelerate.

Doyle Dane Bernbach and the White House liaison complete work on the "definitive plan for the campaign on how to get through to the public." Twelve years after Eisenhower's primitive political commercials, Doyle Dane has created four enduring campaign innovations for Johnson's advertising:

1. The commercials do not show the candidate. Thus Johnson is able to keep his "wheeler-dealer" image out of the public's mind during the campaign. (Toward the end of the campaign some five-minute commercials showing Johnson were produced but were shown infrequently.)
2. The commercials substitute *theatrical* images for the traditional speechmaking images.
3. The commercials are unrelentingly combative and negative toward the opponent.
4. The commercials are intended to serve as surrogates for the traditional, formal, cross-country political campaign, for Johnson has decided he will be "The President" rather than "a candidate." This will enhance the image he is cultivating as a statesman and a humanitarian. (He had unfurled his Great Society domestic program in May and had rammed through Congress many of Kennedy's New Frontier programs that had been stalled at the time of the assassination.) More important, the surrogate commercials will allow Johnson to keep the covert war simmering, out of public view, unhampered by debate from the Republicans and questions from the press, who will continue to report on the line the White House chooses to give them.

July 30, 1964

Under the command of General William Westmoreland, South Vietnamese commandos attack two North Vietnamese islands in the Gulf of Tonkin. While the raid is in progress, the U.S. destroyer *Maddox* steams north into the Gulf of Tonkin on the second DeSoto intelligence mission of the year. There is no evidence that the captain knows in advance about the South Vietnamese raid. But apparently news of it is picked up by the *Maddox* from Radio Hanoi, as are Hanoi's instructions to its torpedo boats to attack the *Maddox.* The Pentagon papers analysis suggests that North Vietnam mistook the *Maddox* for a South Vietnamese escort vessel assigned to the raid. The North believed that the two operations were parts of a coordinated plot, but they were not.

August 2, 1964

North Vietnamese torpedo boats attack the *Maddox.* Two of them are damaged by planes from the U.S. aircraft carrier *Ticonderoga.* A third boat is sunk. The presence of the *Ticonderoga* in waters south of the Gulf of Tonkin is not explained by the Pentagon papers.

Nor is there anything in the Pentagon papers or in other studies of the war to indicate that a conspiracy existed in Washington and Saigon to bring the South Vietnamese raid and the presence of the *Maddox* together. But, as Ralph Stavins has written, "the absence of a conspiracy does not mean that there was no intent to *provoke*" the North (emphasis added). Every covert program was designed in part for that purpose. Tonkin was significant because it taught the United States government that the North could be provoked. As Walt Rostow [McGeorge Bundy's assistant for national security affairs] said in the State Department dining room two days after the Tonkin incident: 'We don't know what happened, but it had the desired result.' The United States government had discovered the way to legitimize the war."

August 3, 1964

President Johnson orders the destroyer *C. Turner Joy* to reinforce the *Maddox* and directs that both ships be sent back into the Gulf of Tonkin. The aircraft carrier *Constellation* is ordered to join the *Ticonderoga.* The Pentagon papers contend that these instructions are a "normal precaution" as a result of the first attack on the *Maddox,* not a plot to use the destroyers as bait for another North Vietnam attack. Nevertheless, on two occasions after that, torpedo boats operated by South Vietnamese secretly attack North Vietnamese coastal installations. The Pentagon papers show that the *Maddox* and the *Turner Joy* were both told that the raids would take place.

August 4, 1964 (Tonkin Gulf time)

North Vietnamese torpedo boats attack the *Maddox* and the *Turner Joy.*

August 4, 1964 (Washington time)

The Pentagon receives word of the attack. Previously planned military operations are activated. The Joint Chiefs of Staff select North Vietnam reprisal targets from a ninety-four-target list. Johnson orders the reprisals, approves readiness of Marine and Army units in the event of North Vietnamese or Chinese retaliation, and meets with key congressional advisers to tell them of the reprisal air strikes and to press for the swift passage of the joint congressional resolution. Later in the evening, aircraft from the *Ticonderoga* commence heavy bombing of North Vietnamese targets.

At 11:36 P.M. (E.D.T.) Johnson, on television, tells the nation of the reprisal raids. He says it is a "limited and fitting" response, and he promises, "We still seek no wider war."

August 5, 1964

The "limited and fitting" response includes readying Army and Marine units and moving an attack carrier group to the Western Pacific, interceptor and fighter bombers into South Vietnam and Thailand, and an antisubmarine task force into the South China Sea.

August 6, 1964

McNamara and Rusk testify in secret sessions of the Senate and House Foreign Relations committees on behalf of a joint congressional resolution granting President Johnson approval and support "to take all necessary measures to repel any armed attack against the forces of the United States and to prevent further aggression."

McNamara denies knowledge of South Vietnamese attacks on the North Vietnamese islands in the Tonkin Gulf. (And, obviously, he does not reveal that the United States inspired and directed the raid or that it was a part of secret U.S. military operations that had grown out of Johnson's National Security Memorandum 273, issued four days after he became president in November 1963 and officially approved by him as covert U.S. policy seven weeks later.)

August 7, 1964

The Johnson government fools everybody on Capitol Hill except senators Wayne Morse and Ernest Gruening, as what comes to be known as the Tonkin Gulf Resolution passes the Senate 88 to 2 and the House 416 to 0. In just three days the Johnson government has obtained two key parts of the May 23 scenario, which called for positioning of major U.S. strike forces and a congressional resolution authorizing wider action—with virtually no public or political debate or criticism.

Hoping to avoid a major escalation in Vietnam, the Johnson government goes into a holding pattern until after the election.

August 10, 1964

Washington and Khanh's weak South Vietnamese government interpret the Tonkin Gulf Resolution differently. To bolster his position, Khanh takes it to mean that he can prepare to invade the North. Washington believes it can bomb the North (and therefore support Khanh), but it does not want to use that authority until after the U.S. election. Although it is unthinkable to Johnson that he could lose to Goldwater, the president knows he must win big in order to make good use of the congressional resolution—or even to use it at all. Without the necessary American public opinion on his side—and *necessary* means the overwhelming majority—Johnson's use of U.S. aircraft, ships, and troops in Southeast Asia will be seriously questioned.

But Ambassador Maxwell Taylor, who has replaced Lodge, tells the Johnson government that if Khanh is not supported, his regime may collapse and a deal may be struck between the North and the South for a coalition government that will kick the United States out of Vietnam as its first order of business. Taylor is instructed by the State Department to oppose any North-South negotiations in Vietnam.

To complicate matters, Goldwater calls for full-scale air attacks on North Vietnam, thereby angering a sizable part of the American public and making many others uneasy. With three months to go before the election, Johnson must be careful not to let Goldwater force his hand.

United States policy during the election campaign will be to use all means short of open war with the North to shore up Khanh. The president's election campaign will provide an ingenious smoke screen; he will present himself to the voters as the candidate of reason and restraint, letting Goldwater prepare the American public for the post-election escalation of the war.

With Johnson having decided months before to limit his formal in-person campaigning (a way to perfect the media image of restraint), it will be up to the president's advertising to do the job.

August 1964, shortly before the Democratic convention

Doyle Dane Bernbach's advertising strategy for the president is approved officially by the White House. This is only a formality; many of the president's commercials (notably the "nuclear responsibility" spots) had to have been already produced, screened, and weighed by the people responsible for approving them, in the White House and on the Democratic National Committee, in order to be ready to go on television by Labor Day.

There are people at the Democratic National Committee who protest some of these commercials, but to no effect. Even if their protests had been successful, it is unlikely that Johnson's "appeals board," Clifford and Fortas, would have allowed them. Both men agreed strongly with Johnson on the vital need for not being defeated in Vietnam. As Richard J. Barnet has pointed out, both "kept feeding his personalized conception of the national interest"—especially Fortas, who almost nightly reminded him, "You do not want to be the first president to lose a war." It seems likely that Clark Clifford and Abe Fortas unreservedly approved Doyle Dane Bernbach's advertising.

August 26, 1964

The Joint Chiefs of Staff tell McNamara that an air war against the North is now "essential to prevent a complete collapse of the U.S. position in Southeast Asia." They disagree with Ambassador Taylor that the United States "should be slow to get deeply involved [in Vietnam] until we have a better feel for the quality of our ally [South Vietnam]. The United States is already deeply involved." The Joint Chiefs add that military responses against the North "must be greater than the provocation in degree [in the Gulf of Tonkin actions], and not necessarily limited to response in kind against similar targets." The memorandum is noteworthy because it marks the first appearance in writing of what has been the provocative strategy of the United States all along.

August 27, 1964

Lyndon Johnson is nominated for president. He tells the Democratic convention that since 1961 "we have carried out the greatest peacetime buildup of national strength of any nation, at any time in the history of the world." Johnson refers to "peace" ten more times during his address and closes with the ironic words, "Let us tomorrow turn to our new task. Let us be on our way."

September 3, 1964

In a memorandum to McNamara, John McNaughton, assistant secretary of defense for international security affairs, outlines a plan designed "to provoke" the North into again attacking the United States, thereby providing the United States with "good grounds for us to escalate if we wished."

But McNaughton is concerned with giving the provocative plan an aura of legitimacy during the president's election campaign. "During the next two months, *because of the lack of 'rebuttal time' before election to justify particular actions which may be distorted to the U.S. public* [which, he has noted, "must support our risk-taking with U.S. lives and prestige"], we must *act with special care*—signalling to the DRV [North Vietnamese] that initiatives are being taken, to the GVN [South Vietnamese] that we are behaving energetically *despite the restraints of our political season,* and to the U.S. public that we are behaving with *good purpose and restraint.*" (Emphasis added.)

September 7, 1964

At the White House, Johnson's senior national security advisers reach general agreement that air attacks will probably have to be launched against the North. The attacks are expected to start early in 1965.

On NBC network television the president's "anti-war" advertising smoke screen begins with the commercial *The Little Girl and the Daisy* (see page 47). Theodore White has written that it and two other Doyle Dane Bernbach commercials "deserve to go down in history as masterpieces of political television." One wonders whether White, who paid scant attention to the role of Vietnam in his account of the 1964

WHITE HOUSE CRISIS PHONE

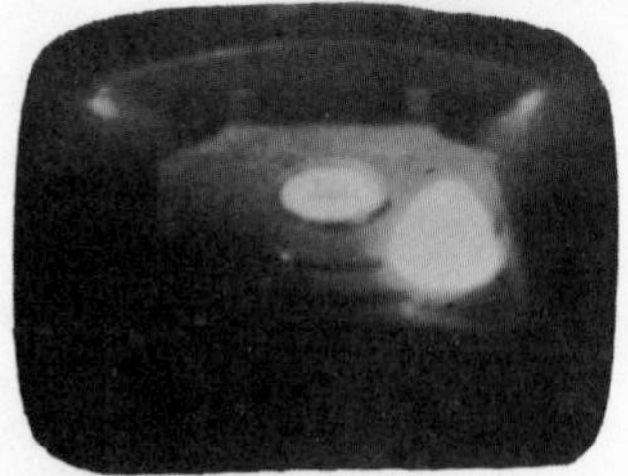

(PHONE BUZZING)
ANNOUNCER: This particular phone only rings in a serious crisis.

Is it in the hands of a man who's proven himself responsible?

campaign, ever came to realize the irony of his description or the deception of the massive advertising campaign.

September 10, 1964

Johnson orders limited covert measures against North Vietnam, including the resumption of covert coastal raids under Plan 34a and the resumption of DeSoto destroyer patrols in the Tonkin Gulf with air cover from U.S. carriers.

Johnson's interim orders represent an important victory for him at this stage of the campaign. As Ralph Stavins has shown, "During the election campaign, the Air Force had lined up in favor of Barry Goldwater for President and continually exerted pressure on Johnson" to take military action against the North. "It was the Air Force view that 'the American public should support any action taken by the United States government against the DRV' and that Johnson should, therefore, put his political fears aside." Despite Air Force pressure, Johnson "succeeded in selling his ' "keep cool" election strategy' to the [Joint Chiefs of Staff] as well as to his senior advisers."

THE LITTLE GIRL AND THE ICE CREAM CONE

WOMAN: Do you know what people used to do? They used to explode atomic bombs in the air.

Now, children should have lots of vitamin A . . . but they shouldn't have any strontium 90. . . .

These things come from atomic bombs. . . . They can make you die. Do you know what people finally did?

They . . . signed a Nuclear Test Ban Treaty, and then the radioactive poisons started to go away.

But now, there is a man who wants to be president of the United States, and he doesn't like this treaty. He's fought against it.

He even voted against it. . . . His name is Barry Goldwater, and if he's elected, they might start testing all over again.

TWO-FACED GOLDWATER

ANNOUNCER: When somebody tells you he's for Barry Goldwater, you ask him which Barry Goldwater he's for.

Is he for the one who said, "We must make the fullest possible use of the United Nations"?

Or is he for the one who said, "The United States no longer has a place in the UN"?

Is he for the Barry who said, "I've never advocated the use of nuclear weapons anywhere in the world"?

Or is he for the one who said, "I'd drop a low-yield atomic bomb on the Chinese supply lines in North Vietnam"? . . .

And how is a Republican supposed to indicate on his ballot which Barry he's voting for?

There is only one Lyndon Johnson. Vote for him on November 3. The stakes are too high for you to stay home.

SOCIAL SECURITY CARD

ANNOUNCER: On at least seven occasions, Senator Barry Goldwater said that he would change the present Social Security System.

But even his running mate . . . admits that Senator Goldwater's voluntary plan would destroy your Social Security.

President Johnson is working to strengthen Social Security.

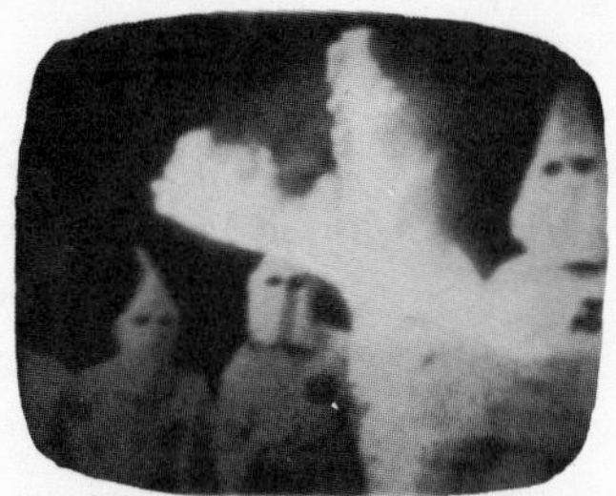

(DRUM UNDER THROUGHOUT)
ANNOUNCER: The majority of people in Alabama hate niggerism, Catholicism, Judaism. . . .

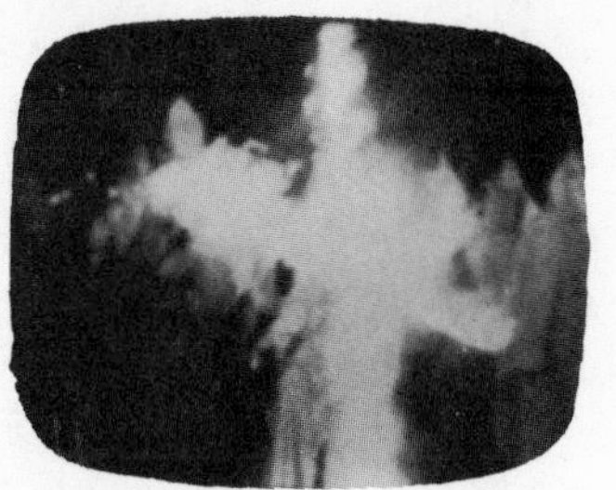

So said Robert Cleal of the Alabama Ku Klux Klan.

He also said, "I like Barry Goldwater. He needs our help."

September 15, 1964

Goldwater's futile advertising campaign begins. In his first television commercial the senator says, "Communism is the only great threat to peace. Some distort this proper concern to make it appear that *we* [the Republicans] are preoccupied with war. There is no greater lie."

September 17, 1964

The second Johnson "anti-war" commercial, *The Little Girl and the Ice-Cream Cone,* is broadcast. Later in the month the famous *White House Crisis Phone* commercial goes on the air.

Early October 1964

The Doyle Dane Bernbach–White House advertising strategy moves into high gear. Johnson's "anti-war" commercials are stepped up with the addition of the *Two-faced Goldwater* commercial. The issue of Goldwater's alleged "national irresponsibility" is added and hung around his neck with the *Social Security Card* and *Ku Klux Klan* commercials.

October 14, 1964

Johnson orders clandestine air strikes on North Vietnamese infiltration routes in Laos, with U.S. jets flying combat air patrol.

The Johnson government worries that negotiations in Paris to arrange a cease-fire between warring Laotian factions is not in the best interests of the United States. It fears that an agreement will lead to a Geneva Conference ending the Laotian war—which could in turn lead to the formation of a neutralist coalition in South Vietnam that would force the United States out.

November 1, 1964

Two days before the election the Viet Cong attack U.S. planes and facilities at Bien Hoa airfield near Saigon. Four Americans are killed and five bombers are destroyed and eight damaged. The Joint Chiefs term the attack "a deliberate act of escalation and a change of the ground rules under which the VC had operated up to now." They urge retaliatory action the same day and include a detailed plan. The president declines to act. He can practically taste his election mandate; he is not going to kick it away now.

However, Johnson appoints an interagency working group under William Bundy to prepare options for military and political action against North Vietnam. This is the one "concrete result" produced by the raid on Bien Hoa, the Pentagon papers say.

November 3, 1964

Lyndon Johnson is elected president by the greatest margin in American history. He beats Goldwater by nearly 16 million votes and wins all but six states. Now he has the mandate he so diligently sought to continue the work of the Great Society.

William Bundy's working group meets even as the votes are counted. Subject: handling world and public opinion—before and after further U.S. involvement in Vietnam.

November 6, 1964

McNaughton draws up three military-political options for U.S. action against North Vietnam. Each contains views established over the past year by the White House and the national security managers and authorized and approved by the president every step of the way:

- *Option A:* "Continue present policies [of covert action]."
- *Option B:* "Fast full squeeze." North Vietnam is to be bombed at "a fairly rapid pace and without interruption until we achieve our central present objectives."
- *Option C:* "Progressive squeeze-and-talk . . . to give the U.S. the option at any point to proceed or not, to escalate or not."

November 27, 1964

National Security Council principals recommend "that over the next two months we adopt a program of Option A plus the first stages of Option C." Option B was ruled out because it "ran the risk of nuclear war and international embarrassment."

December 1, 1964

The president approves the National Security Council recommendation.

December 14, 1964

Operation Barrel Roll begins with attacks by American jets on "targets of opportunity" along the Ho Chi Minh Trail. The National Security Council has previously agreed to "no public operations statements" unless a plane is lost, and then "to insist that we were merely escorting reconnaissance flights."

January 14, 1965

Two U.S. jets are lost over Laotian infiltration routes. A United Press International dispatch reveals publicly, for the first time, American air involvement in Laos—which dates back to May 1964.

February 6, 1965

The Viet Cong attack the U.S. military advisers' compound at Pleiku in South Vietnam and a nearby Army helicopter base, killing nine Americans and wounding seventy-six. The Johnson government now has the provocation it has planned for for over a year.

February 7–March 2, 1965

Johnson's decision is swift. Less than fourteen hours after the Pleiku strike, U.S. Navy jets attack North Vietnamese barracks and staging areas. The Viet Cong retaliate two days later, attacking an American barracks on the central coast. Johnson responds with a second air attack on North Vietnam and decides to launch a sustained air war against the North—code name, Operation Rolling Thunder. Date of first planning meeting: December 1963, one month after Johnson took office. The clandestine war ends; the overt war begins, though the United States will never officially declare it.

By the end of 1965, U.S. forces in Vietnam will number 184,314. By February 1969 the number will have grown to 543,000. By the time of the cease-fire four years later, 56,000 U.S. troops will die, 45,960 of them in combat. More than 303,600 Americans will be wounded, almost 600 will be captured, and no one will know what happened to another 1,300. Some 184,500 South Vietnamese troops will die, and 500,000 will be wounded. Some 927,000 North Vietnamese and Viet Cong troops will die. The permanent damage to the American fabric has yet to be calculated.

The Real Campaign Issue: The Size of Johnson's Mandate

Six television commercials for Lyndon Johnson's election campaign seriously affected the course of United States involvement in Vietnam. Yet not one of them would have been approved for broadcast had they been required to be judged by television standards for product commercials. All six would have been guilty—at the least—of being deceptive, misleading, and unfair.

None of them could have been modified successfully to fit the network code without losing the one thing they all had in common: an unfair and largely unwarranted attack on the Republican candidate. Removing this kind of campaign punch from Johnson's advertising would not have impeded his clandestine war, but it would have seriously affected his decision and his ability to make the war a wider, overt, full-scale struggle.

For the one ingredient that Johnson, his national security managers, and the Joint Chiefs required for the successful prosecution of their detailed plan for a non-Communist South Vietnam was the full and enthusiastic support of the American public and its congressional representatives. No one in the White House and few people in the country believed Goldwater would come close, even in losing. The only issue for the president, and the only task of the advertising, was piling up the votes. Nothing less than a *massive* mandate was required for Johnson to be able to say to the nation and the Congress, "Let us continue," without revealing in what direction.

The task was made easy beyond Johnson's fondest hopes by the perfect political foil, Barry Goldwater. Pressured by the small (in 1964) but articulate elements of the left and center among American public opinion leaders who were against a wider involvement in Vietnam, Johnson could "play off" Goldwater by appearing to be left and center in his advertising images. Pressured by the vocal right who advocated a deeper involvement, Johnson could go about his business secretly, planning for the wider war and knowing that Goldwater would pave the way for him.

Thus, two months after giving Johnson the largest election mandate ever handed an American president, some 43 million Democrats received the first inkling that they had been duped. At the same time, some 27 million Republicans were astonished to find that their wish to "give it to the Commies," if not their choice of who would administer the licking, had been granted. The president was sitting in the catbird seat.

Without the massive mandate, a much different picture would have emerged. Johnson might well have persuaded himself to hesitate in going ahead with his Vietnam adventure. The difficulty of keeping the secret war a secret much longer might well have caused him to reconsider and given him the opportunity to invent a statesmanlike excuse to withdraw with the dignity that would have satisfied his ego and the liberal left and center, while keeping the right at bay.

Without the mandate, the new Congress might have been less intimidated by a president who would not have been so powerful. They might have found the guts to stop themselves from rubber-stamping the wishes of the Pentagon and the strength to use their constitutional rights to check the runaway power of the Executive. They might have been provoked sooner to pass the legislation which would eventually restrict presidential war-making powers—even when a president uses the gambit of not declaring a war.

Without the mandate, the public—beguiled like sports fans by the victory at Tonkin Gulf—might sooner have found the cure to their war fever: the Truth. An angrier public might sooner have found the spark to ignite a bigger and wider public protest and thus might sooner have gotten on the backs of their elected representatives to do the same.

Without the mandate, the Americans who were hurt the most, those who died in Southeast Asia and all the others who served dutifully, would have received a fairer shake in their destiny and would sooner have understood what they were getting into and thus have had more incentive to resist going off to someone else's war like dumb sheep. The economy and social structure of America might have been spared the destruction it would shortly receive. The true nature of the world, and America's proper role in it, might have been better defined and altered.

Without the mandate, the "good" Lyndon Johnson might have been inspired to redouble his considerable energies on behalf of civil rights and poverty, two areas in which he had begun to make major contributions. He might have turned his attention to other serious problems overseas with something other than a warlike stance.

And without the mandate, one ironic twist of history might have been prevented: the return of Richard Nixon to politics.

Through the years it has become popular to believe that the margin of Lyndon Johnson's victory was almost preordained. True, Barry Goldwater could not have done much to lessen it. But challenging the truthfulness of the president's advertising could have trimmed that margin, and by a substantial and meaningful amount.

For two things would then have occurred. The White House smoke screen of peace would have been blown away, causing the president's men to scurry to find other smoke screens. They might have found some they could have made believable, and they might not; in any event, they would have been delayed. And no new smoke screen would have been as inventive and as effective as the "anti-war" advertising.

Even more damaging to the White House mandate scheme would have been the inevitable leaks to the press of the rejections of the commercials. This would have put the White House in the surprising position of being suddenly on the defensive publicly—if not on the run. The press might have decided to do some deeper digging about United States involvement in Southeast Asia. (The Pentagon papers were not published until June 1971 in the *New York Times.*) The public might have decided to wait and see before automatically pulling the voting lever for Johnson.

Rejection of the president's commercials might even have put some life into Goldwater's honest but dopey campaign.

5

THE MAKING OF A STRAW MAN, 1964

Barry Goldwater: Lyndon Johnson's secret image

Vote for President Johnson on November 3. The stakes are too high for you to stay home.

Tag line to President Johnson's advertising

When the White House and Doyle Dane Bernbach decided to make "nuclear responsibility" one of two major issues in the campaign, voters unaware of the facts behind the campaign rhetoric believed they faced a clear-cut choice: between their perceptions of the prudent Johnson and the crazy Goldwater, between the windy but constrained Texas preacher and the gunslinger from the Wild West.

In fact, Johnson and Goldwater were remarkably alike. As Richard Barnet has written, "The irony of the campaign . . . was that Johnson adopted the Goldwater policy. Indeed, the contingency planning actually conducted and put into effect by the Johnson Administration in Vietnam was extraordinarily similar to . . . recommendations prepared for Goldwater in early 1964 by one of his top foreign policy advisers."

Goldwater was no saint when it came to war, or at least to war talk. He was, after all, a major general in the Air Force Reserve. He was also a "religious anticommunist" who believed that American freedom was "imperiled by Soviet Communism" and who received instruction from his campaign advisers on "the virtues of tactical nuclear warfare," presumably to counter the threat.

Whether Goldwater really believed he would use America's array of nuclear weapons if he were elected president is arguable. What counted in the campaign was the talk that was attributed to him—for example, the notion that he would lob atom bombs into the men's room at the Kremlin to teach the Russians a lesson. With nuke craziness permeating the public consciousness long before the candidates were officially chosen, it was easy for Johnson and Doyle Dane Bernbach to portray Goldwater as "trigger-happy."

Part of Goldwater's problem was Barry Goldwater; he provided Johnson with two matchless qualities rarely found in a political opponent: (1) when he opened his mouth, he gave you a straight answer that was not necessarily the answer he meant to give or the answer you wanted to hear, and (2) the people he answered did not always listen to what he said. With a supercharged issue such as the nuclear bomb, Goldwater was in trouble the moment his lips moved.

F. Clifton White, the political media specialist who organized the Goldwater for President draft, realized his candidate's inability to play the political game early in the campaign. "The whole damn nuclear thing in regard to Barry was emotional. Boy, I went through logical arguments with people till I was blue in the face about what Barry had *actually* said. People would stand there . . . agreeing with me for twenty minutes, and when I got all through they'd say, 'But Cliff, we can't [use] the nuclear bomb.' "

Part of Goldwater's problem was that the press did a bad job of research on him, often substituting for facts what they *believed* he had said. Karl Hess, Goldwater's chief speechwriter, discovered that of the hundred reporters covering Goldwater for American and foreign newspapers and television who said they had done research on his views on Social Security, a majority believed that they had first read his views on a voluntary system in his best-selling book, *The Conscience of a Conservative,* published in 1960. "This is very interesting," Hess says. "The subject isn't covered in the book."

Another part of Goldwater's problem was that he sloganized issues instead of providing a full explanation of his views.

Without excusing Goldwater for his communication difficulties or ignoring his Strangelovian view of the world, it is important when reviewing the reasons for Johnson's massive landslide to understand that the sources on which the White House–Doyle Dane Bernbach portrait of Goldwater were based were often questionable, distorted, and untrue. Since (as Lyndon Johnson's advertising solemnly proclaimed) the stakes in the election were high, it is not mere hairsplitting to consider the truth behind several stories that were current during the campaign.

The Kremlin Men's Room Story

This silly story quickly became representative, in the public mind, of Goldwater's thinking. A year before the election Goldwater was asked to differentiate between the *accuracy* and the *reliability* of U.S. guided missiles. He replied in his usual homespun manner that the missiles were accurate enough "to lob one into the men's room at the Kremlin." He added derisively, "If they can be launched."

The supporters of Nelson Rockefeller, Goldwater's chief competitor for the Republican nomination in 1964, took Goldwater's words into the California primary and twisted them to read: Barry Goldwater " 'wants' to lob an A-bomb into the men's room at the Kremlin."

Rockefeller's distortion became famous. All Johnson and Doyle Dane Bernbach had to do was to capitalize on the trigger-happy atmosphere it had created. Though the celebrated Soviet toilet was never used in advertising, it became a major part of the foundation on which the "nuclear responsibility" commercials were based. Fourteen years later William Bernbach would justify the rationale of his commercials by saying, "Almost every commercial that we wrote for Johnson against Goldwater was a pure quote from Goldwater. Always. So we weren't saying anything that wasn't true." As proof, Bernbach remembers solemnly that Goldwater had said, "I would lob an atom bomb into the Kremlin."

The NATO Commander Story

At a 1963 press briefing in Hartford, Connecticut, according to Karl Hess, Goldwater said he would grant "more control over tactical nuclear weapons to 'the' NATO Commander."

But, says Hess, *commander* was multiplied by a reporter to *commanders* (plural), the implication being that Goldwater, as president, would indiscriminately give away his power to control the bomb to several field officers. Under the headline WOULD GIVE NATO COMMANDERS POWER TO USE A-WEAPONS, a *Washington Post* story described Goldwater as wanting "NATO commanders in Europe to have the power to use tactical nuclear weapons on their own initiative in any emergency."

Since the time of Eisenhower, the NATO commander has held the power to use tactical nuclear bombs on his own initiative in the event of an enemy attack if the U.S. president has been assassinated or if communications between NATO and Washington have been cut. In addition, the captains (plural) of America's sizable nuclear submarine fleet, armed to the teeth with nuclear missiles, have the same authority. So do the captains (plural) of America's Strategic Air Command planes loaded with nuclear bombs. Yet Rockefeller, and Goldwater's other rival for the nomination, William Scranton, had a field day with Goldwater's misquoted statement, and Johnson threw it at Goldwater with relish. During the controversy Johnson stated publicly that *only* the president had ever held the power to order a tactical nuclear attack and that *only* the president should have that power. (Not discussed or debated was why the use of nuclear weapons would even be considered.)

In fact there was only a modest difference between the Johnson and Goldwater positions on nuclear weapons and war. But the public did not know this, the press did not enlighten the public by its reporting, and Johnson's political media specialists were obviously not about to do anything to clear up the misunderstanding.

The Defoliation Story

The covert Operation Ranchhand had been defoliating jungles in North Vietnam since Kennedy approved the plan in 1962, undoubtedly with Vice President Johnson's knowledge. However, it was not until May 24, 1964, on the ABC television program *Issues and Answers,* that the defoliation issue exploded into the public consciousness. Again, it was not a deceptive Democratic government that was held culpable but a Republican candidate who, while not directly advocating defoliation, attempted to explain to newsman Howard K. Smith the difficulty of pursuing such measures. The exchange produced some of the most distorted coverage of Goldwater's ideas.

SMITH — Now a lot of [North Vietnamese] supply lines seem to run in on the Laotian border, in any case, through jungles and long trails. How could you interdict those . . . ?

GOLDWATER — Well, it is not as easy as it sounds, because these are not trails that are out in the open. . . . You are perfectly safe wandering through them as far as any enemy hurting you. *There have been several suggestions made. I don't think we would use any of them.* But defoliation of the forest by low-yield atomic weapons *could* well be done. [Emphasis added.]

A wire service report of the television interview had Goldwater advocating the use of atomic bombs in Vietnam. Newspapers played up the story with front-page headlines such as the *San Francisco Examiner*'s "GOLDWATER'S PLAN TO USE VIET A-BOMB." The New York Herald Tribune News Service reported that Goldwater had said he "would use low-yield atomic weapons to destroy jungle cover," the clear implication being that, if elected, he would not hesitate to take the United States into the thick of an atomic war against North Vietnam, Communist China, or any other nation that stood in America's way.

The effort of the White House and Doyle Dane Bernbach to hang a warmonger image on Barry Goldwater, while the Johnson government was itself making clandestine war on North Vietnam and constructing detailed plans for a wider, open war after the election, was as cruel an act of manipulating the public as has ever been perpetrated by a presidential candidate in American history.

Yet apart from the issue of a secret war, the "nuclear responsibility" advertising reflected a cynicism and an arrogance that no politician or political media specialist should be allowed to foist on an unsuspecting public. The extinction of humankind as we know it through the deliberate or accidental misuse of nuclear weapons (and nuclear energy) is not a subject that can be discussed responsibly in a commercial. The subject is so intense, so complicated, so enormous in its implications and repercussions, and so misunderstood, when measured against the everyday lives of most people, that the attempt to encapsule it within a commercial format was as irresponsible a gesture toward the uninformed public as it was damaging to Goldwater's candidacy.

Nuclear warfare and its prevention should have been discussed in 1964, as it should be discussed every year. Lyndon Johnson would have been the ideal person to lead a responsible discussion, using the power of television on behalf of his candidacy if he wished, to demonstrate honestly, ethically, and morally, if he could, his personal and presidential views on nuclear weaponry.

For example, he could have brought the voters up to date on the missions of America's eighteen nuclear-powered submarines and, in general terms, provided a rundown on the range, size, and firepower of the 288 nuclear-tipped missiles they carried as well as a preview of the additional twenty-three submarines and 368 missiles that were then in planning stages. The president could have touched on the unclassified activities of the 500 planes of the Strategic Air Command and the nuclear bombs (capable of far greater destruction than the Hiroshima variety) that they carried. He might have told the television audience something of the four-to-one ratio advantage in intercontinental ballistic missiles that the United States enjoyed over the Soviet Union and what advances had been made in arming U.S. troops with seven types of tactical nuclear weapons. He could have explained why such a nuclear arsenal was required if, as his commercials suggested, he abhorred the whole idea in the first place.

Calling on his famous powers of persuasion, Lyndon Johnson could have told his fellow Americans how many atomic megatons were required for deterrence and what it meant to deter an enemy of the United States. Did a nation use nuclear weapons as a bluffing device, or would the weapons actually be used in certain situations if required? What were the requirements? What would be the result? He could have explained how his views differed from Goldwater's views. No state secrets need have been revealed; he could have simply given the public an overview, as they say in Washington, just a few words of explanation of how and why U.S. tax dollars were being spent on nuclear armaments. That would have been more useful than giving the public the rather slim choice of either loving each other or going into darkness—the darkness, presumably, being the alternative offered by Barry Goldwater.

Of course any politician who would approve a commercial such as *The Little Girl and the Daisy* was obviously not about to tell the other side of the nuclear arms story or anything resembling it. That is where politics veers far from the ordinary truthful instincts that most people use to govern their lives—and why politicians do such great damage to the people they have been elected to serve. On moral grounds alone, the "nuclear responsibility" commercials should have been turned down without ever having been broadcast. Judged strictly as the product commercials they actually were, they would have been rejected for the dozens of network code violations they contained.

The Little Girl and the Daisy
Sixty-second Johnson commercial
Fifteen network code violations

(Illustration and text, page 47)

The violations of the network code by Johnson's commercials are numbered with reference to the list of eighteen typical product advertising violations cited on pages 5 and 6. The only violations there that do not apply to *The Little Girl and the Daisy* are numbers 6, 7, and 18.

1. No satisfactory evidence of the integrity of the advertiser.
2. Product or service (peace) unavailable (under conditions of prevailing U.S. foreign policy).
3. Lack of evidence to support claims (peace from Johnson, nuclear holocaust from Goldwater).
4. Taste of presentation unacceptable. (There is hardly a need to verify the preciousness of children in times of peace or war. But to use a child as a ploy in a one-sided presentation of the most serious issue facing humankind was a cheap shot that did not for a moment come to grips with either the problem of why nations arm themselves with nuclear weapons or the complicated task of dismantling these weapons systems.)
5. Competitor (Goldwater) not fairly and properly identified.

The parties who claim credit for creating the commercial maintain to this day a wide-eyed innocence about its meaning. Political media specialist Tony Schwartz has written, "Many people, especially the Republicans, shouted that the spot accused Senator Goldwater of being trigger-happy. But *nowhere in the spot is Goldwater mentioned.* There is not even an indirect reference to Goldwater." Another political media specialist, Joseph Napolitan, Schwartz's political mentor and frequent colleague, adds, "You know what the daisy spot says? Not one word in there about Goldwater. Not one word in there about whose finger do you want on the trigger. Nothing. It's *just* a girl picking petals off the daisy, the bomb and Lyndon Johnson saying we must love each other or die or some crazy thing like that."

The commercial was not designed to be a religious sermon from Lyndon Johnson. It was a faithful execution of the attack strategy of the White House. There was never a question about the meaning of the commercial or against whom it was directed.

8. Testimonials (on behalf of Johnson) do not honestly reflect in spirit and content the sentiments of the individuals represented (Johnson and Goldwater).
9. Claims and statements, including subjective evaluations of testifiers, are not supportable by facts or are not free of misleading implications.
10. Claims or representations have the capacity to deceive, mislead, or misrepresent. (The commercials deceived the public in not making Johnson's views clear and misled it in seeming to indicate Goldwater's views.)
11. Claims unfairly attack competitor (Goldwater).
12. Unqualified references to the safety of a product (Johnson's—not Goldwater's—policy regarding the bomb and other violent

means of warfare) if the normal use of the product (dropping it on another country) presents a possible hazard (annihilation).

13. The use of "bait and switch" tactics which feature goods or services not intended for sale (peace) but designed to lure the public into purchasing higher-priced substitutes (the war mandate—an unlikely substitute, but a substitute nonetheless).
14. Misuse of distress signals.
15. Scare approach and presentation with the capacity to induce fear.
16. Interpersonal acts of violence and antisocial behavior or other dramatic devices inconsistent with prevailing standards of taste and propriety.
17. Damaging stereotyping (of Goldwater's views).

The Little Girl and the Ice-Cream Cone
Sixty-second Johnson commercial
Thirteen network code violations

(Illustration and text, page 68)

This commercial, which seemed to be about the nuclear test ban treaty and Barry Goldwater's opposition to it, was in effect another White House–Doyle Dane Bernbach "anti-war" commercial designed to give Johnson an image of peace.

Few people are unaware of the dangers of nuclear testing and the potential consequences of radioactivity in the food chain. Yet this commercial addressed the danger in oblique terms, never telling why Goldwater was against the treaty (it might have strengthened Johnson's hand if it had); never revealing that *any* president, even Goldwater, would find it legally impossible to void the treaty on his own (the clear threat of the commercial); never pointing out that the test ban was between the United States and Russia and that other nations (China, for one) were continuing with aboveground testing and were throwing substantial amounts of poison into the atmosphere, including the air over the American dairy farms that supplied milk and cream for ice cream cones; never admitting that Johnson had had nothing to do with the test ban (contrary to the clear implication of the commercial, the ban was Kennedy's achievement); and never revealing that the United States was continuing with underground nuclear testing (the clear implication was that the United States had stopped *all* testing).

Goldwater's position on nuclear testing was fair game, and it should have been discussed—*discussed,* not telescoped into what amounted to sixty seconds of distortion. Thus the commercial was guilty of most of the same violations present in *The Little Girl and the Daisy:* numbers 1–5, 9–11, and 13–17, including taste and integrity of the commercial, unfair identification of the competitor, claims or representations with the capacity to mislead or misrepresent, misuse of distress signals, and scare approach with the capacity to induce fear.

White House Crisis Phone
Ten-second Johnson commercial
Fifteen network code violations

(Illustration and text, page 67)

Particularly underhanded were violations 2 (product offered—peace—unavailable under conditions of prevailing U.S. policy), 12 (unqualified references to the safety of a product—Johnson), and 13 ("bait and switch" tactics featured the lower-priced "peace" in order to lure the viewer into buying the higher-priced "war" substitute).

Two-faced Goldwater
Sixty-second Johnson commercial
Thirteen network code violations

(Illustration and text, page 69)

The violations in frames 6–8 alone included numbers 1–4, 8–15, and 17. Particularly offensive, unfair, and misleading were violations 4 (the tasteless portrayal of Goldwater as a boob, his finger stupidly to his mouth) and 10 (see page 81 for what Goldwater actually said about defoliation on *Issues and Answers*).

The president launched a second advertising front on the American mainland, attacking Goldwater for what were said to be his views on Social Security and connecting him deviously to the Ku Klux Klan. Each commercial in its own way was a landmark. Never before in American history had dirty politics obtained such currency with so many people so quickly. By the end of the campaign, as Theodore White observed, the *Social Security Card* commercial had "probably had greater penetration [into homes and minds] than any other paid political use of television except for Richard M. Nixon's Checkers broadcast in 1952."

Social Security Card
Twenty-second Johnson commercial
Fifteen network code violations

(Illustration and text, page 70)

This commercial was guilty of the same violations of code regulations as *The Little Girl and the Daisy.*

In one month alone in 1964—February—more than 19 million people obtained old age and disability benefits from Social Security. A high percentage of the elderly dutifully turn out to vote, and they tend to vote for the more conservative programs. This was too large a bloc for the White House to let slip away if it were to obtain its hoped-for election mandate.

With Doyle Dane Bernbach producing, the White House took dead aim on the elderly with a commercial showing two hands tearing up a Social Security card—in effect the Social Security cards of the elderly.

Had the commercial been rejected for broadcast for any one of its fifteen violations, the issue, which had been raging for much of the year, would have faded and gradually disappeared as a major campaign topic. Instead the elderly were persuaded that the torn Social Security card was a chilling preview of what Senator Goldwater might do to their retirement money if elected president. The commercial also presented a chilling forecast for some 90 million workers who were paying into the Social Security system and who expected one day to retire on their benefits. It was a false impression that Goldwater could not correct.

The history of the commercial began in New Hampshire on January 6, 1964, when the *Concord Monitor* virtually handed the White House the issue during the state's primary election campaign. A reporter asked Goldwater for his views on Social Security. He said—as he had said for years—that he *supported* the program and added, "I would like to suggest one change, that Social Security be made voluntary, that if a person can provide better for himself, let him do it."

The *Monitor* reported his remarks the following day under the grossly distorted headline, GOLDWATER SETS GOAL: END SOCIAL SECURITY.

No matter how often Goldwater denied that he intended to abolish the Social Security program, his opponents, beginning with Rockefeller and ending with Johnson, kept spearing him on the media-created issue. Goldwater explained his position in major campaign statements twenty-two times and four or five times daily at various quick campaign stops, according to speechwriter Karl Hess. To no avail; the *Social Security Card* commercial was so effective that some people, Hess has noted, believed they saw Goldwater himself ripping up the card.

Ku Klux Klan
Thirty-second Johnson commercial
Fifteen network code violations

(Illustration and text, page 71)

If the president's commercial dealing with Goldwater's alleged views on Social Security was deceptive, his attempt to link Goldwater with the Ku Klux Klan was immoral. So scurrilous were the implications of the Klan commercial that the people who still quarrel over the "honor" of having made *The Little Girl and the Daisy* cannot "seem to remember" the Klan spot at all, let alone want to claim credit for it.

Although the Klan had a membership of only 14,000 in 1964 (reduced from a peak of 5 million several decades before), it was the best-known hate group in America. Its hooded night riders and fiery crosses were the country's most instantly recognizable symbols of terror and fear. An attack by the Klan on black and white civil rights workers in tiny Southern communities still produced the notoriety to attract national media attention. So when Klan Grand Dragon Robert Cleal offered to endorse Goldwater, it was national news. So was Goldwater's rejection of the offer and his vigorous denunciation of the Klan. But when Goldwater's running mate, William Miller, in a politically extraneous defense of free speech, defended the right of anyone, including Klansmen, to support anyone they chose, that was just the incentive the White House and Doyle Dane Bernbach needed to capitalize on the Klan's endorsement. It was an irresistible opportunity to appeal to black and white liberals to make certain they turned out on November 3 to add their votes to Johnson's mandate.

The commercial that resulted was so clearly in violation of the television code that its creators apparently thought it best not to identify it officially as an advertisement for the president—or for anyone else. It simply floated onto the air, broadcasting anonymously and with impunity its message of guilt by association.

And the votes rolled in for Lyndon Johnson.

Three months after achieving his landslide mandate, Lyndon Johnson gave the order to commence the plan for the sustained bombing of North Vietnam that he had kept secret during his campaign for the presidency.

William Bernbach remembers that when he heard the news, he felt "not good, not good. Had I known then [during the election campaign] how Mr. Johnson would perform in the Vietnam situation I would not have done it [his advertising]. . . . I was sorry I did a lot of that stuff for them—for Johnson."

Not sorry enough, apparently; sometime before March 31, 1968—after nearly three years of continuous bombing, napalming, rocketing, and immense losses of civilians and troops from all three armies—Doyle Dane Bernbach agreed again to be the president's advertising agent for his reelection campaign.

But on March 31 a whipped Lyndon Johnson announced to the nation that he would limit the bombing—and then revealed that "I shall not seek, and I will not accept, the nomination of my party."

Doyle Dane Bernbach did not similarly decline to serve. A few months later the agency went to work for Hubert Humphrey.

6

THE UNSELLING OF THE PRESIDENT, 1968

How Hubert Humphrey's fatal advertising strategy put Richard Nixon over the top

What's on the tube is what counts.

Richard M. Nixon

On an autumn day in early September 1968, in an aging office building across from seedy Bryant Park on New York's 42nd Street, there occurred an incident so commonplace and unspectacular in the daily business of the city's advertising community that it does not seem possible it could have decided the outcome of the presidential election two months later.

Squeezed into a conference room at Doyle Dane Bernbach, some of the agency's most talented account executives, copywriters, art directors, and producers had assembled to hear William Bernbach himself present the advertising that they had no doubt would take Vice President Hubert Humphrey to the White House. Although Humphrey was far down in the polls, his campaign disorganized and short of money, Doyle Dane would do for him what they had done for Lyndon Johnson, albeit without a landslide.

Nor did the account team doubt that working for Humphrey was the right and necessary thing to do. The television images of Johnson's illegal war, which many in the room had done so much to perpetuate (however much they had been misled by the disgraced president), were ignored. That they had come to hate Johnson for his lies did nothing to tarnish their collective pride in the advertising they had created for him. Hubert Humphrey was not a Eugene McCarthy or a Robert Kennedy, whom many in the room had once favored and had donated their services to in the primaries earlier that year. Hubert Humphrey was an extension of Lyndon Johnson and the old war managers of the Democratic party. But the alternative was Richard Nixon. Or, God forbid, George Wallace. Working for Hubert wasn't so bad. And they *were* creating good advertising. Besides, electing a president, no matter whom, was still a heady experience, one the agency apparently could not leave alone.

Doyle Dane Bernbach had been retained by the White House when it seemed that Johnson would be running for reelection. An elaborate media strategy had been prepared. A sophisticated computer operation was set up to measure marketing concepts. Arie Kopelman, thirty years old, already a veteran account executive with an acknowledged flair for handling such package-goods accounts as Joy, Bold, Cinch, and Zest, ran the Humphrey account and knew precisely how he was going to advertise the vice president. "When I wrote the media plan, we looked at it as if we were marketing a product for Heinz or Procter and Gamble."

Into the conference room to review what Doyle Dane was going to do for Humphrey stepped the brusque Joseph Napolitan, boyhood friend and former partner of Humphrey's campaign manager, Lawrence O'Brien. Napolitan had worked with O'Brien on the Kennedy and Johnson presidential campaigns and some Senate races, and two years earlier, against the best advice and the worst odds, he had taken Milton Shapp, a "pretty honest," but not "very charming" businessman, and helped to make him governor of Pennsylvania—a Jewish governor, at that. Shapp's underdog victory had brought Napolitan to the crest of the emerging "new wave" of political media specialists, and he was anxious to protect his new reputation by not giving Doyle Dane Bernbach free rein over the Humphrey account, particularly after what he had seen of their work during the initial meeting with Bernbach in Chicago on the eve of the Democratic convention a few weeks earlier.

O'Brien had been frantic in Chicago, even before the bloody confrontation between the students and the police. Although it had appeared certain since Robert Kennedy's assassination in June that Hubert Humphrey would be the Democrats' candidate, no one in the Humphrey organization had prepared a campaign plan. And no one could pin down who in the organization was responsible for creating such a plan; Humphrey was surrounded by many people who worked hard for his nomination, patronage, and affection, but who had neglected to plot an election timetable. Realizing his plight, Humphrey pleaded with O'Brien to pull the campaign together as its manager. O'Brien in turn pleaded with Napolitan to help.

Napolitan's conditions were simple. The one condition that was to be Doyle Dane's undoing and was very likely to affect the campaign was his demand for complete control of the paid media program—the commercials, documentaries, and overall media plan.

When Napolitan had his first look at Doyle Dane's proposals before the convention, he had not yet signed on with O'Brien; he was simply on hand to report on the advertising as O'Brien's trusted and knowledgeable friend. His benign role, however, did not prevent him from making his opinions felt from the moment he walked into the meeting. Doyle Dane's approach, Napolitan wrote in a confidential memo to O'Brien after the meeting, "was typically Madison Ave.: there must have been 20 people there, all set 'to go to work,' and none of them having the vaguest idea of what the hell they are supposed to be doing. (And I don't think there were three Humphrey votes in the whole crowd.)"

William Bernbach presented ideas for twelve sixty-second commercials and one twenty-second spot. Bernbach is an accomplished speaker, smooth, confident, almost courtly, a pixie one moment and a grandfather the next, full of wise humor, with an outward appearance of kindness but as devastating as a finely honed knife. He is also acknowledged as one of the four or five best copywriters in advertising history. In the course of his career, Bernbach had made hundreds of effective presentations to far more difficult clients; he had no reason to believe the Humphrey presentation would be a problem. Then, too, Bill Bernbach had grown to know Hubert Humphrey very well and considered him a good friend.

The first storyboard Bernbach presented opened with a close-up of an elephant's head covered with the letters G.O.P. For the next sixty seconds the elephant is seen walking backward until it has disappeared, while a narrator recites what Napolitan thought was "a lengthy list of undigestible statistics" on the ills of the Republican party.

"That's a terrible use of television," Napolitan said.

Someone from the agency whispered, "*No one* talks to Mr. Bernbach that way."

"I *am* surprised at you," Napolitan told the legendary adman. "I'm surprised that *you* would do anything like this in television."

"*What* do you mean?" Bernbach asked.

"*Well,* you're dealing with a *camera,*" Napolitan said. "*What* you do with a camera—the world is yours. With a camera and movies you can include the world. Millions of things."

Bernbach was incredulous. Who was this man who knew so much about television? And who wasn't even an official part of Humphrey's campaign?

Bernbach exploded. "Look, *Mister* Napolitan, I'm sure you can tell me a lot of things about politics, but *don't* tell me about making an ad. If there's anything wrong politically with this [commercial], you tell me; *don't* give me any lectures on how to operate a camera or what to put in a commercial."

The exchange with Bernbach confirmed the doubts Napolitan had formed as a result of his previous encounters with advertising agencies. In his memo to O'Brien he wrote, "My experience working with other producers and agencies has made me extremely cynical and distrustful of advertising agencies per se, and there was little in what we saw today to cause me to change my opinion. I think it would be a grave mistake to let this agency continue unfettered."

But Hubert Humphrey had no television commercials ready, no radio commercials, hardly any good print material, not much money, and no time. With the election a little more than two months away, Napolitan recommended to O'Brien that men he termed *political* film producers be retained to work on the campaign. Napolitan also proposed that Tony Schwartz be hired and turned loose to create half a dozen commercials for Humphrey on his own. Doyle Dane Bernbach would produce only the few commercials that Napolitan had found acceptable.

Apparently unaware of Napolitan's recommendations, Doyle Dane Bernbach moved ahead briskly with its work. At the agency's headquarters in New York, Bernbach showed a newly filmed version of a storyboard that had been approved in Chicago. Napolitan brought with him a man named Jeno Paulucci, who had made a fortune selling canned Chinese food. (Humphrey was desperate for campaign contributions; that, not Paulucci's political expertise, seems to have explained his presence.)

"I watched the film in disbelief," Napolitan wrote later, describing how his creative view differed from Bernbach's.

Paulucci was less discreet. "Are you guys out of your fucking minds?" he asked Bernbach.

It is not recorded whether Bernbach stormed out of the conference room at that point, but the chances are that little of value would have been accomplished had he remained. Doyle Dane was as good as fired from the Humphrey account at that moment, though the official notification was not to be relayed to Bernbach until a few weeks later, while he was in Mexico.*

Advertising agencies are fired from accounts every day. Accounts move to other agencies, sometimes getting better results, frequently not. For Hubert Humphrey, however, the sudden departure of Doyle Dane Bernbach from his campaign may have been fatal.

Napolitan in effect gave the Humphrey account to himself (though he claims to have received no personal monetary payment from it other than for expenses). The account was moved to Campaign Planning Associates, an outfit that was (to quote presidential public relations observer Melvyn Bloom) "jerrybuilt for the purpose by Napolitan in cooperation with another New York advertising agency, Lennen & Newell [now defunct]." In fact the new media team was composed almost entirely of Napolitan appointees, longtime associates who had worked for him on other political campaigns.

Whether Napolitan's advertising was more effective than Bernbach's is moot. In his original memo to O'Brien, Napolitan criticized Doyle Dane's ideas for Humphrey as lacking "warmth and conviction and emotional appeal" and failing to "indicate that Humphrey is tough and decisive." Some commercials, he thought, "might be too slick."

It would appear that Doyle Dane Bernbach was more than capable

*As so often happens in the advertising business, there seems to have been more to Doyle Dane's firing than what Joe Napolitan thought of its political advertising skills. Napolitan had been as irritated as Bernbach had been about the dispute over the authorship of Johnson's *The Little Girl and the Daisy* commercial for the 1964 campaign. The difference was that Napolitan believed Tony Schwartz was responsible for the commercial, and Tony Schwartz was Napolitan's good friend and frequent political associate.

Napolitan relates this story about what happened when he first met the Doyle Dane people, before the Chicago convention: "They didn't know of my association with Tony because after the presentation they were saying that in 1964 [they] made the daisy spot. And I said, wait a minute, what the hell are you talking about? *You* didn't make the daisy spot, Schwartz made the daisy spot. Oh, no, he didn't [Doyle Dane said]. They called Schwartz [from Chicago] to say that if I asked him, would he please [say] that Doyle Dane had made the spot. *It was another nail in [Doyle Dane's] coffin.*"

The work of Tony Schwartz has had an effect on the political advertising of the Democratic party—and therefore on the party's influence on the fortunes of the nation—that goes far beyond his professional importance. Of all political media specialists over the past sixteen years, he alone seems to have been associated on a nearly continuous basis with the moves of the Democrats. Democratic candidates flock to him for help (Senator Edward M. Kennedy hired Schwartz to create radio commercials for him for the 1980 primaries), and he has helped them—sometimes with political advertising that some consider to be of questionable taste. What is pertinent about Schwartz and other political media specialists, however, is that they demonstrate how major political policy shifts are often the result of the seemingly marginal activities of a handful of people who are not even connected officially with the machinery of the party or the country. In an electronic age the connection is one that political philosophers might do well to ponder.

of making misguided political commercials. Yet few of its consumer advertising competitors in 1968 would have characterized the agency's creative work as Napolitan had. Doyle Dane's reputation, its fortunes, and the fortunes it had brought its clients were built on precisely the opposite attributes.

As it turned out, Napolitan's commercials for Humphrey suffered from the same charges he had leveled against Doyle Dane. In addition, he violated his own cardinal rule of "defining the message we wish to communicate to the voter." While Napolitan realized astutely that Hubert Humphrey was fighting George Wallace as well as Richard Nixon, he did not know how to attack the problem with the political advertising that was supposedly his forte. Napolitan's solution, to combine both enemies within the framework of single commercials, was simply bad advertising in a medium where the cardinal rule is "never build a commercial around more than one idea." In a typical commercial for Humphrey, Napolitan had the off-camera announcer talking pejoratively, first about Nixon on Vietnam, then Wallace on law and order, then Nixon on Medicare, then Wallace on taxes, then Nixon on international politics. Not until the final seconds of the commercial did the viewer learn that the commercial was about Hubert Humphrey. It was murky, directionless advertising.*

Bernbach never again committed his agency to political advertising. But time does not seem to have soothed his ego from the effects of the loss of the Humphrey account. Years later, his voice rising between contempt and embarrassment, Bernbach felt no need to be diplomatic in describing the caliber of Doyle Dane's successors. "The people surrounding Mr. Humphrey were . . . not second-rate people, they were third-rate and fourth-rate people."

Bernbach's observations may be correct. But in the 1968 presidential campaign, as far as Hubert Humphrey was concerned, it may not have been the quality of the advertising that cost him the election but the fact that there was too little advertising of *any* kind. Not until five weeks before the election did the first Humphrey commercial appear on television. One month of valuable time had been lost to what amounted to a bitchy, personal, and ill-advised feud. The smallest degree of con-

*Interestingly enough, much of Humphrey's advertising, had it been required to pass a television code of taste and ethics, would have done so. However, two commercials that were neither murky nor directionless but unfair and disparaging would not have passed. And that might have been just as well for the Democratic candidate. For the commercials attempted to make light of what was mistakenly perceived by the Democrats to be a Republican liability, Spiro Agnew. The strategy probably lost more votes than it gained.

ciliation between Napolitan and Bernbach might have made all the difference to the Democrats.

In the meantime Richard Nixon had had a battery of well-produced and (for his purposes) perfectly targeted commercials hitting away on all fronts at the Democrats during prime television viewing time. Most of what the nation saw of Hubert Humphrey on television in September were repetitious snatches of him on the news programs, shouting hysterically at anti-war hecklers who were on his tail everywhere he spoke. The contrast between the low-keyed, confident Nixon commercials and a Humphrey who had lost his composure could not have been more devastating to the Democrats' cause.*

The packaging of Richard Nixon in 1968 became an instant part of American political and advertising lore. Yet had there been a television code for political advertising, his commercialization would have failed it. Forcing the Nixon advertising people to correct code violations in the candidate's key commercials on poverty, law and order, and Vietnam would have been tantamount to changing the political strategy of his campaign—and this they could not have done and still hoped to win.

The idea of viewing Nixon as a neatly tied package is too simple. He was not one package but many, each one designed to suit the dreams and demands of different groups, not to mention what appears to have been his own deep desire to possess many faces without seeming to be two-faced.

The mistake of viewing Nixon merely as a political package lies in the assumption that the images projected on television had nothing to do with his intentions upon reaching the White House. If Lyndon Johnson had used political advertising to obscure his intentions, Richard Nixon used it to provide some very generous signals about his. That the signals were as malicious and deceptive as Johnson's camouflage only demonstrates the remarkably flexible ability of unregulated political advertising to do damage to the political system.

For example, Nixon made no bones about his intentions to break the Democrats' antipoverty program, although at a conscious glance his commercials did not *seem* to convey such a message.

*This is not to say that the pictures and sounds on television of an America frustrated by Vietnam did not produce a refreshing breath of air in the history of the illegal war. Humphrey, freed of Johnson, began to move away slightly from the administration's war policies. But he never took on the issue where it would have counted most, in his commercials. Nixon, on the other hand, having lost none of his cunning, used his advertising to sell the *illusion* of ending the war. Many voters were willing to believe him.

(MUSIC THROUGHOUT)
NIXON: . . . We've been deluged by government programs for the unemployed . . . for the cities . . . the poor.

And we have reaped from these programs an ugly harvest of frustration, violence, and failure across the land.

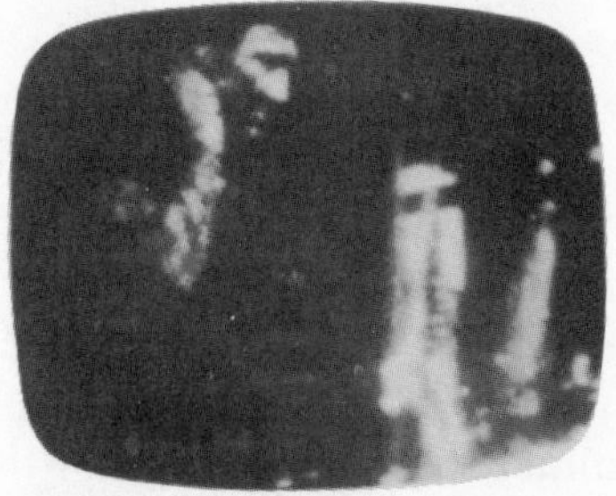

Now our opponents will be offering more of the same. . . .

It's time to quit pouring billions . . . into programs that have failed.

What we need are not more people on welfare rolls, but more people on payrolls. . . . we should enlist private enterprise which will produce progress, not promises, in solving the problems of America.

(SILENCE)

(SILENCE)

In one commercial ostensibly aimed at the problems of blacks, Nixon spoke of rescuing the ghetto from its despair, but not "with the old solution, the handout." He claimed to advocate a program he called Black Capitalism, which would result in more "black ownership of business and land and homes." This, Nixon said, would "end our racial strife." How the impoverished blacks would become capitalists was not specified.

In another commercial Nixon described an America deluged by government programs for the unemployed, the cities, and the poor and the "ugly harvest of frustration, violence, and failure" that he claimed the programs created. Once more, private enterprise would solve "the problems of America."

But Nixon was not talking to blacks, other ethnic poor, and working-class citizens. He knew that they rarely if ever voted for him. He did not think he could convert them to his cause, nor did he try. And Nixon surely was not talking to the traditional audience who felt obliged to "help" minorities: the urban liberals and the former urban liberals who had transferred their dreams and their guilt to the suburbs. Nixon laundered his message in the commercials, addressing not the blacks but "his people" from the smaller towns of America, and Democrats who longed to be conservative.

When Nixon spoke of America's problems, did he mean the problems of the ghettos or the problems the ghettos were causing white middle Americans who considered they had pulled themselves up by their own bootstraps without anyone's help? When he spoke of "our racial strife," did he mean the harm done to the entire country by race war, or the harm done only to Nixon's white constituents? It would appear that Nixon meant to keep poor and black America separate from middle America, and he was signaling middle America that, if elected, he would "protect" them from the welfare cheats, youthful hoods, and other shiftless people on the dole.* Theodore White has written that Nixon "conspicuously, conscientiously, calculatedly denied himself all racist votes, yielding them to Wallace." *Overtly* racist

*Once in office, Nixon, true to his advertising signals, impounded urban renewal and model city funds generally earmarked for "big city voting areas." Impoundment of previously allocated federal funds was a favorite Nixon tactic (as it was to his predecessors) for outflanking the Congress; he intended to use it as "a method for reshaping social priorities along the lines he wished"—not necessarily what the people needed. In the long run, say Nixon's critics and foes, what was important to him was not a specific program, social or military, but *how* he could use a program to further tighten his grasp on the reins of government for the power and privilege he believed was due the office of president and was necessary to run the presidency—virtually a fourth branch of government that since the time of Franklin Roosevelt had been accruing power outside the constitutional system of checks and balances.

votes perhaps; hidden in the images of these commercials were barely concealed appeals to the silent racist votes belonging to Spiro Agnew's Silent Majority.

Yet in appealing to the silent racists, Nixon's poverty commercial, for example, was guilty of nine violations of the television code. The commercial misled viewers in general with the unsupported claim that violence in the country was the result of a deluge of government programs. It misled the poor and blacks by indicating that they could be helped by private enterprise. It misrepresented its case by suggesting that private enterprise take over from the government—typical Republican rhetoric but clearly an impossibility on the massive scale that would have been required. Nixon knew this and did not support his message with facts because he could not. The commercial was unfair to Humphrey when Nixon accused his opponents of offering more of the same kinds of programs, which was not necessarily the case. The commercial was also guilty of misusing distress signals, trading on interpersonal acts of violence for Nixon's own purposes, and using unsupported or exaggerated promises of employment or earning. Together, these violations brought the most serious charges of all: lack of integrity of the advertiser and unacceptable taste of the advertising presentation.

In a series of three commercials ostensibly aimed at solving the problems of crime, Nixon again preempted for himself the imagery of the big city, but not, as we have seen, for the votes he knew he would not receive in the traditional Democratic strongholds of New York, Chicago, Pittsburgh, Detroit, Philadelphia, Boston, and Washington.

When, in a commercial his political media specialists called *Crime,* Nixon pledged that "the wave of crime" would not be "the wave of the future in America"; when, in a commercial called *Order,* he charged (against a background of rioting mobs and burning buildings) that "there is no crime that justifies resort to violence"; when, in a commercial called *Woman* (featuring a middle-aged woman walking by herself on a lonely street on a rainy night while a figure lurked behind her), he vaguely announced a campaign to take the "offensive" against robbery, mugging, and murder, Richard Nixon was not speaking to those who regularly took the most punishment from urban criminals: namely, their ghetto neighbors. Instead he was crusading on the backs of inner-city slum dwellers to appeal to the law and order votes that were in the hands of those who existed outside the dark and dangerous places.

If subjected to the network code for product advertising, all of Nixon's law and order commercials would have been rejected by the networks in the first instance for using a blatant scare approach with the capacity to induce fear.

While Nixon's staff believed that law and order was his bread-and-butter issue, Nixon himself always thought that the issue was Vietnam and America's strong desire for peace—a peace that he, not Humphrey, would make. Nixon summed up for his speechwriters the Vietnam strategy in both party camps: "If there's war, people will vote for me to end it. If there's peace, they'll vote their pocketbook—Democratic prosperity."

From early September, as the Humphrey propaganda machine stood dead still on the rails while awaiting the switch in advertising agencies, Nixon banged away at the mismanagement of the war and the great loss in lives and prestige. His vague solution, "an honorable end to the war," simply called for the country "to turn to new leadership," and his lead in the polls climbed week after week. Yet hovering beyond his reach was the specter of Lyndon Johnson's last hurrah.

For much of that spring and summer and into the fall of 1968, the venerable Democratic politician Averell Harriman and his deputy, Cyrus Vance, had been negotiating with the North Vietnamese in Paris for a halt to all American bombing in the North and the involvement of South Vietnam in peace negotiations. The discussions and the proposed terms were kept secret to the best of anyone's ability and fancy. In October the Soviets secretly entered the diplomatic scene, believing that an end to the war was in their best interests. After months of stalemate there was a swirl of peace activity, and a breakthrough in negotiations appeared possible.

On October 16 Johnson phoned Nixon, Humphrey, and Wallace to tell them that a settlement was near. Johnson "asked all three candidates to think of 'what was best for their country' and drop Vietnam from public debate."

Nixon might have been excused for thinking that Johnson's phone call was directed wholly at his candidacy. His well-advertised, deliberately cloudy solution to the war was, in his mind, about to pay off in the public consciousness. Every day that he could propagandize Vietnam meant points he could deny Humphrey in the polls and votes for himself on election day. Thus Johnson's secret peace initiative seemed to Nixon to be a typical, calculated Democratic trick to snatch the White House from him at the last minute. Still, Nixon felt he had no choice but to delete the war theme from his campaign. Nevertheless, although his lead in the polls began to narrow almost immediately, Nixon had already made sufficient use of the war in his *Vietnam* commercial, in speeches, and in his "spontaneous" question-and-answer television programs to accumulate great political capital—and the margin of victory.

Vietnam
Forty-second Nixon commercial
Six network code violations

In this commercial Nixon was guilty of hitching a ride on the war-weary backs of American soldiers and Vietnamese peasants. This brand of taste, by network product standards, was unacceptable. So were his scare approach, his use of distress signals, and his use of interpersonal violence. What was Nixon's solution in Vietnam that was not "tied to the policies of the past"? He did not say, and therefore he earned another violation for not supporting a claim. All these violations combined to make the commercial grossly unfair, not just to Humphrey but to the American people, and therefore it was not qualified for broadcast.

There was another fascinating aspect of almost all of Nixon's commercials that may have had a powerful effect on viewers without their being in the least conscious of it. At least one of the key people who worked on the commercials suspected that this was true.

"Have you noticed?" he says to journalist Joe McGinniss. "The same faces reappear in different spots. The same pictures are used again and again. They become symbols, recurring like notes in an orchestrated piece. The Alabama sharecropper with the vacant stare, the vigorous young steelworker, the grinning soldier."

McGinniss asks whether this is "insidious."

The filmmaker smiles. "Yes: the effect of the stills can be almost subliminal. In less than a minute you can get up to forty images, each with a different time, place and face, so you can create an impression that is altogether different from what is being said."

Nixon and his men had learned much about using television in the years since his loss to John Kennedy in 1960, when media cult leader Marshall McLuhan had written, "Without TV, Nixon had it made."

Hubert Humphrey's month-long advertising silence left television viewers with a choice of three negative impressions: Humphrey did not have a Vietnam policy that he wished to talk about, he was afraid to

VIETNAM

(SOUNDS OF WAR)

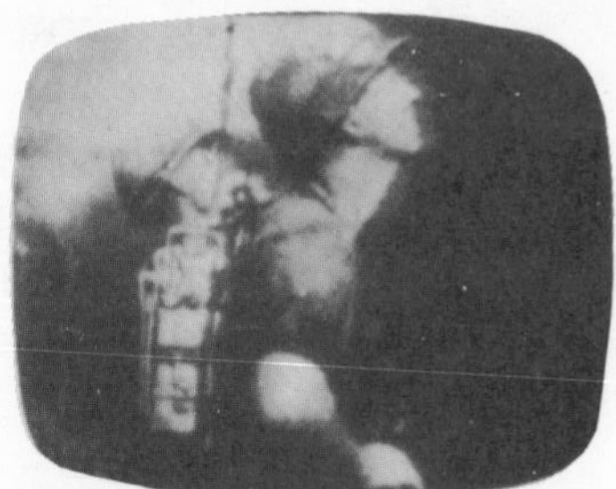

NIXON: Never has so much military, economic, and diplomatic power been used so ineffectively as in Vietnam.

If after all of this time . . . sacrifice and . . . support, there is still no end in sight . . .

I say the time has come for the American people to turn to new leadership

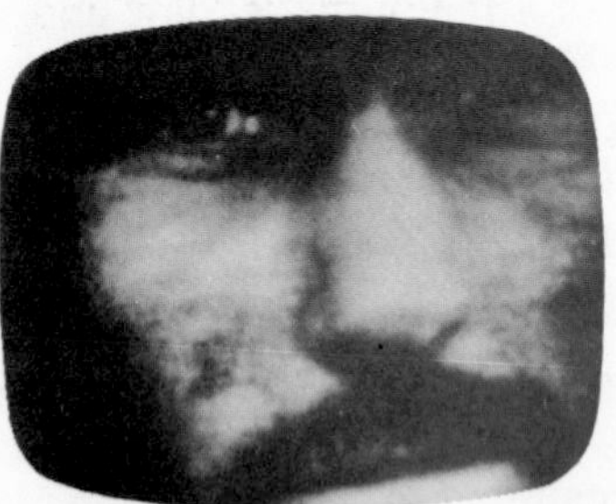

not tied to the policies and mistakes of the past. I pledge to you we shall have an honorable end to the war in Vietnam.

(SILENCE)

disagree with Lyndon Johnson's policies, or he in fact agreed with the castrated but spasmodically powerful president.

If is treasured above all words in the vocabulary of political losers. For Hubert Humphrey in 1968, the difference between the ifs that were to work against him and those that might have been converted to his political gain came down in the end to a heartbreaking fraction of the 72 million votes cast.

If 336,371 votes had shifted to Humphrey out of a total of 13,140,804 votes cast in four states that Nixon won narrowly—California, Missouri, Alaska, and Ohio—Humphrey would have won the required electoral votes to be elected president.

If 100,077 votes had shifted to Humphrey out of a total of nearly five million cast in Ohio, Alaska, and Delaware, or 3 percent of the vote in California alone, enough electoral votes could have been taken from Nixon to have thrown the election into the House of Representatives, where most political analysts believe Humphrey would have won.

If Eugene McCarthy, whose showing against Johnson in the New Hampshire primary made him a serious presidential candidate for much of 1968, had even tacitly endorsed Humphrey at the Democratic convention, his legions of youthful supporters might have turned out for Humphrey in far greater numbers.

If Martin Luther King had not been assassinated, there would not have been the rioting, burning, and looting in the black ghettos that was induced by King's death and that gave Nixon a ready-made "law and order" issue.

If Humphrey had spoken out against the bombing of Vietnam earlier than September 30 in Salt Lake City, he might have won the votes he needed, particularly from young people, many of whom simply did not vote at all.

If Lyndon Johnson had halted the bombing of North Vietnam earlier than October 31, Humphrey would have profited enormously.

If Johnson had not chosen Chicago as the convention city for its promise of security and Mayor Richard Daley's political patronage, the tone of the street demonstrations might have been altered sufficiently to have avoided the bloody confrontations between the young and the police. And without the albatross of the most savage convention in American political history, Humphrey might well have obtained the votes he needed.

If Humphrey had had the wisdom and the guts to talk about the reasons for the anger of the young and the hostility of parents toward their children, he might have bridged the generations and won more votes in the same families.

If Nixon's advertising had been exposed by the press for the injustices it contained, his campaign strategy would have to have been altered—to Humphrey's benefit.

If; more ifs and more crucial extrapolations from them than in any national election in recent memory. The combination of ifs working against Humphrey should have been devastating to his campaign, for he had neither the power nor the ability (nor the luck, for the most part) to control their effect on his candidacy. Yet he almost won, and that makes the focus all the more critical on the one if which was independent of political tides and collisions of fate and which Hubert Humphrey could have controlled completely but let slip from his grasp: his advertising.

Judging by every known measurement of the power of television, if there had been even a little advertising for Humphrey in the right place at the right time—in key counties in key states—his narrow loss could have been converted into a narrow victory.

But advertising is costly, and for the Democrats the lack of campaign money was a serious concern. The nervous, disorganized party, beset by internal squabbles and Vietnam, found it hard to raise money. Most of what came in was used to keep Hubert Humphrey and his staff going—traveling, speaking, meeting the faithful. That, not the media, was the main thrust of his old-fashioned campaign.

Not until the final week of the campaign, with Humphrey running neck and neck with Nixon in the polls (despite the ifs), was there a half million in additional funds for television. Too late; the detailed television media schedule prepared by Doyle Dane Bernbach before the convention in August, but never implemented following the switch of the Humphrey account to Napolitan's people, reappeared as suddenly as the newfound money to haunt the Humphrey drive. "Humphrey campaign managers found themselves literally unable to buy television time in California—all the time available for politics had been bought up by local and state candidates previously."*

*After the election Napolitan seemed to have second thoughts about the people at Campaign Planning Associates/Lennen & Newell who bought television time for Humphrey. He wrote that the job the time buyer does in a major campaign "can make the difference between winning and losing an election. I'd go so far as to say that if Ruth Jones [an astute time buyer who usually worked for Republicans] of New York had been buying time for Hubert Humphrey instead of Richard Nixon in 1968, Humphrey would have been elected president, or at least the race would have gone into the House of Representatives." Doyle Dane, it should be noted, has always employed some of the best time buyers in the business.

Joseph Napolitan believes that an expenditure of as little as $50,000 on media advertising in certain states during the final campaign week could have swung the necessary votes to Humphrey. But it would be a mistake to think that the Democrats' inability to spend money when it was needed was the last straw in Humphrey's defeat. Had key Democratic campaign managers not held what seems to have been an unconscious bias against television, hundreds of thousands of dollars could have been rechanneled at any time during the campaign from Humphrey's heckled stump speeches to television advertising. Instead, Napolitan and Bernbach, the two people who could have lobbied best for television funding had they acted together, fought like proud lions for their piece of the campaign turf while the campaign dribbled away.

The irony is that the more Humphrey had advertised, the greater his chances would have been to project a more positive and possibly a more correct image of himself, the higher he would have stood in the polls at an earlier date, and the easier it would have been for him to raise more money to buy advertising.

Thus Richard Nixon's well-advertised victory was not so much the product of his packaging as it was the failure of Hubert Humphrey's campaign managers to utilize television effectively.

7

INSIDE THE NOVEMBER GROUP, 1972

The White House starts a private advertising agency, and the dance of the leaders goes on

"There were four basic personnel groupings for undercover operations," Deep Throat said. The November Group, which handled CRP's advertising; a convention group, which handled intelligence-gathering and sabotage-planning for both the Republican and Democratic conventions; a primary group, which did the same for the primaries of both parties; and the Howard Hunt group, which was the "really heavy operations team."

Bob Woodward and Carl Bernstein,
All the President's Men

White House staffs have always influenced presidential advertising, but never before 1971 had an advertising group actually been an organizational arm of the White House—in this case a White House in which manipulation, bribery, threat, theft, extortion, money laundering, and war was a way of life. Because George McGovern's campaign for the presidency was so inept, it will never be known how dangerous to the political system this unregulated advertising agency, the November Group, formed and supervised by the White House and fed by the unlimited cash gathered by the bagmen of the Committee to Re-elect the President, could have become. With Watergate as a measure, however, it takes only a little imagination to paint a picture of a White House not only manipulating the media but actually *creating media*—in effect a state-run advertising/propaganda mechanism, unauthorized by the public or its representatives and with much greater power than the White House press office or the public relations departments of the various government agencies, able to "create the truth" without prior restraint, able to plant advertising seemingly signed by "other" sources, able to use its own transmission facilities to beam its messages onto home television screens during an election campaign—or at any other time—without initial suspicion or interference or regulation by other government bodies.

It is very much a *1984* vision, and one which has not disappeared with Richard Nixon's demise. That the November Group was duped by the White House, along with the voters it sought to persuade of Richard Nixon's good intentions, does nothing to alter either the vision or the danger.

To appreciate the danger posed by an agency such as the November Group, one must remember what Nixon expected to achieve in his second term and how his creation, the Committee to Re-elect the President (CREEP), was to help him obtain it.

Nixon—the poor boy with the second-rate college degree, the political novice with the brilliant instinct for and the need to practice dirty politics, the wounded political pro who forced himself down the throat of a party that despised but required his tactics in order to survive—seemed to believe with Hegel that "leaders are exempt from moral obligations if they are great enough." Nixon, the eternal bench sitter, saw for himself the chance to be great and perhaps uniquely powerful. His ability to gain power would be checked only by his inability to circumvent a federal bureaucracy which was dominated by its own regulations, self-interest, and unwritten codes.

To further his ambitions, Nixon hired a staff composed of unquestioning men drawn from the FBI, the CIA, the military, law firms, and, notably, advertising agencies. No senior White House staff in history had contained advertising people; Nixon's had them in key positions. It was no accident.

During Nixon's first term, as Marcus Raskin has pointed out, his men were "assigned very specific tasks" that were "calculated to liberate the President, in his second term, from dependency on either the Republican party, the recalcitrants in the bureaucracy and the Congress, or the citizenry."

Among the tasks and assignments, according to Raskin, were:

> The congressional Republican party was downgraded and shunned. (Ehrlichman and Haldeman)
>
> The Democrats were cast as enemies of the state and sovereign. They were surveilled, confronted, and, if necessary, personally discredited. (Colson, Chapin, and Haldeman)
>
> Phones were tapped, with an increase in break-ins, burglaries, entrapment. (Mitchell, Mardian, and Ehrlichman)
>
> Political dissidents were controlled through limited martial

law, informers, harassment, and entrapment. (Rehnquist, Mardian, Kleindienst, and Mitchell)

Universities and schools were encouraged to adopt stringent rules of behavior and admissions standards, expelling students who did not comply. Grants and federal contracts were withheld from unfriendly university administrations. (Agnew and Colson)

National security became a justification to eliminate any type of politics deemed threatening. (Mitchell and Kissinger)

Members of the bureaucracy were watched and bugged for any signs of disloyalty. (Haldeman, Ehrlichman, Mitchell, and Kissinger)

Secret wars were fought and secret negotiations were carried on without the knowledge of the Congress and without any form of accountability. (Kissinger, Laird, and the Joint Chiefs of Staff)

Police budgets were substantially increased with federal funds used for equipment, centralization, and quasi-militarization of the police. (Kleindienst and Santarelli)

Millions of dollars collected through CREEP were controlled by Nixon's personal lawyer. The funds were used for any purpose the President and his clique deemed necessary. (Kalmbach and Ehrlichman)

When and where necessary, such activities were hidden with the claim of executive privilege. (Kleindienst and Dean)

The media were intimidated. (Agnew, Buchanan, and Whitehead)

Under the guise of saving money, congressionally appropriated funds were not spent except for projects which the President had cleared. In other words, the President would set and enforce his own social priorities in the face of laws and acts of Congress. (Weinberger, Shultz, Malek, and Ash)

CREEP was to be Nixon's means of controlling the bureaucracy. After his 1972 landslide victory, he obtained the resignations of two thousand government officials. Raskin notes that he "left hundreds of policy-making offices empty through the first year of his second term, although he filled more than a hundred positions with CREEP people."

Forming a mechanism as unique as a White House advertising agency to reelect the president no doubt seemed a natural and fundamental extension of CREEP to H. R. Haldeman, Nixon's chief of staff and the former manager of the Los Angeles office of J. Walter Thompson, the world's largest consumer advertising agency. The advantages of the November Group over a traditional advertising agency, according to its senior staff, were that (1) it could obtain the services of top advertising people; (2) the people would be totally committed to Richard Nixon's reelection; and (3) the people would work only on Richard Nixon's reelection, having been freed from the distractions of working on consumer advertising. It was never noted that once such a group was in place it could, if the White House wished, use its talents on many more serious issues once the business of the election was over.)

The November Group was started in the fall of 1971. CREEP hired Peter M. Dailey, an advertising executive little known in the business beyond the West Coast, to be its president. Over the next months, after screenings at the White House (usually attended by Leonard Garment, Nixon's counsel; Gordon Strachan, Haldeman's assistant; and Jeb Magruder, CREEP's deputy director), other advertising professionals were hired to fill positions as executive vice president and heads of the November Group's account services, creative, media, finance, and promotion departments. The group soon grew to include some forty-five writers, art directors, account executives, producers, time buyers, and secretaries—not an immodest agency by Madison Avenue standards.

*Meanwhile, Watergate. . . .**

At about the time the November Group was being formed, Howard Hunt, G. Gordon Liddy, and others broke into the office of Daniel Ellsberg's psychiatrist in order to film Ellsberg's psychiatric files. Ellsberg was a defendant in the Pentagon papers case. The Nixon White House wanted to "nail" him, according to the transcript of a telephone conversation between Hunt and Charles Colson, Nixon's special counsel, held the previous July 1. A memo recommending the "covert operation" had been approved on August 11 by John Ehrlichman, Nixon's domestic affairs adviser. On August 27, Ehrlichman sent Colson a memo regarding the Hunt-Liddy operation, asking for a "game plan" on the use of material from Ellsberg's files. Later in the fall, James McCord, who was to be convicted for participating in the Watergate break-in, began working part-time for CREEP. In January, McCord would become CREEP's security coordinator. (One of the November Group remembers the irony of hearing that McCord had come to its

*The history and the direct quotations in the Watergate episodes are derived from news reports of the break-in and the subsequent testimony of the various figures, and from the text of the recorded conversations of President Nixon and his aides—the Watergate tapes—submitted to the Judiciary Committee of the House of Representatives. For this research, *The White House Transcripts,* prepared by the New York Times (Bantam Books, 1974), including Linda Amster's chronology of Watergate-related events, was a valuable reference source.

offices during the height of the Watergate heat to check *them* out for "bugs.")

The November Group rented office space in New York (two floors on Third Avenue) as a concession to its top people, who had eagerly taken leaves of absence from their regular advertising jobs but were reluctant to move to Washington.

It was also thought that the physical separation from Washington would enable the November Group to maintain an independence from CREEP and the White House. The Group seems to have had a notion that the two hundred miles between the cities would provide an effective buffer. The notion was illusory. With the November Group's president, his assistant, and its vital research function based at CREEP headquarters around the corner from the White House (and not far from the surveillance of John Mitchell,* who would officially become CREEP's director on March 1, and Magruder), and what with the Group's frequent excursions to Washington for long briefing sessions with CREEP and the White House staff, to say nothing of the White House's famous telephone connections, the November Group in reality got as much independence from CREEP as the White House decided it was useful to give them.

In fact, CREEP and the White House were in the thick of everything. "Christ, their requests were insane," a November Group official remembers, forgetting the independence he claims the Group had. "Every day they would ask for stupid things . . . I mean there were 180 people involved in this . . . everybody asking for something else at the Committee to Re-elect and the White House: 'Why don't you do an ad on this? Why don't you do this? Why don't you do this?' "

The November Group official was asked if by "White House" he meant the inner circle: that is, Haldeman and especially those who had advertising backgrounds.

> Exactly. Dwight Chapin [Nixon's appointments secretary] and Gordon Strachan and all the people who worked with Haldeman and Colson and Ehrlichman . . . it was a client like you've never seen. I went to briefings down there and there used to be forty-one people sitting there, including Nixon's brother, the black sheep man . . . he was sort of involved in that. And there was that old guy, Murray Chotiner [political adviser to Nixon since the early

*Deep Throat told Woodward that Mitchell had such "tight control of the money" at CREEP that he "was getting details almost to the point of how much was spent on pencils and erasers."

> California days], who died soon after, that nasty political figure . . . he was there giving advice. . . . And Len Garment was involved and he was giving advice. And these weren't even the Committee [CREEP] . . . these were just extra people. I don't know where the devil they came from.
>
> Boy, we needed the buffer, because once it got going . . . the Committee or the White House three or four times a day would say, "Gotta get this out." And [the November Group's executive vice president] would say, "Yeah, I'll take care of it" and hang up and pay no attention. He wouldn't even tell us.

Of course the November Group's people in New York had no way of knowing how many of the White House and CREEP requests were conveyed to them. With Richard Nixon and his men a "request" was not idly disregarded. As Magruder told some of the Nixon workers, "You've got to do what the hierarchy wants, that's why you're here."

To this day people from the November Group do not seem to understand that if the election campaign had proved close, and if the White House and CREEP had not been embroiled in trying to keep a lid on Watergate during the campaign, the November Group's advertising would have come under heavy and continuous scrutiny from the White House instead of merely being heckled three and four times a day and subjected to long meetings attended by the president's men (not precisely independence in any event). With so many professional advertising men at Nixon's side, and with his well-known belief that elections were won through media manipulation (political commercials and meaningless but publicly effective staged media events), it would be naïve to think otherwise. The reason some people at the November Group believed they had independence was that they were simply very good at following orders and coming up with ideas and executions that the White House and CREEP could be enthusiastic about. These are the roles many people, in and out of politics, play while imagining that what they are doing is synonymous with freedom.

By the winter of 1972 the November Group had put together an advertising strategy to reelect Richard Nixon which, years later, some of them would still staunchly maintain was *their* creation, but which might have been cleanly superimposed on a Haldeman memorandum:

1. The president would be presented as The President. He would not be brought down to do battle as a candidate. He would be "positioned" as being *above* the opposition.
2. The president would not be shown talking directly on camera.

3. The president's television commercials would be *about* him, not *by* him.
4. The president would be presented only in a "presidential stance," never as a candidate "attacking" his opponent.
5. The advertising would emphasize Nixon's foreign policy leadership. (This seemed to be the only decision which could have been made, since Nixon had recently effected what seemed to the public to be major diplomatic coups on trips to Russia and China.* Besides, the November Group knew—or were instructed—that the successes of Nixon's domestic programs ran from weak to questionable.)

Meanwhile, Watergate. . . . On January 27, 1972, Gordon Liddy presented his $1 million "broad-gauged intelligence plan" in John Mitchell's office to Mitchell, Magruder, and John Dean for what Mitchell would later describe as "mugging squads, kidnapping teams, prostitutes to compromise the opposition, and electronic surveillance." Mitchell asked Liddy to create a more "realistic" plan.

The four met again on February 4 to review Liddy's more limited proposal (at half the cost), which emphasized wiretapping and photography. Mitchell delayed making a decision. But Magruder later would claim that Mitchell selected the Democratic National Committee headquarters at the Watergate apartment house complex as well as other targets for the surveillance. Mitchell denied it.

On February 15, former secretary of commerce Maurice Stans became chairman of the Finance Committee to Re-elect the President. Stans and his colleagues would eventually raise $75 million in legal and illegal contributions, some of it given freely by corporations seeking to butter up Nixon for the next four years, some of it collected through high-level extortion. (Upon hearing charges by Senator George McGovern that his administration was "the most corrupt in American history," Nixon said it was "not necessary for me to respond.")

"Do you really believe George McGovern has a chance at being nominated?" one of those who had originally coaxed the senator into the race was asked in the spring of 1972. "George McGovern," his

*Nixon was the most traveled president. One of the November Group's commercials showed the pages of his passport and reported proudly that in "his four years in office, Richard Nixon has visited six continents and forty-seven countries." For a man who did not wish to come out of the White House during the campaign because of the press of state affairs, Nixon certainly was away from it enough of the time when he wasn't campaigning.

supporter answered very deliberately, "is going to shove his nomination down the Democrats' throats whether they like it or not."

The White House, who knew the man only by reputation (which was sufficient eventually to earn him a place on its enemies list), thought he was right, hoped he was right, and drooled at the prospect. Yet the White House played it safe and privately feared everybody.

Of all the Democrats that spring, only Edward Kennedy was thought to be strong enough to take on the president and maybe win, but no one believed that Kennedy would be foolish enough to waste a shot at the office so soon after the Chappaquiddick incident of July 1969. As for the rest of the Democrats, Hubert Humphrey was a dead duck. Edmund Muskie had been a threat; he had led Nixon in the polls for much of the previous year, so decisively that the White House's dirty tricks people were assigned to sabotage his campaign.*

That left George McGovern, and the White House had George McGovern beat before he was nominated. George McGovern was a populist, for God's sake! George McGovern hung around with those damn radicals on the New Left, picked up on their ideas, made them into his own. To make matters worse, the November Group official said, "he was a softy. Soft image and soft voice and less tough and hard-hitting than the president. All compassion and no guts, just the opposite of Nixon."

The November Group official flew down to Washington many times that spring to have the Nixon litany hammered into him: "I'm hard and tough. I'm a good businessman. Maybe you can't see my humanity, but I know how to run a country. I know how to do foreign policy. I know how to stand up to the Russians. I know how to get inflation down. I know how to get jobs." Anyone who didn't see McGovern as a soft-headed radical certainly would by the time CREEP was finished with his image. This job they would leave to the November Group, who would have plenty of time to do it now that it had been determined that the president's image needed so little polishing.

For obvious reasons, certain policies were probably not spooned out to the November Group to be used as a part of their introductory course on Richard Nixon's domestic accomplishments: Nixon was dismantling the poverty program; Nixon was impounding funds author-

*Two examples from Woodward and Bernstein: "a Muskie fund-raising dinner . . . had been harassed, as unordered liquor, flowers, pizzas, cakes and entertainers arrived COD. . . . [And] before the Florida primary, a flier on bogus Muskie stationery was distributed, accusing both Senator Humphrey and Senator Henry Jackson of illicit sexual conduct." Such was the early schooling of the people who worked for CREEP.

ized by Congress for the cities; and with the help of the Federal Reserve, Nixon was holding down the discount rate in order to rev up the economy for his reelection. For low discount rates meant more housing starts and more corporate spending on new plant equipment, which equaled more jobs. (After Nixon's reelection, when inflation took off, the discount rate was nonchalantly raised—and nearly doubled.) Also unrecorded was an eighteen-year low on Wall Street.

Of course these were all facts that members of the November Group could have read about in their hometown newspapers—and they would have been woefully ignorant if they had not. Yet the chances of impressionable advertising people disputing the Nixon litany while sitting in a chandeliered White House conference room are not very good. So, after a while, the falsehoods and the half-truths of the litany conveniently merge into a new truth. At this point they are advertised as accomplishments and promises kept.

Meanwhile, Watergate. . . . On April 3, 1972, a $100,000 contribution was made to CREEP by Gulf Resources and Chemical Corporation, Houston. Because the contribution came directly from a corporation, it was against federal law, and the money was "laundered" to disguise its source. The $100,000 was transferred to the corporate account of a Mexican subsidiary of Gulf Resources, and a $100,000 "legal fee" was then given to a Mexican attorney representing Gulf Resources' interests in Mexico. The following day the attorney converted $89,000 of the sum into four checks, each payable to himself and drawn on his account in a Mexico City bank. On April 5 the attorney's checks and $11,000 in cash were taken back to Houston by courier, to the office of the president of the Pennzoil Corporation, who was also the head of a group of Texas fund raisers for CREEP. The checks and cash, plus an additional $600,000 in cash and negotiable securities, were put on a Pennzoil plane, flown to Washington, and delivered to the office of Hugh W. Sloan, Jr., treasurer of the Finance Committee to Re-elect the President.

On or about April 7, Sloan later said, Liddy told him he would soon need $83,000—his first payment of an authorized quarter-million-dollar budget. Magruder, backed by Mitchell, confirmed that the money to Sloan should be given to Liddy.

On April 12, McCord later testified, Liddy gave him 650 $100 bills—numbered in sequence—from the $83,000 he had gotten from Sloan. Liddy also told McCord that Mitchell had approved surveillance of the Democratic National Committee and wanted it accomplished within thirty days. Eventually $58,000 was spent on electronic surveillance equipment to be used at the Watergate.

On May 22, Hunt, Liddy, McCord, and a "break-in team" from Miami made final plans to break into the DNC offices at the Watergate and McGovern's headquarters. Three break-ins then failed—two at the DNC and one at McGovern headquarters—but on May 28 the team managed to get into the DNC, where documents were photographed and wiretaps planted on phones. Shortly thereafter a former FBI agent hired by McCord for the Watergate burglary team began monitoring the DNC from the motel across from the Watergate. He made transcripts of the conversations he picked up and gave daily reports to McCord, who gave them to Liddy.

On June 8, Liddy gave Magruder photographs of DNC documents made during the break-in and the subsequent wiretapped conversations. Magruder later testified that he gave Mitchell the photographs and transcripts the next day and that Mitchell objected that there was "no substance to them" and said Liddy should get better information. (Mitchell dismissed this testimony as a "palpable, damnable lie.") When a second break-in at DNC headquarters at the Watergate was attempted in the early hours of June 17, McCord and the others were caught by the police, who took possession of their cameras, surveillance equipment, and the sequenced $100 bills that had been part of the original money Sloan had given Liddy. At 8:30 A.M. Liddy called Magruder in California to report the Watergate arrests. The following day Haldeman, in Key Biscayne, called Magruder and told him to fly back to Washington to deal with any problems concerning Watergate.

On June 19 it was stated that McCord had been ousted from his job with CREEP. John Mitchell described his "apparent actions . . . wholly inconsistent with the principles upon which we are conducting this campaign." The same day, John Dean would later testify, Liddy told Ehrlichman about Watergate. According to Gordon Strachan, Haldeman told Strachan to "make sure our files are clean," and Strachan complied by destroying the "political matters" files. Haldeman later denied that the instruction came from him. The same or the following day, Dean later testified, he told Attorney General Richard Kleindienst that he was concerned "this matter could lead directly to the White House." He also discussed it with Henry Petersen, the assistant attorney general who would head the Justice Department's Watergate inquiry, and believed that Petersen "realized the problems a wide-open investigation of the White House might create in an election year."

* * *

Charles Guggenheim, whose political commercials for George McGovern had captured perfectly his candidate's image of unraveled do-gooding, finished his lecture to a group of Yale undergraduates on the art of political advertising (deception was presumably not on the program, at least not from the podium) and turned to introduce an official from the November Group. Guggenheim had not met the man before his visit to New Haven, but he seemed genuinely to like the novice with whom he had sparred and been knocked out a few weeks before. Richard Nixon had won the election by 18 million votes, grabbing everything in the electoral college but seventeen electors from the District of Columbia and Massachusetts, and Watergate was half a year away from becoming the country's favorite television show. Guggenheim knew better than to make excuses at Yale in the winter of George McGovern's embarrassment.

"I want to give this man the respect his commercials deserve," Guggenheim said. "They are some of the best political commercials ever done. And whether you agree or not, he's talking as a pro to you, and I think you should treat it that way." It has not been noted whether the November Group official, rising to show the commercials to the long-haired and beaded undergraduates, reported to them that making Richard Nixon's advertising had been "great fun," as he was later heard to describe it.

It had been that; the official was no more immune than anyone else making that first entrance into the White House, the old mansion rearing up in the brightness and blue sky, nothing like the tourist's instamatic view; the guard on the gate quickly approving *his* name on that day's official visitors' list ("I'm here to see Jeb Magruder," he said with much less difficulty than he thought he might); the white-gloved Marine holding open the oversized doors for him in deferential silence, as if he really was expected. With such approval he might have been excused temporarily for considering himself important—anointed to make a contribution to a president and to his nation's place in the world. To do that *and* have "great fun" *and* receive his usual high pay was to find himself in a lovely spot in life, all the more so since it had not been sought.

So it is perhaps understandable that the memories of those times with the November Group should have remained intact, unmarred; perhaps pardonable that they could be recalled as "great fun" long after the punishment of the famous and the powerful with whom the official had walked and discussed and argued and counseled, whose approval he had earned and cherished, to whose rooms he had been granted admittance. What the memories are not allowed to reveal is why the official, a smart and sensitive man, believed that Richard Nixon was different in the summer of 1972 from the man he had ever been. Even when the official dreamed up the president's campaign slogan, the irony of the admittedly silly creation slipped by him.

As usual, the meeting in Washington at which the November Group presented the choice of proposed slogans was packed. "My God, you wouldn't believe the people who got into it from the White House staff and the Committee." (He could never bring himself to call it CREEP.) It was a long meeting, and afterward "there were all sorts of memos and analysis" of the slogans. But in the end they picked the one he liked, "Nixon, now more than ever." The people at CREEP must have smiled at the *double entendres* available in such a description.

The November Group plastered the slogan everywhere, on lapel buttons, posters, placards, automobile bumper stickers (where it would be impossible to scrape off after Watergate), and in print advertisements. Yet it was to television that CREEP and the November Group naturally gravitated to spend the bulk of the advertising money. Television was now the president's medium. ("Certainly I am the world's living expert on what television can do for a candidate and what it can do to a candidate," Nixon once told the National Association of Broadcasters).

Not surprisingly, the question of advertising money would not come up at the November Group, although the official, who was used to dealing with consumer accounts that spent $10 million and $15 million a year, would regard the Nixon money as "amazing." (The amount did not amaze him; it was the uninterrupted flow of it.)

"We would get leads on subjects and information sheets from the Committee to Re-elect, and from the White House [he would keep referring to them as separate bodies], and suggestions for commercial subjects. We picked the ones we liked and wrote commercials and went ahead and filmed them [unheard of in consumer and political advertising]. Money was no problem whatsoever. Nobody ever said, 'Save money.' "

The November Group created and produced twenty-seven Nixon commercials, an abnormally high number for a political campaign of nine months or even a product campaign lasting years. Only seven ran.

In the beginning they concentrated on making five-minute commercials because the networks offered the longer time periods, "pushed by those who believed political advertising needed more time (than thirty and sixty seconds) to be honest and truthful and meaningful," the November Group official said.

Q: What do you think?
A: I think it's a lot of horseshit. I don't think time has anything to do with the content of a political message.

It would have been impolitic for the November Group to refuse the networks' gesture. Thus they produced five-minute commercials on older Americans, environment, and youth and on Nixon's trips to Russia and China, editing from thousands of feet of official film they had purchased from the Navy Department (price not disclosed).*

The November Group then hired David Wolper, the television producer, to make three long documentaries on the Nixons "at an incredible price, negotiated really," the official remembered, "by the Committee more than us . . . they knew Wolper was very good and he came up with this huge price and they said, 'Do it.' "†

Q: So money was really no problem?
A: No problem.
Q: Had it ever occurred to you that political campaigns traditionally are always looking for money?
A: Well, it occurred to me, of course. But I knew money was no problem, and we didn't worry about it.

If the official was unconcerned about the status of money from CREEP, his sense of morals began to be tweaked during the making of the five-minute commercial on youth.

> In the commercial we spent a lot of time on Nixon ratifying [signing] the bill giving the vote to eighteen-year-olds. He's there [on film] with the pens, and the kids are all clapping, and he's making a speech about how he welcomes them, and if eighteen-year-olds can fight and die, they can vote, blah, blah, blah. We

*In every case but one, film of Nixon used in his campaign commercials was obtained by the November Group from existing file footage. The exception is something of a historical document. In the spring of 1972 Nixon allowed a director and a small camera crew into the White House to film what the November Group official described as Nixon's "supposedly normal working day." The commercial which resulted shows Nixon talking to John Ehrlichman about federal revenue sharing, property taxes, and a forthcoming trip by John Connally. Included as part of any normal working day in the Oval Office, of course, was the operation of the hidden microphones which recorded what was being spoken there. Thus the commercial—which the November Group official is not certain was ever broadcast—turned out to be significant not for its advertising value but because it provided a superbly produced record of Richard Nixon in the act of bugging himself.

†One documentary on Nixon was thirty minutes long, and one on Mrs. Nixon was fifteen minutes long; they were shown *once* each at the Republican convention. The other thirty-minute film on Nixon was broadcast *once* on national television.

didn't think anything of it, but later I did. I mean, Nixon damn well *had* to ratify [sign] that bill. He spent a year and a half fighting it and *Congress* had given them the right. *He* didn't want the damn eighteen-year-olds to vote. At the time [the White House] thought the eighteen-year-olds would kick him out. So when he *had* to put his signature on the bill, there we were having a commercial about taking credit for giving them the vote. Is that fair to do?

At about the time the Democrats nominated McGovern, John Connally defected to the Republicans and was immediately snapped up by CREEP. With the Democrats holding an edge of more than a million in registered voters, and with the eighteen-year-olds thought to be for McGovern (they may have been, but most of them did not bother to vote), CREEP believed it had to convert Democrats to its side in big numbers to win the margins they thought necessary for their purposes.

"When he [Connally] came out for Nixon, that was a lovely thing," the official remembered. "When McGovern was in place, [our] people saw a great weakness in the man and his record and they saw we could do attacking commercials—our stated policy was not to have *Nixon* do attacking commercials. So Connally started an organization called Democrats for Nixon."

Q: Did he really start it?
A: Ah, it was under his name: John Connally, president, Democrats for Nixon. You couldn't tell it from the Committee to Re-elect the President . . . and in a financial sense of who paid for the commercials, you couldn't tell the difference.
Q: It was a pre-set deal?
A: Probably so. Supposedly Connally said he was independent and was going to raise his own money, but I'm sure it was all mixed up in there [with CREEP].

With Connally "we could do commercials that slammed McGovern and his record, never involve President Nixon, and sign it with the official title, Democrats for Nixon. We weren't trying to fool anybody," the November Group official explained.

But that is precisely what CREEP and the November Group *were* doing, simplistic and harmless a move as it then appeared to be. Pretending to the vast and impressionable television audience (how were they to have known otherwise?) that Democrats for Nixon was separate from the Committee to Re-elect the President was like the White House's pretending in the days after the Watergate bugging was discovered that CREEP was "a private company set up by supporters of Richard Nixon who were intent on drafting him for re-election and contracting his campaign to a consulting firm."

But to the November Group official, "When you simply had to turn a couple million Democrats around to vote for Nixon, [it] was a marvelous idea [doing attacking commercials], led by someone as *respected* as Connally. Half the Democrats think their grandfathers will turn over in their graves if they dare vote for a Republican. This suddenly legalized or gave them a nice excuse for doing it. They could stay Democratic and be for Nixon."*

Using Connally as Nixon's point man, the November Group would create three "attacking" commercials against McGovern that summer, capitalizing on the regularity with which the Democrat put his foot in his mouth, yet resorting to unfairness and deception in order to portray his mistakes. CREEP got its money's worth from John Connally's name, and Connally was later rewarded with a series of high administrative positions.

Most of the November Group's work was completed by the time Richard Nixon was renominated in Miami in August. "But we kept putting off the actual expenditures on television," the official said.

Q: What do you mean, you kept putting it off?

A: As time went by, everything McGovern did was wrong. There was the Tom Eagleton affair. Then he [McGovern] started the strange stuff about the welfare schemes he had. And the polls kept coming in showing Nixon getting better and better. And I think they [CREEP] knew it [the election] was over but they didn't tell us. But they kept delaying the start of our major TV burst and it was only a month and a half before the election before we spent any big money doing television. They would have started *much* earlier and spent *twice* as much [$8 million] if they were terribly worried.

Perhaps that may have been the rationale for CREEP's delay in Nixon's advertising. On the other hand, the better campaign strategy that uncertain summer would have been for Nixon to remain out of sight as much as possible, in person and in advertising, and hope that Watergate would blow itself out. With the artful but potentially controversial

*The official could never make up his mind about Connally. Later in his reminiscence he referred to him as a man "I wouldn't trust . . . never admired him that much." It would have been interesting if even one person with the November Group (or, for that matter, in the press) had stood up before the Connally imprimatur was transmitted to between 30 and 60 million people at a crack and asked, "Do we know enough about this man to do this? Is what we are doing correct?"

Connally "attacking" commercials as its most important campaign weapon, CREEP might have thought twice before calling more attention to the White House than was necessary at the time and thereby providing the Democrats with a source of ammunition that could have inadvertently set off the Watergate powder keg. It was Nixon's good luck that he could afford to coast on McGovern's weaknesses and—except for Woodward and Bernstein—the modest coverage of Watergate in the press.

If the Democratic candidate had been a forceful individual and had legitimately attacked Richard Nixon's most glaring weakness—his long, nasty, and overripe political record—Nixon might well have been smoked out of his official residences and retreats and been made to confront his opponent, in person and on television. Who can tell how much faster Watergate might have been made public had there been a genuine political punchout before the election?

Meanwhile, Watergate. . . . On June 20 the contents of Howard Hunt's safe were turned over to John Dean. Included were forged diplomatic cables implicating officials of the Kennedy administration in the murder of South Vietnamese president Diem (the cables spliced together by Hunt at Colson's suggestion in September 1971) and files on the Pentagon papers and Daniel Ellsberg. Ehrlichman, according to Dean, told him at this time to destroy the documents and get rid of a briefcase containing electronic equipment. Around June 21, Sloan later testified, Magruder warned Sloan that he might need to lie under oath about how much money was given to Liddy.

The next day President Nixon held his first press conference in three months. He denied any White House connection with the Watergate break-in and said that attempted surveillance "has no place whatever in our electoral process or in our governmental process." On June 24, according to Magruder, Mitchell and Magruder talked to Stans about problems concerning money given to Liddy.

On June 28, at a meeting of acting FBI director L. Patrick Gray, Dean, and Ehrlichman, Dean handed Gray two files from Hunt's safe, describing them as "political dynamite" that "should never see the light of day." That same day, Dean later testified, he, Frederick LaRue (assistant to Mitchell at CREEP), Robert Mardian (deputy manager of CREEP), and Mitchell met to discuss "the need for support money in exchange for the silence of the men in jail" (the Watergate burglars). Also that day Magruder got Herbert Porter (scheduling director of CREEP) to agree to lie under oath that the disbursal of $100,000 to Liddy was something "more legitimate-sounding than dirty tricks," such as a program to infiltrate radical groups.

On June 29, when Herbert Kalmbach, the president's personal attorney, had told Stans, "I am here on a special mission on a White House project and I need all the cash I can get," Stans responded with $75,000, paying the first installment of nearly half a million dollars that eventually found its way to the Watergate defendants and their lawyers.

On July 5, Magruder asked Sloan to corroborate false information on the sum of money disbursed to Liddy. Sloan at first agreed, then changed his mind the next day.

On July 21, circumventing the attorney general and in violation of the regulations of the Justice Department, Gray sent an FBI report on its Watergate investigation to Dean. The report indicated that CREEP had attempted to obstruct the FBI investigation.

On August 11 the U.S. District Court in Washington rejected CREEP's request to defer the $1 million civil suit brought against it by the Democratic National Committee. On August 16, rehearsed by Dean, Magruder lied under oath in a grand jury proceeding.

On August 22, Nixon was overwhelmingly renominated in Miami at the Republican National Convention.

During the festivities the November Group official found himself dancing with Magruder's secretary, "a nice kid from Florida. I said, 'What are you going to do after the election? Are you going to stay in Washington?' She said, 'No! It's the dirtiest, filthiest place you've ever seen. There are things going on you wouldn't believe.' I said, 'Oh, really?' And went on dancing."

It did not occur to the official to ask Magruder's secretary why she would say such a thing. He did remember that "two or three weeks before . . . federal investigators had been around to see Magruder . . . but nobody [at the November Group] knew anything."

> As the summer went on, it [Watergate] built a little. We kept hearing about it, but we knew absolutely nothing about it. I always maintained that treasurer who we had at the November Group was an absolute godsend. He was an old-line stiff guy and if we wanted to get forty dollars out of the damn thing [the Group], we had to sign our name eight times. I think he probably saved the November Group from real involvement in that [Watergate].

Q: In what way?
A: I think money would have gone through us and things would have been paid by cash.
Q: How would you [the November Group] have laundered money?
A: Oh, I don't know anything about how that's done. . . . I *do* remember we paid the *New York Times* for an ad in cash once —I heard that.
Q: Which was a phenomenal thing to do [since placement of advertising from accredited agencies—which the November Group certainly was—is traditionally done on credit].
A: Yeah. Now I wonder in retrospect . . . where that cash came from?

On August 29 Nixon said at a news conference that Dean had completed a thorough Watergate investigation and "I can state categorically that his investigation indicates that no one in the White House staff, no one in this administration, presently employed, was involved in this very bizarre incident.* . . . What really hurts is if you try to cover it [wrongdoing] up." Dean later testified that this was the first he had heard of his investigation.

The anti-McGovern commercials the November Group's competitor so admired—which the beaded young men of Yale had the manners to applaud, which the president's top aides had initially "fallen in love" with, then acclaimed as "the greatest thing in the world," and finally "cheered"—went on television at the end of September.

Unless you were covering up in Washington—like Fred LaRue, delivering $210,000 in payoff money to Howard Hunt's attorney, or John Mitchell, denying a *Washington Post* story that he had been in charge of a secret fund while serving the nation as its chief law enforcement officer—the last week of September was not particularly notable in American political history.

It was certainly not notable for George McGovern, who wanted to move his people as badly as they wanted to be moved but who knew three weeks into his campaign that it was not going anywhere.

It was not publicly notable for Richard Nixon except that it marked one week less that he would have to wait until the annoyance of the election would be over. The federal grand jury had already

*As of the date of the news conference, Hunt, McCord, and Liddy had been fired, the last by Mitchell. Mitchell had quit as director of CREEP for "the welfare and happiness of my wife and daughter." And Sloan had resigned.

returned an eight-count indictment against the Watergate burglars and Hunt and Liddy. Dean would later testify that the president told him and Haldeman that he was "pleased that the case had stopped with Liddy."

If Nixon had decided that he did not have to campaign for reelection to the office of president of the United States, the public did not appear to mind very much. His decision may actually have been a relief for people who had been rubbed raw by what would that week be nearly eight years of an overt political war they did not understand and for which they still could not get a believable explanation, by a rattling economy whose only merit had been to prove the textbooks right for once about the inability of guns and butter to coexist, and by a consuming fatigue from too many images of nightsticks and guns that left them wishing to shut it all out with sleep.

Anti-McGovern was the label Nixon's men gave to the commercials, but it would be a cover-up of another kind to let the description rest in its already mellowed place in campaign annals.

The commercials are still spoken of as though they were somehow separate from something called the bad Nixon (as though there were something called the good Nixon with which to compare it). The commercials were not separate from Nixon and his men; they were dangerous commercials, a perfect extension of devious minds. It is not surprising that H. R. Haldeman, "straight and tough and staring you right in the eye when you presented to him," as the November Group official said with a certain fondness, could "fall in love" with them so easily.

The commercials, whatever the November Group believed, were not anti-McGovern. That label has been mistaken for many years; George McGovern was no more than a convenient straw man for the Democrats for Nixon. The commercials were in fact anti-American. They were anti-American in the way they continued to mislead and deceive the public about the policies of their rulers. And the people Nixon deceived the most were the middle Americans he claimed to respect so much—as much as one can bestow respect from behind the velvet fortresses of the White House and Camp David, Key Biscayne and San Clemente, Fifth Avenue and privately owned islands in the Bahamas. He also deceived the rich in the nonessential industries, those in the pale outside military and diplomatic procurement. (The rich who manufactured weapons and war understood what he was doing and were his silent partners in the deception.) Only the poor were not taken in; few politicians fooled them anymore. For the record, Nixon would occasionally commend to them the rewards of hard work, but they knew he had impounded their bootstrap money.

The issue of advertising in the 1972 campaign was not so much how it helped Nixon to his landslide—which he would have achieved, more or less, against a candidate like McGovern—but how advertising reinforced in the public mind the myths that Nixon continued to use as a means and a mandate to rule.*

That the myths were reinforced by a landslide made them and the landslide all the more dangerous. Huge winning margins tend to bond mythology to the public mind until long after an election is over. Despite ample evidence to the contrary, the public automatically reasons that if so many people voted for the winner, his principles and programs must be just and true. Many who vote for the loser come to believe this, too. Thus the public, having come under the influence of the main source of alleged campaign information, the unregulated political commercial, unwittingly becomes a rubber stamp, not only for the perpetuation of the mythology but for the continued erosion of its own individual rights.

Using the considerable skills of its private advertising agency, the White House was able to advance the myth of national security in the commercial it called *The McGovern Defense Plan.* The White House and the November Group were unexpectedly aided in their effort by Hubert Humphrey, who had attacked McGovern in a similarly misleading manner in the California presidential primary the previous spring. Going into a debate with Humphrey, McGovern held a wide lead in the polls. Humphrey, making a last-ditch attempt to capture the Democratic nomination, shamelessly resorted to cheap demagogic tactics in a state that was in hock economically to the military-industrial complex. "Humphrey knew better," said a man who had known him for years, an expert on military armament and destruction.

Humphrey was not entirely wrong about McGovern's defense plan; he just conveniently forgot to say *how* McGovern's proposed reduction of the military would actually weaken the United States. So did Nixon's advertising men. Both would have had a difficult time proving such a case—but then they didn't want to.

When national security becomes a campaign issue, the Pentagon's extravagant budget is usually defended in tough but simplistic and

*Myths are easily transferable in the presidency and do not observe party lines. Nixon inherited his share from predecessors from both parties, and even in disgrace he left legacies which presidents from both parties will not reject.

THE McGOVERN DEFENSE PLAN

(DRUM ROLL OVER TOY SOLDIERS) ANNOUNCER: The McGovern defense plan. He would cut the Marines by one-third. The Air Force by one-third . . . Navy personnel by one-fourth.

(HAND REMOVES TOY PLANES) . . . interceptor planes by one-half.

(HAND REMOVES TOY SHIPS) The Navy fleet by one-half.

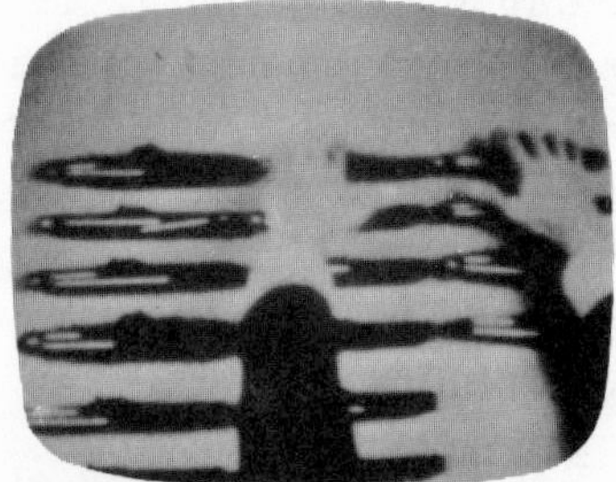

(HAND REMOVES TOY CARRIERS) . . . carriers from 16 to 6.

(TOYS FALL IN A JUMBLE) Senator Hubert Humphrey had this to say about the McGovern proposal: It isn't just cutting into the fat . . . it's cutting into the very security of this country.

(MUSIC: "HAIL TO THE CHIEF") President Nixon doesn't believe we should play games with our national security. He believes in a strong America to negotiate for peace from strength.

(MUSIC OUT)

misleading ways. Rarely does a major candidate choose to go against the misinformation and folklore that have arrogantly cloaked national security since the creation of the National Security Act in 1947.

For three dangerous decades, national security myths have kept an unquestioning public in the dark, giving it no choice but to be an automatic check-writing machine for the expansionist ambitions and economic greed of the military, their industrial suppliers, their baronial patrons in Congress, and presidents and their national security managers.

It is much easier to defend or ignore this amorphous creature called national security than to struggle to see it for what it is—and what *we* are as a people. When a McGovern, inept as he may be, tries to shed some light on the subject, the power elite (led by Nixon in 1972) rises up to swat down the "soft-hearted" liberal. The issue can be buried faster and more efficiently with misleading and demagogic television commercials (such as *The McGovern Defense Plan*) than by any other form of propaganda. That is why this kind of commercial, while "great fun" for its naïve creators to make, presents the public with an insidious danger.

The McGovern Defense Plan
Sixty-second Nixon commercial
Eight network code violations

There is so much more to this clever piece of work than meets the eye. In order to have even a basic understanding of its implications, the commercial should be seen on three levels: (1) how it misrepresented McGovern's statistics and intent; (2) how it misrepresented what U.S. military strength would have been if its forces were decreased along the lines the commercial purports; and (3) how it misrepresented U.S. political and military intentions.

On the first level, the commercial was guilty of at least eight major violations of the network television advertising code. Those violations would have caused its rejection, had such a code been applicable to it.

- It unfairly attacked McGovern (and was unfair to the public in the process) because it strongly implied that he was for unilateral disarmament, which was not the case. It implied, by the examples it chose and the manner in which it portrayed them, that conventional warfare was the backbone of the nation's "national security," which was not the case and which McGovern had never claimed. The commercial conveniently ignored the real backbone: nuclear submarines and nuclear-tipped Intercontinental Ballistic Missiles, which McGovern had not indicated he would scrap.

- The commercial was dangerously misleading and deceptive. In two instances, statistics attributed to McGovern were incorrect: he would have cut the Marine force by 29 percent, not 331/3 percent, and the Navy by 21 percent, not 25 percent. To the eye these are small differences, but they are enormous when translated into taxpayer dollars. [Even if the Nixon commercial's personnel statistics were correct, the cuts were made to appear as a crippling blow to the nation's defenses.] McGovern's plan to cut interceptor planes, implicitly criticized here, was in fact comparable to Nixon's own timetable. The example of the carriers was a classic case of the half-truth, a distortion by omission. Only "five of sixteen existing carriers were being maintained on active duty." The McGovern plan called for "a force of six, with three on active duty."
- The commercial was guilty of using distress signals.
- The label "Democrats for Nixon" tended to suggest that this was an organization independent of and separate from CREEP (when in fact, as the November Group official revealed, "you couldn't tell the difference"). The label could therefore be questioned on grounds of fairness.
- The commercial was guilty of damaging stereotyping—in this case, of military myths.
- It used scare approaches and presentations with the capacity to induce fear. (The November Group would not disagree with this charge. On the contrary, referring to the commercial, the official said it was "effective because it *scared* people." He thought that was "perfectly fair.")
- It did not support its claims.
- It lacked advertising integrity and taste.

"President Nixon doesn't believe we should play games with our national security," an announcer intoned gravely over the playing of "Hail to the Chief" while the television picture showed Nixon greeting one of his admirals.

But playing games with national security is precisely what Nixon did, just as presidents had done before him and have done since. It is difficult to imagine that Nixon, his national security managers, and the Pentagon really believed that McGovern's proposed cuts would weaken the nation's security. This can be seen by focusing only on the examples the commercial gave—the Pentagon no doubt had thousands of others.

Cutting the Marines. The Boston Study Group has pointed out that "the Marines have become in this century specialized forces for beach landings." In 1972 there were approximately three Marine land-combat divisions, not counting Marine air wings and amphibious ships. (A division in the U.S. military is formed of about 16,000 to 17,000 men, supplemented by many support units, which brings the total to about 45,000.) In 1972 the Vietnam War was winding down (though not for the poor men who were being used as American political pawns). A cut of 29 percent, or 39,150 Marines, as McGovern had recommended, would have had little effect on a force whose mission had been largely reduced to providing embassy guards and shipboard security. The *only* justification for maintaining three battle-ready Marine divisions would have been for a future interventionist assault landing on a third-world country. After Vietnam it would be difficult for a president to obtain congressional and public sanction for such an imperial ambition. But of course Richard Nixon never knew the limits of ambition.

Cutting the Air Force. Most of the interceptor planes that McGovern proposed cutting had been gathering dust on runways "around the periphery of the forty-eight states" since 1960, waiting to defend the United States from enemy bombers that had never come. In addition to their age, the mission of the interceptors in North America was very much in doubt by 1972, the likelihood of enemy bombers being sent on such a mission having further diminished in the missile age. In fact, as the Boston Study Group has observed, "Aircraft especially designed for interception have not been particularly important in the U.S. force structure." Thus McGovern proposed only obvious cuts in planes and personnel. Nixon did not think that it served him politically to agree. The public remained in the dark.

The commercial became tricky where it claimed that McGovern would cut the Air Force by one third. The implication was planes and pilots, but McGovern probably had in mind Air Force personnel who never leave the ground. For example, a squadron of twenty-four F-4E fighters is supported by some 720 ground personnel. It stands to reason (though not by November Group standards) that for every interceptor cut, thirty to forty Air Force support people could theoretically be cut too. But without this information, the viewer cannot know what such a cut means to his or her security (i.e., nothing). Nor could the viewer know that both McGovern and Nixon's commercial excluded approximately 5,000 Navy and Marine aircraft and their personnel, which are separate from the Air Force.

Cutting the Navy. When McGovern proposed reducing the size of the fleet, a large part of it was either obsolete or unnecessary to the U.S. military mission in 1972. Consider the economics: "At $200 [million] to $1,500 million apiece (compared with $1 million each for tanks and $15 million each for tactical aircraft), ships are by far the single most expensive item of military equipment." Ships take years to build, rather than months and weeks. The sizes of their crews are enormous. Training costs are high. Ships have a limited sea life, and they are highly "vulnerable to crippling damage by vastly cheaper and more numerous missiles, torpedoes, and bombs."

Knowing this better than anyone, the Navy nevertheless had (and has) three primary missions for its general-purpose ships (excluding missile-bearing submarines):

1. to provide floating air bases for light and medium bomber aircraft . . .
2. to provide troops and their arms (principally the Marine Corps) for amphibious assault landings on overseas beach areas . . .
3. to provide antiaircraft and antisubmarine defense of war-supply shipping from the United States to Europe in the event of a prolonged non-nuclear war with the Soviet Union in that theater.

The third mission was of dubious value even in 1972, given the slim chance of a *prolonged* non-nuclear war with the Soviets breaking out and in light of the increasing number of new Russian missiles with the ability to knock out large surface ships from a distance of up to twenty miles.

The second mission, Marine transport, was meaningless. In 1972 there were over sixty amphibious ships. What would be their function if Marine forces were cut or used only to protect embassies?

The first mission, that of the aircraft carriers, was nearly obsolete except to "show the flag." With a flight deck area of some six acres, the extraordinarily costly carrier ($5 billion to build and outfit) was highly visible and a sitting duck for the new "smart" missiles being deployed.

In addition to its own vulnerability, each carrier drags in for its alleged protection a convoy of at least eleven fighting and supply ships. The convoy is protected by five more ships.

It is no wonder that the Navy spends *more than half of its budget* in some way to pay for its carriers. This budget and the one for amphibious landing ships would have accounted for most of McGovern's proposed slash in the fleet and in Navy personnel. If anything, his figures were conservative.

If Nixon used McGovern as a straw man to argue against conventional force cuts, the conventional forces themselves had become the straw men for the new age of the microelectronic "smart" weapons. These weapons, operated by sensitive miniaturized circuitry very much on the order of tiny pocket calculators, gave "the individual soldier or small teams of soldiers the odds-on probability of being able to destroy with one shot a formidable target: a tank, an airplane or even a ship."

In May 1972, at a time when McGovern was beginning to rail against the excesses of the military, Nixon showed what a few "smart" weapons could do in the air war over North Vietnam. Since 1966 the Air Force's best-equipped fighters had failed to destroy the fortified Than Hoa bridge with conventional weapons. The first Paul Doumer bridge *had* been destroyed in 1967 after many attempts, but at the cost of eighteen aircraft. Yet on a single day in that presidential campaign year both the Than Hoa and the rebuilt Doumer bridge were taken out with "smart" weapons in single air strikes. No U.S. planes were lost.

George McGovern could have cut into the military establishment, and cut and cut some more, and the United States would not have lost a notch of its military supremacy. The Pentagon would have lost only its archaic military pieces and the supernumeraries it maintained out of public funds.

In fact most of the conventional equipment could have been dumped in the sea for all the good it would do in a nuclear attack. But that was a subject Nixon did not want to discuss with McGovern or with the voters.

Most of the people who watched Nixon make fun of McGovern's defense plan had no idea that their country soon would have "1,054 land-based missiles, 656 submarine-based missiles, and 380-plus long-range bombers [that] could theoretically deliver more than 6,500 megatons of nuclear explosive on more than 11,000 targets." Nor did most people know or remember that in the spring of 1972, following the Salt

I agreement that Nixon proudly signed with the Soviet Union, the United States would begin to add to its nuclear warhead stock "at the rate of more than 100 per month, three times the rate achieved by the U.S.S.R." Nor did they know that the United States would accumulate over 30,000 nuclear weapons by 1978. Nor did they know of or wish to remember the possibilities of nuclear annihilation that even a handful of these weapons could cause.

Only about four years earlier, Secretary of Defense Robert McNamara had estimated that just five American submarines could wipe out 37 million Russians and 59 percent of their industry. McNamara did not provide an estimate of what Russian nuclear bombs could do to the United States. The devastation, it may be assumed, would have been no less extensive.

If Richard Nixon knew all these terrible things, if he knew that the nation's national security was not threatened by McGovern's proposals or by what McGovern had not even said, why did Nixon's most trusted aides approve so joyously the November Group's dangerously deceptive commercial?

One answer is that the commercial was the perfect fulfillment and extension of CREEP's dirty campaign mentality (although it is probable that the naïve November Group never caught on).

But another explanation is more dangerous than the first. Vast sins are committed in the name of national security, which has long since become "a modern incantation," in the words of arms critic Richard Barnet. "In the name of national security, all things can be threatened. All risks can be taken. All sacrifices can be demanded. Break-ins, wiretaps, deception of Congress, assassination attempts on foreign leaders—indeed, the Watergate cover-up and the intervention in Vietnam—were all ordered in the name of national security."

The price the public has paid for this mentality has been very high. By 1972, America's cold warriors had spent well over $1.5 trillion of the public's money (since the end of World War II) in the name of national security. Yet no spectrum of the country, unless it was the military, felt secure. Older Americans who had retired on adequate savings began to have trouble paying bills. Middle-aged Americans were being eaten up by taxes and inflation. The poor, penned up in the cities, were making the streets violent in their desperation, Nixon's campaign rhetoric notwithstanding. The treasure of America was producing national insecurity.

McGOVERN WELFARE

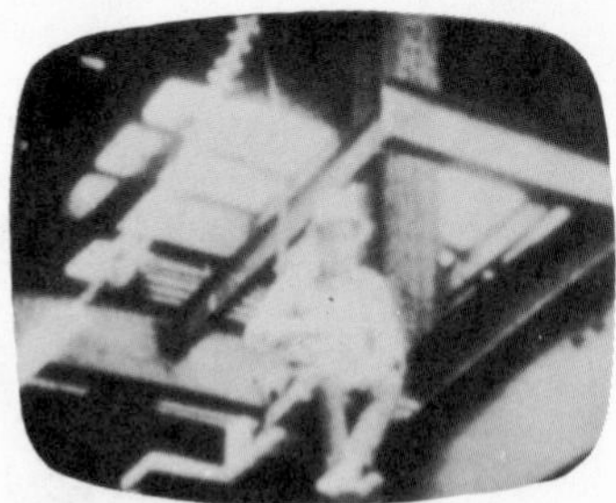

(FACTORY WHISTLE)
ANNOUNCER: Senator George McGovern recently submitted a welfare bill to the Congress. According to . . . the Senate Finance Committee,

the McGovern bill would make 47 percent of the people in the United States eligible for welfare. . . . Almost every other person . . . would be on welfare.

The Finance Committee estimated the cost of this incredible proposal at $64 billion the first year. . . .

And who's going to pay for this?

Well, if you're not the one out of two people on welfare, you do.

(SILENCE)

(CAMPAIGH SIGN)
ANNOUNCER: . . . Last January, Senator McGovern suggested a welfare plan that would give a thousand-dollar bill to every man, woman, and child in the country.

Now he says maybe the thousand-dollar figure isn't right.

Throughout the year, he has proposed unconditional amnesty for all draft dodgers. Now his running mate claims he proposed no such thing.

In Florida he was pro-bussing. In Oregon he said he would support the anti-bussing bill. . . .

(SIGN SPINS)
Last year, this year. The question is what about next year?

(SILENCE)

* * *

The November Group had other tales to spin before the election.

In the famous *McGovern Welfare* commercial, it claimed that a bill McGovern had recently submitted to Congress "would make 47 percent of the people in the United States eligible for welfare." "And who's going to pay for this?" the commercial asked, hardly able to restrain itself. "Well, if you're not the one out of two people on welfare, *you* do," it answered, as the hardhat in the television picture looked in disbelief. Well he might have.

With White House approval, the November Group had substituted in the public mind figures from a bill proposed by the National Welfare Rights Organization (which McGovern was prevailed upon to sponsor) calling for a $6,500 guaranteed annual income for poor families with a short-lived McGovern *campaign* idea which proposed paying everybody in the country $1,000 annually.

McGovern's own welfare plan was intended to provide economic and psychological uplift for the poor, using money to be raised by taxing the well-off. What merit the plan may have had was quickly sabotaged by McGovern and his aides, who could never explain it to the media, who then made it into a national joke. The real joke was that McGovern's proposal was similar to Nixon's Family Assistance Plan, which the president had once called "White House priority number one." For three years Nixon had tried to push through Congress a bill giving poor families $1,600 a year (later increased to $2,400 a year). The Nixon bill eventually died in Congress, but with so many other legal matters on its mind during the election campaign, the White House appeared not to mourn its death.

To further confuse the public on the subject of welfare, the November Group created a third commercial, *McGovern Turnabout,* whose centerpiece *was* McGovern's $1,000 welfare plan, albeit presented in a misleadingly simplistic way. The public naturally assumed that the $1,000 welfare misunderstanding was what both Nixon commercials talked about. On this matter the November Group official's conscience began jabbing at him again.

> When McGovern was a senator, just six months before he got the nomination, the Americans for Democratic Action [the official confused the ADA with the National Welfare Rights Organization] had come to him and said, we have a bill for a welfare scheme and we want to have you introduce it to the Congress. And McGovern purportedly—this is what I heard—said, "I am *not* in favor of this. I won't vote for it.

But I want to get a hearing to see what kind of reaction it gets in Congress, so I will introduce it."

Q: Is this the thousand dollar [plan]?

A: This wasn't the thousand dollars to every man, woman, and child, this was another one. . . . Is it right if the man did it under that guise—he wanted this bill discussed and thereby he in a sense sponsored it and introduced it to Congress even though he didn't think it was practical or right—is it right to *hang* him on it? I don't know. This one makes me wonder.

Q: Why did you do it?

A: Because I knew it would be effective and at the time I didn't really worry that much about it. In retrospect, I wonder if it's absolutely fair.

Q: How did you feel [the November Group official was asked] when Haldeman and Ehrlichman were indicted?

A: I was absolutely crushed and entirely disillusioned, and so were most of the people who had worked for Nixon, because most of us sincerely believed he should be reelected. . . . It was just absolutely crushing, as it was to everyone in the country, but to us it was just a little sickening. . . . I used to watch those damn hearings every day . . . everybody I worked with, all those people, one by one, would testify. The Ehrlichmans and the Haldemans and Garment and Magruder and Strachan and Mitchell . . . and some of them I liked. I sort of liked Haldeman, who was the one we dealt with. . . .

Q: Do you regret having done it, in light of what happened afterward?

A: I—I don't regret in a personal sense because it was a wonderful experience and an ego trip and great fun. I regret I helped . . . that I had helped that man, who was an awful man. But I take comfort in the fact he would have been reelected anyway.

A few years later the November Group official was back in the political advertising business, this time "working only for Democrats." The neophyte political media specialist who bore a responsibility for "some of the best political commercials ever done" apparently viewed Watergate as a singular event—a political aberration—temporary. "I've only worked for Democrats since," he reiterates, "three or four Senate campaigns . . . a lieutenant governor."

Q: Why did you want to do that?

A: Because I enjoy political advertising and I was very against the Nixon stuff [presumably referring to Watergate, not to the advertising] and it was a chance to make some money and I agreed with these candidates that I was supporting. . . . I wouldn't do it again for Nixon, of course, but I'd be happy to do it [presidential advertising] again because it's a strange place, Washington . . . I like it.

8

HONEST JIMMY VS. HONEST JERRY, 1976

A campaign as American as apple pie, motherhood, and Machiavelli

Men in general are as much affected by what things seem to be as by what they are; often indeed, they are moved more by appearances than by the reality of things.

Machiavelli, The Prince

"I voted for everyone on the ballot except president," the middle-aged man, his face heavy with commuter's fatigue, explained to the passenger in the next seat. "When I got to Carter and Ford, I couldn't make a decision. First, I put my finger on the Ford lever, then I took it away. Then I put my finger on Carter's lever and took it away. Christ, I froze in there; I didn't know what to do. I kept looking under the curtain at the feet of the people waiting to vote. They're shifting from one foot to another and coughing and clearing their throats, and I know it's to tell me I've been in the booth too long. Hell, I knew that. I was actually beginning to sweat, for God's sake, but I just couldn't seem to make myself vote for either prick. I wished to hell I'd walked out without pulling the fuckin' lever."

"Did you?" the second man asked.

"No, I voted," the first man admitted. "And I probably will again," he said in mock disgust, turning to peer out the dirty train window for a sign of his station in the winter gloom.

Americans are perhaps more resilient about their form of government than they have the right to be. Or they understand it less well than they think they do.

Researchers professed shock when they discovered that only 53 percent of those eligible to vote in the 1976 presidential election had bothered to do so.

What is shocking about that figure is not that it is so small but that so many people actually turned out to vote.

Of the 53 percent, by far the largest bloc of voters were people who, regardless of station, had taken an almost continuous mental drubbing throughout most of their lives.

Born during or before the Depression years, perhaps weaned on the Bank Holiday, they had lived with fear and sellouts, without letup, through World War II/atomic bomb/Iron Curtain/Korea/Cold War/Berlin Wall/Cuban missiles/Vietnam/family disintegration/impersonality/unemployment/inflation/recession/unmitigated taxes/trade deficits/multinational profiteering/OPEC/Middle East/Africa/third-world revolution/terrorists/political assassination/urban riots/bankrupt cities/drugs/degradation/decay/pollution/poverty/mugging/murder/waste/welfare/Watergate—the crises coming at them and coming at them in such an unrelenting blur that they confused what had become a permanent state of debilitation with normalcy. And everywhere, and onto everyone, the soil of political arrogance, political lies, political deception, and broken political promises permeated their lives and their dreams.

Still the voters came back to vote in 1976—little more than half of them, but an imposing 80 million nonetheless—gnawed by feelings that they were about to be duped again (if not by one candidate, by the other) yet harboring a homespun hope based on real and imagined memories of an America that was quieter, gentler, kindlier, and more decent, and praying that *somebody* would fix things up again. *Somebody,* for God's sake, would come and save them, and their troubles would be over, at least for a little while.

It was a tantalizing market for a presidential candidate who knew how to pick it off.

Political analysts believe that Jimmy Carter's genius lay in his ability to preempt for himself those qualities that pollster Pat Caddell found that people craved the most: honesty above all else, followed by honesty's political bedfellows: trust, reliability, goodness, caring, responsiveness, and—perhaps for the first time in American political history—love. Sweet, tender, sentimental, unabashed, old-fashioned, revival-hall love. Since Carter never had much in the way of original ideas to run on, or urgent proposals of state to advance, he grabbed eagerly at the republic's cries for help and converted them into his own campaign tactics.

But Gerald Ford, about whom the public knew not much more than it knew about Carter, his two years as tenant in the White House notwithstanding, old, funny, bumbling President Jerry, the cartoonists' delight, was learning to play the game faster than even Jimmy Carter might have thought possible. After trailing Carter 62–29 in the Gallup Poll in the days before his nomination, Ford rapidly made up ground during the final weeks of the campaign. By election eve he had pulled into virtually a dead heat.

It was in those final weeks that a startling though subtle change occurred in the American political system: The candidates ceased to oppose each other in the flesh as their political commercials took over and "ran against each other." The campaign for president had become a contest of cinematic surrogates.

It was a natural outgrowth of twenty-four years of political advertising on television, one that required only two evenly matched candidates (however weak), lacking the leverage of bona fide incumbency, to become automatically *the* election process.

It is comment enough on the frightening implications of such a change to note that neither the press nor the 80 million people who voted had realized that it was happening before their eyes.

After the election, political researcher Michael Barone confirmed that the commercials of Ford and Carter were the one media element that actually changed voters' minds in the last month of the campaign.

Barone's thesis was that the highly touted debates did not determine the result of the election. The debates were a test of the candidates' competence and ability to think fast (or to give that impression) in the whirl of television lights and cameras. But, Barone points out, "honesty" and "responsiveness" more than "competence" were the qualities voters wanted in 1976, as Carter and Ford had discovered earlier. These qualities cannot be portrayed in televised pseudo debates nearly as well as they can be in skillfully controlled television commercials.

The debates did alter the flow of the campaign. "For several days before each debate," Barone reports, "the candidates would prepare, and afterward they would rest while their entourages proclaimed them the victors and the pundits picked over their mistakes. So during the debate periods, the only real campaigning that was done, aside from the debates themselves, was in television advertising."

To prove his thesis, Barone cites the Harris and other private polls which he says showed that although Carter was credited with having beaten Ford in debates two and three, it was Ford who rose in the polls during this time. Barone also cites the Gallup Poll, which calculated that Ford lost points following debate two, then gained points, while Carter's standing remained more or less stationary. "Whichever figures you rely on, it is clear that Carter, acclaimed winner of the second and third debates, did not gain during this period, and that Ford, the acclaimed loser, did not lose ground."

Yet there is a terrible irony about Michael Barone's research. For if he has verified what political media specialists have always known about the power of television advertising, he has also inadvertently proved how dangerous it can be. In addition to the advertising discussed in chapter 1, other key commercials for Carter and Ford would similarly have been barred from television for serious violations of the network advertising code had they been required to observe it. In a campaign in which the political commercials themselves were the leading players, holding center stage almost entirely on their own during the crucial closing weeks of the campaign, who can tell how adherence to the code would have altered not only the election of 1976 but, because of the power of the incumbency, perhaps the election of 1980 as well?

Creating the Carter Advertising Image: The Coca-Cola Connection

It is said that within weeks of the start of Jimmy Carter's occupancy of the White House, Pepsi-Cola, Richard Nixon's favorite drink, was banished from the mansion's vending machines and replaced by Coca-Cola. The change was not so much a gesture for past favors as it was a clue to things to come.

The relationship between Coca-Cola chairman J. Paul Austin (and his chamberlains at Coke, his attorneys at King & Spalding, his bankers at the Trust Company of Georgia, his international colleagues and fellow tycoons on the Trilateral Commission) and candidate Carter had been strong and enduring since the time of Carter's governorship. With the presidency in hand, there were potential new benefits in the relationship.

It may be that Austin helped open the right doors for Jimmy Carter because he liked the idea of a fellow Georgian and former governor sitting in the White House. Even a man who has easy access to the most important corporate and banking boardrooms in the world likes to flatter himself as being a "good friend" of the president of the United States. But the head of a multi-billion-dollar multinational corporation built around the most famous product in history perhaps had a more fundamental reason for having so generously extended his friendship and campaign help over the years to the "unknown" candidate. Coca-Cola is, after all, something more complicated than an ice-cold bottle of Coke.

Few people who are accustomed to quenching their thirst with a swig of Coke may know that the company, built as much on lore as on sugar, is involved in a big way in many other businesses—wine in New York, oranges in Florida and South Africa, bottled water in the Northeast, sewage in Canada, protein drinks in Latin America, coffee in Europe, management trainees in Washington—in addition to selling the sweet syrup that is the base for "the pause that refreshes" to nearly every country in the world. Nor is it common knowledge that Coca-Cola has carved out for itself these international positions: "world's largest consumer of granulated sugar, world's largest privately owned truck fleet . . . world's biggest retail sales force, world's leading producer of citrus concentrate, world's most extensive franchise system, world's first multinational corporation of consumer products, world's best-known product, world-wide supplier of private-label coffee and tea."

Like any upstanding industrial giant, Coca-Cola must not only protect itself from competition, it must keep a resolute eye out for the chance to expand—for greater profit, to be sure. But as much as the money involved, there is the call and the intoxication of holding the raw power that manipulates people, nations, and empires.

Not long after Jimmy Carter was installed in the White House, Coke was awarded the franchise for the China market, 900 million strong.* Potentially, China represented the largest single market in the world, a bigger and thirstier market even than Pepsi-Cola's Russia.

To maintain a lock on its position of international dominance, Coca-Cola budgets the largest advertising expenditure in the world for any single product. Over the years Coke's advertising, concentrated

*Peter Meyer notes another reward for Coke: "In May of 1977, because of plummeting world sugar prices which were threatening the existence of domestic producers unable to compete with the cheaper foreign imports, Carter decided to give the processors a government subsidy to keep them in operation. The real beneficiaries of the new policy, however, were the sugar users, who were saved from increased prices by the infusion of government money." (Remember, the world's largest consumer of granulated sugar is Coca-Cola.)

largely in television, has been exceptionally attractive, catchy, clean-cut, rich in color and evocation, and striking for its eminently hummable music. But perhaps its most interesting characteristic is that it is almost never annoying. It has what the industry calls high "wear rate." People actually seem to *like* Coca-Cola commercials. Of all the accolades heaped on Coke advertising over the years, however, probably its greatest accomplishment is its absolute mastery of image manipulation. Nobody at Coke, of course, would admit openly to such a thing, and a lot of people employed specifically to manipulate images for Coke are not aware that that is the direct result of their labors. And, dollar for dollar, those labors have made Coke commercials probably the best producer of sales for any product in the marketplace. All the more fascinating when you consider that there is no more substance to them than there is in the fizzy, sugared water they sell in such remarkable quantities.

If there was one favor J. Paul Austin's company could do for Jimmy Carter it would be to give him instruction in the art and science of image manipulation—the myth message. Journalist Bob Hall, who has closely followed the history of Coca-Cola, points out that "Austin legitimized Carter for the Northern banking centers" and that "candidate Carter used Coke's international sales network, instead of the State Department, for his foreign trips." Peter Meyer has noted that Austin provided "seed money for Carter's second [successful] gubernatorial bid; Coke executives chipped in with campaign contributions while he was governor; the corporate aircraft whisked him around the country as he made his political contacts while ostensibly drumming up business for the state; and J. Paul Austin was there again to host a lucrative New York City fund-raiser on behalf of the Carter presidential campaign." But beyond these niceties, Coke might be able to teach Carter and his advertising director, Gerald Rafshoon, some tricks of the advertising trade.* That kind of help would be of inestimable value for a fellow with Jimmy Carter's background, no

*As the head of a very small Atlanta advertising agency, Rafshoon, though a cool operator, did not appear to have had much experience handling accounts of national advertising class, which good presidential advertising must be. In 1975, when Carter's "formal" advertising began, the Standard Directory of Advertising Agencies shows that Gerald Rafshoon Advertising, Inc., placed only $7 million in advertising for its clients. According to *Advertising Age,* that made it the 226th largest agency in the country. Only one third of its advertising was for television; all but one of Rafshoon's clients were from Georgia and included such accounts as Adair Realty, Getz Exterminators, Tacoa Jewelry Distributors, and Discount Wallcoverings. However, one of Rafshoon's clients did achieve national fame of a sort: First National Bank of Calhoun, president and controlling stockholder, Bert Lance.

matter how many contacts he had made over the years; that kind of advice would give him the type of image that would gently but firmly sell to the voters.

With so much riding on a Carter victory, it stretches credibility to believe that J. Paul Austin's marketing department at Coca-Cola never "chatted" with the Carter camp about the cold realities of advertising. After all, marketing departments of all famous corporations often do extra duty for the boss, whether it be to turn out a program for his country club dinner-dance, to teach high school kids about business basics as a part of the corporation's community relations, or to throw tidbits of campaign advice now and then to a friend who just happens to be a prospective president of the United States. It would have been highly unusual, as a matter of fact, if Coke had never talked to Carter and Rafshoon. Certainly there has been speculation in Washington that the financing and concerns of the "soft message" for Carter's basic campaign advertising came from Coca-Cola.

The advertising strategy that cast Carter as an unknown peanut farmer who had "risen up" from the byways of the South to give the country back to "the people" was brilliantly conceived. For more than a year and a half it worked, first along the primary route and then in the general election.

But in the last weeks of the campaign, as the Carter and Ford commercials dueled, Carter's lead in the polls began to melt. There are two views as to why this happened.

One view is that Carter's strategists and patrons made the classic marketing error of relying more on their instincts than on research to measure the pulling power of their commercials. Joseph Napolitan believes that the Carter people gambled on trying to run the same kind of campaign in the general election that they ran in the primaries. "You can't do that," he believes; "they're entirely different ball games."

A second view is that Carter's people, suddenly panicked by what they saw in the polls, made the classic marketing error of switching advertising campaigns at the wrong time.

In the last twelve days of the campaign, Carter's advertising changed momentarily. It may have been that the Coke people thought they could halt the declining fortunes of the candidate by suggesting he make use of the talents of political media specialist Tony Schwartz, who had worked on dozens of Coca-Cola commercials as a creative consultant; in any case, Schwartz went to work for Carter.

Schwartz thought he saw the problem. He took Carter "out of the fields," as he later described his strategy, dressed him in the usual candidate's suit and tie, sat him down in a "library" setting, and had him speak lines attacking Ford's voting record that Schwartz had hurriedly written.

Schwartz offered further authentication that there is no difference between political and product commercials. "Whether it's Coca-Cola or Jimmy Carter," he said, "what we appeal to in the consumer or voter is an attitude. We don't try to convey a point of view, but a montage of images and sounds that leaves the viewer with a positive attitude towards the product regardless of his perspective."

But some of Schwartz's commercials did not seem to sit well with the Carter people, in particular Rafshoon. They were concerned that, far from creating "positive" images, Schwartz's advertising was negative.

"In my mind, there's no such thing as 'negative' advertising," said Schwartz.

The powers behind Carter were not so sure. At least four years of preparation, expenditures, and hope seemed about to go down the drain. Schwartz's new commercials were yanked and the old Carter commercials reinstated, probably just in time. Carter still held a lead, however precarious; better to keep pitching soft images of him at viewers than to risk alienating them further (which seems to be a logical explanation of what the Schwartz advertising was doing) by attacking a president whom nobody really disliked.*

The strategy or the luck (probably a little of each) paid off. Two years later President Carter gave a glittering state dinner for Chinese Deputy Prime Minister Deng Xiaoping, in honor of the resumption of diplomatic relations. Of all the guests carefully selected for the historic and politically important occasion, none could have been more pleased and less surprised to be in attendance at the White House that evening than J. Paul Austin, the soft drink executive from Atlanta. A few months later in Peking, at the reception marking the opening of the U.S. embassy, Chinese guests were

*A third view of the Carter marketing error says that it lay not in making new commercials but in making the wrong commercials. New advertising might have been created, using the same themes and the same rural setting, but with a variation on the approach and the words. The original themes were not necessarily worn out; the way the camera viewed them may have been. When product managers from the giant soap and food corporations change commercials in the midst of a successful campaign, they do it to freshen the images, not the themes.

served ice-cold cans of Coca-Cola—just like in the commercials. Appropriately, most people in the United States saw the first pictures of the reception on television.

It's the Real Thing?

If the influence of Coca-Cola's advertising on Carter's advertising was not purely intentional, it may have been the greatest coincidence since the joining of politics and advertising.

No Carter commercial better demonstrates its debt to the Coke style of image manipulation than his *Walls Around Washington* spot. Consider the similarities:

In Coke commercials there are no middle-upper-class executives from the world of power and decision making, no professional women with jobs outside the home, no young people plagued by anything more serious than a Tom Sawyer infatuation. No one who would upset the rhapsodic scenes of yesteryear is allowed. The people who populate Cokeland affect the pace of dappled sunlit days and new-mown fields. They are smiling people, clean-cut and mannerly. They never speak in the commercials, but there can be no doubt that their speech is soft and friendly, for not a lick of harsh reality intrudes. These people are not from the rough-and-tumble city centers where decisions they cannot control are made for them without their knowledge or approval (by, among others, the Coca-Cola Corporation). They might be populists; the rank and file, the God-fearers, the good, uncomplaining workers, the first to volunteer for military duty in time of need without asking why. They are hometowners, small-towners, farm boys and girls and moms and dads and close-knit kin. Here is a cherubic, gangly high school football hero suddenly smitten by the cheerleader who has taken off her glasses. Here is the little girl trying on her mother's bridal gown. Here is the community turned out to paint the old lady's house. Here is the hard-boiled world of the ghetto playground, beautified, falsified, and converted symbolically into the carefree froth of the drink these suddenly unangry, nonviolent street kids have been handed. These are giggly children, frolicking on a homemade raft on a lazy summer day on a slow-moving Southern stream.

"Coke goes with life," said a commercial at the time of the Carter campaign. The life that Coke conjures up has been generally missing for some time—if indeed it was ever around to the extent portrayed in

ANNOUNCER: If there's one thing that can bind our country together . . .

[it] is a president who's in touch with the American people. A man who understands our needs and our strengths. Such a man is Jimmy Carter.

CARTER: We've seen walls built around Washington, and we feel that we can't quite get through

to guarantee the people . . . a government that's sensitive to our needs. And if there are things that you don't like in your own government,

if we've made mistakes that you don't want to see made again,

or if there are hopes . . . in your own lives

or in the lives of your children that you'd like to see realized, I hope that you will join me in a personal commitment to change our government for the better.

ANNOUNCER: Together, we can make our country strong again. . . .

any but our dreams and Coke's. But it is pretty to think about, and it is very, very good for sales.

You see the identical symbols in this political commercial for Carter. The crowds are Coca-Cola people. It is as if the camera that made the product commercial, instead of being turned off after the last shot of the Coke bottle, was left running as candidate Carter entered the scene. In fact Carter's role in his own commercial is not unlike that of the soft drink.

Like those of a Coca-Cola production, the techniques of a Carter for President production seem designed to create the illusion of slaking the public's thirst—in this instance for honesty and trust, for responsiveness and caring—with the chance, we are led to believe, to participate in our own destiny.

Run it through your mind:

Fade-up: People longing for love again.
Cut to: Product shot of the smiling new face, the "pause" on the political scene "that refreshes."
Cut to: Crowd drinking in the candidate's promises.
Cut to: Candidate promising.
Cut to: Crowd.
Cut to: Carter.
Cut to: Crowd.

Back and forth, back and forth, the crescendo building within the commercial and in the heads of the true crowd, the millions in the television audience.

What did the commercial say? More important, what did it convey? For like the cloying aftereffect of the syrupy soft drink, the residue left by Carter, bubbly personality and all, was a mess of sweet images —Coke images: the "outsider" come to save the "outsider" lurking in the hearts and minds of every person; the Bible-loving deacon come to rescue his populist brothers and sisters from the evils of Washington; the "country boy" come back to speak to his "country people," many of them deteriorating in slums as rancid as those of any city; the "farmer" spinning out dreams not for the benefit of working fellow farmers, who could hardly make ends meet, but to supplement the "farm reverie" of people who had never worked the soil; and the "small-towner" appealing to the small-town nostalgia of people who had forsaken the loneliness of an idea-depleted countryside a generation before or who had never been there. And though the nation had been bent out of recognizable shape from decades of bad times (induced in large part by its elected leaders), and though bad times were what the candidate *appeared* to address himself to, the symbolic imagery which lingered in the mind long after the commercial had vanished from the television screen was that of "good times" in which the ending (the election) would be as sweet and uncomplicated as the last drops of the candidate's soft-drink model.

One year after the election Jimmy Carter was sinking fast in the polls. Of five immediate past presidents, only Gerald Ford had fallen farther faster. By the spring of 1978 Carter's low standing was only a few points above Richard Nixon's at its lowest.

The problem, Carter pollster Pat Caddell theorized, was that the president was still a remote, distant figure to many Americans. "After fifteen months in office they are still not sure who he is."*

Journalist Tom Wicker saw the problem less simplistically:

> Jimmy Carter's record so far suggests the danger inherent in the era of media politics: candidates who get elected primarily by their successful use of television and imagery may not have, or may gain too slowly, the skill and experience necessary to manage the political offices they have won. And the danger is doubled when such candidates arouse expectations that cannot be met by political performance.

Yet the expectations planted in the public mind by Carter's image-manipulating commercials, for all their sugary promises, would have been challenged by the networks for dozens of advertising code violations had product guidelines been applied to them. Correcting the *Walls Around Washington* commercial to make it conform to the television code would have effectively destroyed the intent of its creators. The television code would have substantially altered other Carter commercials and many of Gerald Ford's as well. In looking at these violations we should ask, Where would the country—and the world—stand today if the key commercials from both sides in the 1976 campaign had been booted out of the network standards offices for their serious breaches of the advertising code?

*Carter, the media invention, turned to a typical media solution: Gerald Rafshoon was called in to develop and publicize "the themes of the presidency." In one of those coincidences for which Washington is famous, he was given the office in which the Nixon tapes were "accidentally" erased.

Four Unacceptable Carter Commercials

Like Carter's workhorse commercial *My Own Campaign* (see chapter 1), four other key campaign commercials were guilty of making "claims or representations which have the capacity to deceive, mislead, or misrepresent" and therefore would have failed the network test for integrity of the advertiser.

If integrity is missing, it follows that the taste of the presentation is unacceptable; also unacceptable was the "lack of evidence to support the claims" made in the advertising.

And since Carter's commercials were testimonials on his own behalf, his advertising violated that section of the code which requires that "all claims and statements, including subjective evaluations of testifiers, be supportable by facts and free of *misleading implications.*" There was a minimum of five violations per commercial, any one of which would have been sufficient to disqualify the commercial from broadcast.

Walls Around Washington
Sixty-second Carter commercial
Five network code violations

Walls Around Washington was in violation because Carter failed to support his claims by explaining *how* he would be "in touch with the American people" as president, *what* it was he possessed that would enable him to understand the country's "needs" and "strengths," *what* those needs and strengths were, *what* the nature of the guarantee was that would enable him to give the people "a government that's sensitive to our needs," *how* he would go about the task of changing "our government for the better," *what* "better" meant, and *what* precisely Carter meant when he asked the people to join him "in a personal commitment" to effect that change.

Some may ask, Why carp at what has been viewed historically as the politician's harmless propensity for campaign gloss? An answer lies in asking further questions: Is it any longer harmless? Is the rhetoric of politicians, particularly those who would be seriously considered for the office of president of a powerful yet vulnerable nation, affordable still to people living under the threat of instant catastrophe that they neither created nor sanctioned? And how much longer will issues of life and death be relegated to half-baked puffery?

CARTER: . . . I don't think we'll ever have a solution to our present economic woes as long as we've got eight and a half or nine million people out of jobs and looking for jobs.

And another two or three million who have given up hope of getting work.

And another million and a half on welfare that never have worked but are fully able to . . . .

ANNOUNCER: If you want to put America back to work, vote for Jimmy Carter. . . .

Jobs
Thirty-second Carter commercial
Seven network code violations

The rhetoric of the *Jobs* commercial offered more of the same. It is a long way from verifying the obvious fact that millions are unemployed to putting teeth into the airy claim that, as president, you can provide work. How? Through a Civilian Conservation Corps program? By coming to grips with technology and restructuring the concept of work? If Jimmy Carter knew a way to put people to work, he did not even hint at it in this thirty-second commercial. Had he taken a full minute —or five minutes, or thirty—to have a more detailed discussion, it is doubtful that he would have had one more thing to say on the subject (though the longer length would have allowed the public to see this).

It appears that Carter's intention was only to mimic concern—a cruel deception of the millions who had "given up hope of getting work" yet went to the polls to vote for the new savior, especially the poor and low-income blacks whose votes gave Carter his majorities in several states in the Deep South.

Had the *Jobs* commercial been required to comply with the television code, Carter would have been prevented from *implying* solutions, for his advertising would have been in violation not only on the five counts cited earlier but also on the grounds of "service [jobs] unavailable" and "unsupported or exaggerated promises of employment or earnings." It will be an interesting day indeed for Democracy when the public either decides to remove from the politician's campaign repertoire the phony issue of employment or insists that candidates explain what they mean.

Arab Oil and Israel
Sixty-second Carter commercial
Five network code violations

This commercial, designed to entice the important Jewish vote, was in violation of the code because the claims that Carter could (or would) prevent the Arab nations from attempting another oil embargo by withholding food, weapons, and oil-drilling equipment were not substantiated. Nor could they be. What food does the United States export to Arab oil-producing nations that they could not buy from other eager-to-please countries? The rice, wheat, and canned goods that Saudi Arabia imports? *Le Monde,* the Paris daily newspaper, also notes that "the Saudis produce more than half their meat consumption" and "could in the short term fill half their wheat needs."

How can the United States prevent France, Britain, Italy, West Germany—or the Soviet Union, for that matter—from selling weapons to the Arabs in the face of a threat of a similar embargo being imposed upon them? (After all, West Germany refused to let U.S. supply planes bound for Israel during the Yom Kippur War refuel at its airports for fear of incurring Arab wrath.) And how can the United States prevent a multinational corporation, despite its American base, from selling oil-drilling equipment to the Arabs if the firm is clever and prudent in its operations?

CARTER: I would make it clear to the Arab countries . . . that if they ever again try to blackmail this nation as they did in 1973 . . .

that we would consider . . . an economic declaration of war . . .

not give them any foods, no weapons, no spare parts for weapons, no oil-drilling rigs, or oil pipe, no nothing.

I think this would prevent their trying to bring this nation to its knees again with an oil embargo. . . .

ANNOUNCER: As president, Jimmy Carter will never risk our security or sacrifice the survival of Israel in return for barrels of oil. . . .

CARTER: When I was elected governor, I went into office not as a politician but as an engineer, a farmer, a businessman, a planter.

We had 300 agencies and departments in the state government. We abolished 278 of them. . . . That saved a lot of money. . . .

With a new budgeting technique called zero-base budgeting we eliminated all the old obsolescent programs.

Put into effect long-range goals, planning, and cut administrative costs more than 50 percent.

And shifted that money and that service . . . toward giving better government services to our people.

ANNOUNCER: What Jimmy Carter did as governor, he'll do as president. If you agree that government should be reorganized, vote for Jimmy Carter.

Government Reorganization
Sixty-second Carter commercial
Five network code violations

Carter's *Government Reorganization* commercial was one of the rare instances in which he cited facts. The facts, however, were used in ways that were deceptive and misleading.

Carter used the reorganization of the Georgia state government when he was governor as proof that he could reorganize the federal government—without indicating what he would reorganize in Washington, how he would do it, or why. It was in the *telling* of his accomplishments as governor, however, that the most serious violations occurred, for, as Carter very well knew, he was fudging the facts he kept reciting as gospel.

First, Carter again misrepresented his background when he claimed that he was not a politician when he was elected governor. In fact he had been a member of the Sumpter County School Board in 1961 and subsequently its chairman; he was elected to two terms in the Georgia Senate, beginning in 1962; and in 1966 he lost in his first try for the nomination for governor and immediately began working for the 1970 gubernatorial election, which he won.

Second, while as governor he abolished "278 of the 300 state agencies and departments," his reorganization was by and large a paper reshuffling. Most of the agencies he eliminated either were not funded by the state or were not in operation. Then Carter converted 65 "budgeted" agencies which were funded by the state into 30 superagencies, a step which in the view of some Georgia officials did not necessarily guarantee anything more than further bureaucratic confusion and slowness.

Third, Carter's claim that his "reorganization" had "saved a lot of money" is not substantiated; it is further open to question in view of a second claim that his "zero-based budgeting . . . cut administrative costs more than 50 percent." When journalist Steven Brill was researching a magazine article on Carter in December 1975,* he questioned the candidate about the 50 percent savings. Carter directed Brill to a campaign aide who could not suggest spe-

*Brill's article appeared in *Harper's Magazine* of March 1976. He was one of the few political writers to challenge the basis of Carter's facts and programs early in the campaign, and the Carter forces quickly attempted to discredit Brill and the article.

cific items which would have accounted for the already well-publicized cuts.

But many specifics were known about the cost of running Georgia during Carter's four years as governor. The cost of running the governor's office, for example, *grew* by 49 percent. Georgia's total budget *grew* by 58 percent, its (outstanding) debt *grew* by nearly 25 percent, and the number of employees *grew* by 30 percent. Possibly inflation and hiring additional people to strengthen social programs accounted for much of the increase in budget and employees, but neither was cited in the commercial. Instead, Carter used his "cost-cutting" figures to bolster the illusion of the outsider who would straighten out Washington's bloated bureaucracy just as he claimed he had done in Georgia.

Ford vs. Carter—Frame for Frame

While Carter's *Government Reorganization* commercial was running, Ford challenged it with a counter commercial that used much of the information just cited. The result demonstrated vividly how it was the opposing commercials, rather than the candidates, that ran against each other in the last weeks of the campaign.

The commercials also demonstrated what a public disservice political advertising has come to be. Here were two contradictory sets of claims thrown against each other without the substantiation that would allow voters to make a decision based on reason and fact. Although the facts in Ford's commercial were correct, there was no way to know which commercial was telling the truth.

There was, however, a disingenuous tone to Ford's plea not to "let Jimmy Carter give us more big government," in view of the federal government's spending habits under Ford. On taking office, Ford submitted a revised budget of $302.2 billion for fiscal 1975, with an estimated federal deficit of $34.7 billion for that year. For fiscal 1976 Ford sent Congress a federal budget of $349 billion, with a deficit of $51.9 billion, the largest "peacetime" deficit in U.S. history. For fiscal 1977, Ford submitted a budget of $394.2 billion.

The Carter and Ford commercials again met head-on on the issue of help and health for the elderly. Ford's commercial was first on the air. The president, taking a cue from earlier Carter advertising, appeared in sweater and sport shirt and boasted, "Under the proposals that I recommended, no person would have to pay more than $750 a

ANNOUNCER: [Jimmy Carter's] ads say that he will do the same thing as president that he did as governor of Georgia.

Then you should know that during his one term as governor,

government spending increased 58 percent. Government employees went up 25 percent.

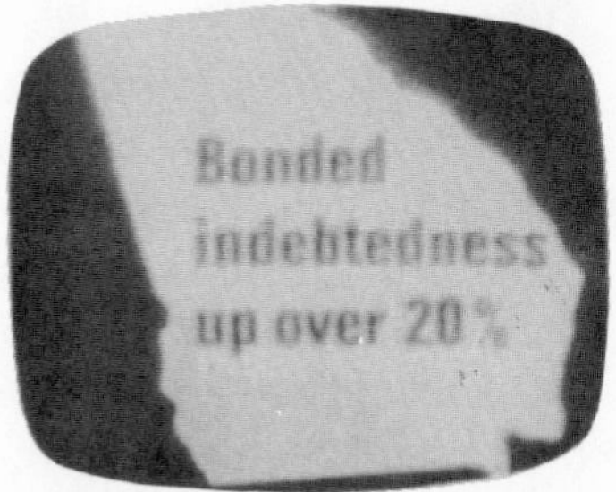

. . . Georgia went over 20 percent deeper into debt. Don't let Jimmy Carter give us more big government.

Keep President Ford.

year for both hospital care and medical care." Even if $750 was a manageable sum for the elderly, the idea itself was guilty of nine separate violations of the television code, beginning with the "integrity of the advertiser."

Gerald Ford posed in his commercial as a person who was sensitive to the needs of the elderly and the ill. Yet in 1975 the Ford administration bore down on health benefits and programs in an attempt to reduce costs, took a hard stand against amending health plans needing more federal money, and decided not to back a bill for national health insurance. On July 26, Ford vetoed the health services legislation, though his veto was later overridden by substantial majorities of Democrats and Republicans in both houses.

The Ford government then proposed so-called cost-cutting measures for Medicare and Medicaid (referred to in part in the commercial) which it claimed would really benefit the elderly and the poor (all too frequently the same people). The idea was to dissuade them from what the government termed "unnecessary hospitalization." Medicare patients would be responsible for the costs of day one of their hospitalization, plus 10 percent of the charges incurred for each day thereafter until they had given the hospital $750 of their own money. The Ford government's proposal was to amend the law under which patients would be billed at the national average hospital rate for the first day and excused from paying anything from day two through day sixty. The Ford government also wanted Medicare patients to pay a higher deductible before Medicare took over its coverage of their physicians' charges. This is hardly what Gerald Ford was chatting about with the old people in his commercial. Groups such as the National Retired Teachers Association and the American Association of Retired Persons vigorously challenged the Ford idea, charging that it would add to the burden of hospital and health costs on the people least able to pay. Congress gave Ford's proposal the cold shoulder.

This took place one year before Ford's *Elderly* commercial went on television with what was made to appear to be a new idea—a violation of that section of the television code which prohibits using commercial claims when conditions on which the claim is based no longer prevail. The commercial also smacked of " 'bait and switch tactics' which feature goods or services not intended for sale [defunct health legislation] but designed to lure the public into purchasing higher-priced substitutes [Ford]."

At this point Carter attempted to capitalize on old people with a

FORD: We should in the field of health

take a major step to protect older people from what I call catastrophic or prolonged illness. Under the proposals that I recommended

no person would have to pay more than $750 a year for both hospital care and medical care.

With that kind of protection, then nobody really has to feel all of their resources being depleted. . . .

I say frequently, and I mean it, there's no reason why somebody should go broke just to get well.

ANNOUNCER: Sensitivity, concern. A willingness to listen and to act. Let's keep President Ford in charge.

CARTER: Gerald Ford voted against Medicare.

Against food stamps for the elderly. . . .

Isn't it bad enough that older people are the worst victims . . . of hoodlums and criminals?

Must they also be victimized by their own government . . . ? . . . I could not live in the White House without helping them.

heart-wrenching plea for their votes that perfectly utilized media theories of Tony Schwartz. Schwartz had written earlier that "the question of truth is largely irrelevant when dealing with electronic media content," and that "the best political commercials are similar to Rorschach patterns. They do not tell the viewer anything. They surface his feelings and provide a context for him to express these feelings."

An example of this occurs in the first frames of Carter's commercial accusing Gerald Ford of voting against the sick and the elderly. The accusations were sneaky. The implication was that Ford's record as *president* was under attack, but the record that was referred to belonged to Ford the *congressman.* The commercial deserved to be thrown out for using "claims that unfairly attack competitors" and for not "properly identifying competitors." Having implanted the unfair notions in an effort to "surface" the feelings of the elderly in the viewing audience, Carter abruptly shifted the focus to himself as the potential occupant of the White House, implying that he would provide the necessary programs for the elderly without telling the viewer anything about such programs.

For both commercials, a larger question should be asked: Was either actually directed to an audience of elderly people? Or were the Carter and Ford strategists looking for bigger game, the multimillion-strong, middle-aged, reasonably healthy voter market—the vital center for any campaign victory—who would not be affected directly by either advertising message but who would be pleased with what each candidate suggested for their future retirement?

Two Doubtful Ford Commercials

The "people on the street" commercials contained some of Ford's most damaging advertising. Carter is said to have complained about their effect on his campaign; he was right to do so.

In using this technique, a producer and a cameraman go out on a street, supposedly chosen at random, and look for people who are willing to appear on camera and say something favorable about a product in a few seconds. The technique has suited the purposes of many product advertisers in recent times—for soap, laundry detergent, denture polish, and the like—because stiffer advertising regulations (and sometimes lazy advertising writers) have made it difficult if not impossible to advertise product superiority in any real detail in those categories in which all products are more or less identical. Thus a montage of people appears on the television screen, people talking in rapid-fire bursts about a laundry detergent that makes clothes "brighter," "whiter," "cleaner," "nicer," "fresher," "sweeter." And this is probably about the extent of anyone's vocabulary when it comes to describing the effects of soap on bedsheets and socks.

However, one might wish for a somewhat deeper thought process when describing a candidate for president of the United States. After all, "honest," "trust," "trust," "decent," "faith," "trust," "honest," "best," "best," "honest," "straightforward," "honest," "best," and "downright decent" in a sixty-second commercial do not provide one with much to think about. Honesty is a fine quality, but one would like to think that every candidate for president possesses at least a little of it, however whimsical that daydream may be. Simply to state these qualities with deliberately calculated repetition will not make them so; it only *appears* to make them so, as Ford's advertising chief, Malcolm MacDougall, understood.

The honesty of this technique has been suspect for years, though

WOMAN: An honest man . . . I trust him.

(FORD FAMILY)
WOMAN: I'm voting for Ford because I trust him . . . he's a decent man.

WOMAN: . . . I have faith in the man. I trust the man.

MAN: He's an honest man. And that's the kind of guy that I want representing me. . . .

WOMAN: He's the best president that we had. And he's going to be the best president . . . we're going to have.

WOMAN: I like him very much. He's a very honest man. . . .

MAN: He's about the most straightforward man I know. His policies are sound. . . .

WOMAN: He's just a downright, decent, honest person, seems to me.

we have MacDougall's word that there was no rigging in his commercial.

> It's quite true that anyone can go out on the street with a camera and find people who are willing to praise one candidate and criticize another. Give me a week and I can probably make a film full of people praising Adolf Hitler. [But] nothing was staged. The people were not selected in advance.

MacDougall maintains that the commercials "accurately reflected an existing national attitude towards Jimmy Carter." That may be, but there is no way that the undecided voter could be certain of it. There is no way for one to know how many people were filmed before enough were found who could be edited effectively into a commercial that would be shown again and again to millions of people.

It is one thing to use the "people on the street" technique for products that play trivial roles in the lives of people; it is something quite different to make it a major tactic in election campaigns.

Newspapers for Ford
Thirty-second Ford commercial
Seven network code violations

In *Newspapers for Ford,* papers from Carter's home state that had endorsed Ford were announced as the name of each passed quickly in review on the television screen—so quickly that it appeared there was not enough time to mention them all. "Like most of our best commercials, this was *deceptively* simple," MacDougall said. "And it's not *all that misleading,*" said his campaign associate, Doug Bailey (emphasis added). MacDougall was right.

The commercial was designed to make it appear as though a landslide of Georgia newspapers had come out for Ford, and this impression was false. A private survey of twenty-two of Georgia's major newspapers, including those noted in Ford's commercials, found that twelve papers with a total circulation of 306,347 did endorse Ford. One, the *Atlanta Daily World,* was touted as though it were *the* paper in the state's largest city. But with a circulation of just 23,000, it was not precisely a major political voice.

Only ten newspapers in the survey endorsed Carter, but one of them was the powerful and influential *Atlanta Constitution.* If the vital

NEWSPAPERS FOR FORD

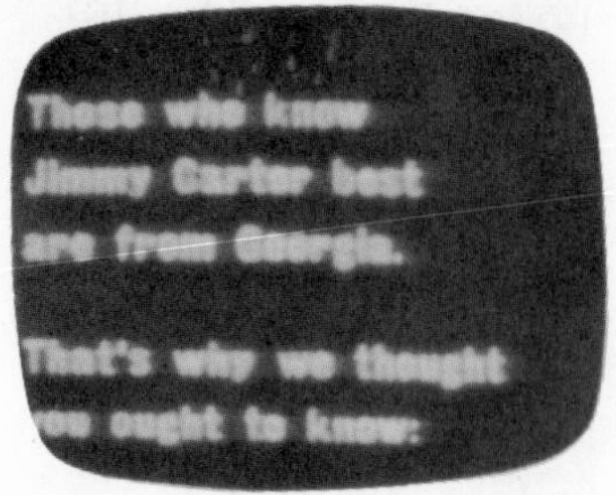

ANNOUNCER: The Savannah Georgia News endorses Gerald Ford for president. . . .

The Atlanta Georgia Daily World endorses President Ford.

The Marietta Georgia Journal endorses President Ford.

The Albany Georgia Herald endorses President Ford.

The Augusta Georgia Chronicle endorses President Ford. . . .

Sunday circulation of the *Constitution* is counted, the circulation of the ten newspapers endorsing Carter totaled 956,700.

Newspapers for Ford was clever political advertising, all right, but it was guilty of no less than seven code violations. For once in the campaign Carter had a legitimate beef.

9

SHOULD POLITICAL ADVERTISING BE BANNED?

The rights of politicians vs. the rights of voters

> *Congress shall make no law . . . abridging the freedom of speech or of the press; or the right of all people peaceably . . . to petition the Government for a redress of grievances.*
>
> The First Amendment to the Constitution

> *That whenever any Form of Government becomes destructive of these ends, it is the Right of the People to alter or to abolish it, and to institute new Government, laying its foundation on such principles and organizing its power in such form, as to them shall seem most likely to effect their Safety and Happiness.*
>
> The Declaration of Independence

The political television commercial, far from being just another powerful campaign technique in the long history of dirty politics in America, is a dangerous weapon in the hands of the unscrupulous, one with a proven record of instigating and inflicting great harm on an unsuspecting public.

That being the case, the obvious solution is to ban the political commercial. Yet such an act would appear to violate the First Amendment. The Constitution provides for unlimited protection, short of seditious and treasonable ideas, for what the Supreme Court refers to as ideological speech—political speech. When political speech turns up in the form of a television commercial, freedom of speech is extended implicitly to whatever the candidate wishes to say and show, no matter how false, deceptive, misleading, or unfair it may be.

Politicians have ducked behind the free speech clause of the First Amendment ever since it took effect in 1791. But in a time when campaign rhetoric was transmitted at the speed of horseback, the theory of the amendment served as a pretty good brake against their bad habits. With the "mighty caldron of free expression and ideas" literally at its feet, on the village green, the public had the time and a place to size up candidates in the flesh and winnow the honest and creative from the charlatans and crooks. Public questions, dissatisfaction, and rebuttal could be vented in town meetings (unlike the contrived media events held today) and in fiery newspapers unbeholden to a corporate board of directors. Even in the era of the railroad whistle-stop—when the backs of trains were used for serious campaign speeches, not as a campaign gimmick—crowds could still get close enough to the candidates to challenge the facts and the ethics of what they had to say. A fraud was easier to spot, and frauds could be told off to their faces. Moreover, people then were less reluctant to do so. And word got around.

But the public's ability to challenge directly the intentions and the veracity of political candidates began to fade with the emergence of radio as a campaign device in the thirties, and it disappeared almost entirely with the advent of the Eisenhower television commercials in 1952. Since the joining of politics with television and advertising, politicians (who may prove to be foolish once in office but who are certainly not fools when it comes to manipulating the media to get there) have used the privilege and protection of free speech with virtual immunity as a cover not only for broadcasting deceptive and misleading information but, worse, for creating deceptive and misleading impressions. There is always the chance that false information can be corrected; false impressions are next to impossible to eradicate.

Does this mean that political commercials can *never* be banned? After all, the television networks ban many kinds of advertising that are similar to political commercials yet much less harmful: fortune telling, astrology, phrenology, palm reading, numerology, mind reading, character reading and other occult pursuits, tip sheets, and the sale of franchises.

The television networks have also banned the advertising of products considered hazardous to the public's health and welfare: hard liquor, firearms, fireworks, and cigarettes. The Federal Trade Commission is considering a ban on commercials (during children's programs) for pre-sugared cereals and snacks and violent toys. The FTC has also wondered whether advertising for milk should not be reviewed because of milk's possibly unhealthful butterfat content.

Television commercials for hazardous products have been thought by the courts and by Congress to be hazardous in themselves because of their power to spread harmful information. That is why cigarette advertising has been banned from television but not from newspapers and magazines.

Each time the question of banning the advertising of hazardous products arises, it is thrown into the free speech debate. The cigarette advertising case posed the classic question of health vs. the First Amendment and produced the now classic reply from the court.*

The question, as former television executive Fred W. Friendly has noted, was, "Does the state have the power to protect the health of its citizens, even if it means violating freedom of speech and 'the sanctity of the First Amendment,' as the broadcast industry put it?"

Writing the majority opinion for the court, Chief Judge David L. Bazelon recognized that issues beyond the First Amendment needed to be considered. On the decisive question of "public interest versus public health," Bazelon was firm. "Whatever else it may mean, however, we think the public interest indisputably means the public health. . . . The power to protect the public health lies at the heart of the State's political power. . . . The public health has in effect become a kind of basic law."

What is the definition of health? Webster's says it is "the condition of an organism or one of its parts in which it performs its vital functions normally or properly: the state of being sound in body or mind."

What does common sense say? Is it too frivolous to argue that the political commercial is unhealthful? Is it farfetched to reason that nearly three decades of electronic deception, bamboozle, and outright lying about war and peace, national security, the right to work, to minimum wages, nutrition, and health care, the right to clean air, to adequate and safe energy and drinking water, among other inherent rights, have caused the vital political and mental functions of the public organism to perform abnormally and improperly?

Yet it is unlikely that the political commercial as the instigator and purveyor of deceit will be banned. The power to protect the public health may lie at the heart of the state's political power, but it is perhaps too much to expect the state to rid the public of the very instrument that has helped it to power.

**Banzhaf* v. *FCC,* U.S. Court of Appeals for the District of Columbia, 1968.

If the political commercial cannot be banned, can it be regulated, like the product commercial, for false and deceptive claims?

No, not as things stand now. But serious questions remain to be asked, and the Supreme Court may have inadvertently provided some clues to the answers.

Against the background of a decade of intensive product advertising regulation, the court entered the scene with two landmark rulings that catapulted product advertising into the free speech arena of the politicians.

In 1975, in *Bigelow* v. *Virginia,* the court ruled that an advertisement in a Virginia newspaper announcing the availability of abortions in New York (illegal under Virginia law) not only was legal but "did more than simply propose a commercial transaction. It contained factual material of clear 'public interest.' "

The following year the court expanded on the concept of First Amendment protection for commercial speech. In the *Virginia State Board of Pharmacy* case the issue involved a Virginia statute that prohibited pharmacists from advertising prescription drug prices. The court held that, assuming that an advertiser's interest is "a purely economic one," that "hardly disqualifies him for protection under the First Amendment. . . . Advertising, however tasteless and excessive it sometimes may seem . . . is nonetheless dissemination of information. . . . It is a matter of public interest that [private economic] decisions, in the aggregate, be intelligent and well informed."

The court, however, set limits on the application of the First Amendment to product advertising. "In concluding that commercial speech, like other varieties [political advertising, for example], is protected, we of course do not hold that it can never be regulated in any way. . . . Untruthful speech, commercial *or otherwise,* has never been protected for its own sake." (Emphasis added.)

Has the court not left room for an overdue review of the nature and status of the political commercial? For example:

- Are all forms of political speech identical? Is there no difference between political debate, political addresses, political commentary, and political advertising?
- Does political advertising give up the right to absolute free speech when it behaves like product advertising: that is, when it is identical in concept, creation, and production, in length,

> sales pitch, and sloganeering; when it is transmitted in the identical manner and received in the identical environment; and, most important, when it is perceived in the identical way by the brain?

Is there not an opening in the *Virginia State Board of Pharmacy* ruling to apply its doctrine *in reverse* to political commercial regulation? For example:

- If product advertising can be given First Amendment protection yet be regulated for truth because the consumer cannot be expected to know the validity of advertising claims, why shouldn't the voter expect equal protection under law when politicians sell themselves like products?

It should be unnecessary to have to point out that the consumer and the voter sitting before the television set are the same person. Yet electoral folklore and conventional First Amendment wisdom persist in dividing the viewer in two. That is not the situation, and it never was. Perhaps one day a valid test case will be brought before the courts in an effort to do away with this folklore, and someone will have the courage to ask:

- What are the First Amendment rights of television viewers who receive the bulk of their information about politicians through television programs and commercials?
- At what point does the political commercial infringe on the public's First Amendment rights when the information and images the commercial conveys are distorted and untruthful?
- Is the political commercial, which has become as much a part of the television medium as the product commercial, *never* subject to similar restraints and challenges?

These are serious questions that concern virtually every facet of a citizen's life, including the sanctity of citizenship. Who will come forward to pursue them?

In the meantime, unfortunately, all questions are academic; the political television commercial cannot be regulated. Section 315 of the Communications Act (approved in 1934, eighteen years before the first political television commercial) leaves no doubt about that.

> If any licensee shall permit any person who is a legally qualified candidate for any public office to use a [radio] broadcasting station, he shall afford equal opportunities to all other such candidates for

> that office in the use of such broadcasting station. . . . *Provided,* That such licensee *shall have no power of censorship over the material broadcast under the provisions of this section.* [Emphasis added.]

Whenever the act has been amended to take into account the effect of television on the electoral process, the provisions have always concerned the rights of the politicians and the responsibilities of the broadcasters—usually to the politicians. Viewers have been legislated into nonparticipants in their own electoral process. For example, when Congress amended the Communications Act in 1959 to make certain exemptions to the equal time rule,* it included every way a political candidate could use television except the most powerful way, the commercial.

> Appearance by a legally qualified candidate on any—
>
> (1) bona fide newscast,
> (2) bona fide news interview,
> (3) bona fide news documentary (if the appearance of the candidate is incidental to the presentation of the subject or subjects covered by the news documentary), or
> (4) on-the-spot coverage of bona fide news events (including but not limited to political conventions and activities incidental thereto),
>
> shall not be deemed to be use of a broadcasting station. . . . Nothing in the foregoing sentence shall be construed as relieving broadcasters, in connection with the presentation [of the above], from the obligation imposed upon them under this Act *to operate in the public interest and to afford reasonable opportunity for the discussion of conflicting views on issues of public importance.* [Emphasis added.]

What constitutes "reasonable opportunity" and "public importance" has been left to the interpretation of the broadcaster and the FCC. But there is only one way to decide if a station can "operate in the public interest" while at the same time broadcasting false and deceptive political commercials: It cannot.

*The equal time rule should not be confused (as it usually is) with the fairness doctrine, which contains some of the same language. The fairness doctrine requires broadcasters "to devote a reasonable amount of broadcast time to the discussion of controversial issues; and to do so fairly in order to afford reasonable opportunity for opposing viewpoints." The fairness doctrine supposedly applies to any subject at any time; the equal time rule applies only to elections.

When it comes to the political commercial, the station by law is merely the electronic distributor of false and misleading information and images that, increasingly, are counter to the public interest.

A station intending to carry out what it may consider to be its public interest duties could reject a political commercial, demand revisions from the campaign organization, or make the revisions itself in order to bring the commercial up to the level of broadcast standards applicable to its product commercials and general program material. However, should the "offended" politician make a complaint to the FCC about the station's action—and that would almost certainly happen—the station in all likelihood would be fined, perhaps heavily, or have its license revoked, or both.* Faced with this economic risk, what station will decide to exercise its conscience, even if it has bona fide knowledge that what is being broadcast on behalf of a candidate is untrue?

This does not mean that a station or a network's conscience does not occasionally and discreetly surface, though when it does, it is never on a level higher than that of under-the-table negotiations with the campaign organization or the advertising agency responsible for the offending commercial.

David Adams, the esteemed former vice chairman of NBC (now retired), points out that when a political commercial seems to go beyond the bounds of "decency, veracity, taste . . . what we try to do is deal with the advertising agency. . . . And all we can do is to try to use persuasion."

"We will never turn [a political commercial] down because of content," says NBC attorney Stan Kaufman. "We *will* often raise a question with an agency: Do you really want to say this? Or do you really want to say it *this* way? Or do you really want [the candidate or the opponent] to look like this? Is [what is being said in the commercial] really accurate?"

On occasion a commercial is withdrawn after a "heart-to-heart" discussion with the station or network; most often it is not. One talk that failed to bring about the withdrawal of a commercial concerned Right to Life candidate Ellen McCormick in her race for governor of New York in 1978. Her main issue—her only issue—was abortion and what she considered its illegality and immorality.

*There are rare circumstances under which a station can indeed reject a political commercial: when the commercial does not include at some point the candidate's likeness or voice, when it preaches sedition, treason, or overthrow of the government, or when it makes an obscenity.

To make her point, Kaufman said, "she showed in some of her commercials, four-week-old and six-week-old fetuses being born. It was pretty grizzly, gruesome stuff. And we raised questions from a taste standpoint—'Really, this stuff is going to offend a lot of people and do you really want to show this?' 'Yes, we do,' was the answer."

When a network does question the standard of taste in a political commercial, it may ask the campaign organization to state in writing that its candidate knows about the commercial—because sometimes the candidate does not know, according to NBC's former vice president for broadcast standards, Herminio Traviesas. Traviesas believes that the practice stems from the time a questionable commercial for Ronald Reagan was broadcast. "He just never knew it was being used, and when he saw it he was embarrassed and pulled it. So we want to be sure."

But these are the exceptions that prove the FCC's rule on censorship. Undoubtedly the television stations and networks could be much more aggressive without running afoul of the FCC—relentlessly aggressive if they chose—in questioning political advertising, and not just for taste but for content, for the claims made about a candidate's background, accomplishments, and plans for the nation's political, social, and economic future. That kind of questioning and investigation, once politicians understood that it was standard procedure at a television station and that the questions and answers could find their way to the news department and to other news media, could go a long way toward dealing with present practices.

One wonders—to take the most recent example—how the 1976 presidential election would have turned out if some television station near the beginning of Jimmy Carter's primary trail had called in media specialist Gerald Rafshoon and asked, "Do you really want to say in this commercial that your candidate had no political organization when the campaign began? Do you really want to say that Mr. Carter did not have much money? It's none of our business, of course, but we understand that the candidate has a great many connections in Atlanta, as well as a substantial peanut business of his own, and, after all, you must have the money to pay for the air time for this commercial."

Asking hard and reasonable questions of candidates of course requires broadcasters to get off their behinds and do a little research. It also requires guts. Consequently the questions are not likely to be asked very soon, for the truth is that as many broadcasters hide in safety behind the provisions of Section 315 and the First Amendment as do politicians. Stan Kaufman is very clear about NBC's feelings:

> We're schizophrenic about it [Section 315]. We don't like being put in a position of saying that we don't have any control whatsoever over any segment of the broadcast day. We like to think we are responsible people and we should be permitted to exercise responsibility. On the other hand, [Section 315] is a kind of buffer for us. We don't have to make certain decisions which are often very tough, and to the extent that [it can be] your excuse for [not] making tough decisions, I guess it can be considered to be an advantage.

What Kaufman could not ask but is keenly sensitive to, like executives from all television networks, is the question, What could happen to the licenses of networks and stations when the candidate whom they have "given a hard time" wins? More than a few presidents and senators have tried, directly or through the FCC, to bring pressure on stations they thought were being "too aggressive" in their political policies and views. Franklin Roosevelt tried to take newspapers that opposed his third term out of the broadcasting business. Lyndon Johnson used to pick up the telephone and chew out network heads for reporting news he didn't like. Charles Colson liked to visit the networks in New York to let them know how unfair he thought they were to Nixon.

There is a great deal of talk about the First Amendment rights of the politician and the broadcaster. Very little is said about the rights of the viewer.

If the political commercial cannot be regulated, can a television station refuse to sell time for a political commercial it believes is false, deceptive, or unfair?

Not any more. Until 1972 a television station might have used a loophole in Section 315 to avoid selling time to candidates running for a federal office if the station believed that (1) it was in the best interest of the public not to see *any* commercials for any candidates because the commercials for *one* candidate would have an unfair effect on the election; (2) serious irregularities existed in the commercials for *all* the candidates, which would have an unfair effect on the election; (3) the political commercial was not the proper time unit or forum for serious and objective discussion and debate or viewer enlightenment.

The loophole in Section 315 said: *No obligation is imposed under this subsection upon any licensee to allow the use of its station by any such candidate.*

That loophole was closed by Congress (whose members, after all, spend an inordinate amount of their elected time on the business of getting reelected) with the passage of the Federal Election Campaign Act of 1971, specifically Section 312(a)(7), which required broadcasters *to permit the purchase of reasonable amounts of time for the use of a broadcasting station by a legally qualified candidate for federal elective office on behalf of his candidacy.*

Why did Congress believe it needed a law to make sure it could purchase time for political commercials? Because, as the FCC noted in its 1978 report concerning an inquiry of Section 312(a)(7), "many candidates have found the broadcast of spot announcements to be the most effective way of reaching the voters." One of the great understatements in American political history!

If additional evidence were needed to prove the power and the necessity of the television commercial in the careers of politicians, it is in this act, which the Senate-House conference report called a bill "to promote fair practices in the conduct of election campaigns." In fact the bill institutionalized misconduct in political advertising.

If a television station must sell time for a political commercial it considers false, deceptive, and misleading, can it mandate the length it believes a commercial must be for a fair examination of the candidate and the issues?

No. The law requires that television stations offer political candidates the same commercial time units they offer corporations for product advertising, which means units of ten, thirty, and sixty seconds, with thirty seconds being the basic buy today.*

Perhaps there exists a politician blessed with the dual gifts of fierce intellectualism and brevity. Should one be discovered it would still be difficult to imagine how that person could successfully define for the viewer, in thirty seconds or less, not only his or her real origins but also his or her stand on subjects that threaten to bury the country in a daily avalanche of panic and despair.

A viewer can learn all he or she needs to know about chewing gum in thirty seconds. To think that the credentials and the character of people who seek high office can be examined in the same length of time is absurd. Electing people in this way has proved disappointing again and again. But it is one thing to elect a fool or an incompetent (however "legally qualified") as a result of commercials whose length compresses the complexity and danger of the issues being "discussed." Someday

*Occasionally a candidate will try to buy time for five-minute commercials, but this is rare, costly, and difficult to negotiate. Networks and producers dislike shortening their programs to accommodate this length.

someone is going to sneak into elective office behind a shield of these hit-and-run commercials who will make Watergate look like child's play. For all anybody knows, that person is already in office—somewhere.

If the political commercial cannot be banned, regulated, refused broadcast time, or have its length mandated, are there other ways to check its runaway power?

We are trained as children to believe that, in our constitutional system of checks and balances, fair-minded representatives, judges, and others who operate the machinery of state in the public interest will keep an eye on each other in order to curb corruption of government power and excesses of personal privilege. But if checks and balances in recent years have deteriorated into a checkmate of government by corporate interests, and a contest with government and corporation opposing the citizen, they are next to nonexistent in the new system of election by television and advertisement.

Traditionally there have been three basic antidotes to counteract the effects of misleading political information, unfair political persuasion, and political lies. The first antidote has shown that it cannot be relied upon; the other two, like so many venerable political theories, have proved to be sentimental myths when exposed to the light emanating from the television set.

The First Antidote: A Free Press*

The revelations of the Pentagon papers and Watergate were a reaffirmation of the duties and abilities of the press to expose fraud, duplicity, and perhaps even possible mental illness at the topmost reaches of government. But for every brilliant investigation and exposé, there are hundreds of examples daily of press delinquency, and many of them have serious implications for the country. The reasons for this are not obscure; they are simply rarely discussed.

The decrease in the number of newspapers. Since the rise of television, hundreds of newspapers have gone out of business, thereby reducing the public's access to balanced reporting and investigation. Today television stations greatly outnumber newspapers in most cities. Ironically, it is hard to find much in the way of news in many of the surviving

*"Press" in this context includes newspapers, television, radio, magazines, and all other news gathering and publishing organizations.

newspapers. In an attempt to recapture readership, newspapers imitate television by using suggestive pictures and brief, rapid-reading stories that are long on gore and gossip and pitifully thin—where they exist at all—on news analysis and government and corporate investigation.

The decrease in the number of independent newspapers. A handful of powerful newspaper chains control the editorial positions of scores of newspapers in large and medium-size cities throughout the country. If a politician, party, or cause is on the wrong side of that position, they are out of luck. So is the public.

How the public gets the news. Survey after survey shows that most people get most of their news—or what is doled out to them as news—from television. But the amount and depth of the news contained in an average television news program is infinitesimal compared to that of even a modestly published newspaper. The word count of a half-hour news program would not fill up much more than one column of one page of the *New York Times.*

Television news is basically people reading headlines and obvious captions to pictures, much of it sandwiched into short segments of network time under the arch heading "world news roundup."

Television has a knack of taking complex stories that have been played out over hours, days, weeks, and even years and telescoping them into simplistic featurettes, each one calculated, where possible, to contain something to grab the viewer's attention, if not his or her mind.

Violence, confrontation, blood, and tears are the television editor's indispensable tools. They are unrelentingly spliced into story after story, frequently out of all proportion to the underlying and more significant factors causing the event. True, the world is a violent place. But on television the elements of violence are edited too easily and too often in such a way as to make them appear to be the event rather than the symptom or the effect of it.

Much of the less violent news that the viewer receives is not really news at all but an obedient reflection of what the subject of the report wishes the viewer to know. Government and corporate press releases, handouts, and quotes from "highly placed sources" are dutifully read into a television camera against a backdrop of the White House, the Capitol, or an international landmark by terribly serious network reporters, with hardly a lifted eyebrow, word of caution, disclaimer, reservation, or statement suggesting that the so-called fact may not be quite that.

One of television's better reporters, Bob Schieffer of CBS News, illustrated the problem:

> Carter's White House operation is about the same as the others, but these people are more clever. They know when it's to their advantage to be helpful to us. Like the joint swearing in of an anti-war guy (Sam Brown, director of Action) and a disabled Vietnam veteran (Max Cleland, head of the Veterans Administration). You know you're being had, but you do it exactly the way *they want it done* because they're right, *it's good television.* [Emphasis added.]

Viewers tend to take this kind of "objective" reporting at face value, especially when it deals with complex news such as inflation, energy, or disarmament. Since the viewer has little or no means of evaluating what is received from the television set, distorted, incomplete, and phony news *becomes* the news, and few are the wiser.

Television newspeople know what they are up against. Walter Cronkite has been quoted as saying, "In the compression process forced upon us by the severe limitations of time, the job is incredibly, almost impossibly, difficult. I'm afraid that we compress so well as to almost defy the viewer and listener to understand what we say." Cronkite reportedly admitted also that distortion was the inevitable result of news compression.

The limitations of time do make broadcasting the news an almost impossible task. Yet that is only one reason why news programs resemble an airborne *People* magazine. Perhaps a more important reason is that television's news, like its quiz shows and vapid comedies, is a full partner in the ratings game. As such, news producers who would like to keep their jobs will cater to management's craving for high ratings because high ratings naturally bring more revenue from the sale of advertising time. In the opinion of television management, high ratings and news analysis do not mix, so there is little analysis. Management also has a low opinion of the concentration powers of the "average" viewer, whoever that may be, believing the viewer incapable of sitting still for a news story for much more than sixty seconds—a self-fulfilling view, for television trains people *not* to concentrate. Thus, given the choice between showing a few seconds of a surging mob and offering a reasoned explanation of the mob's anger, everybody along the television chain, from reporter to editor to producer to manager, will give you the mob scene nearly every time.

Television's unwillingness to investigate. The excuse most often given by the networks for their dismal record of investigative programming is the fairness doctrine, which requires them to "devote reasonable time to the discussion of controversial issues" but to "do so fairly" and to provide "reasonable opportunity for opposing viewpoints" in the process.

The fairness doctrine is perhaps the fuzziest section of broadcast law. Their attempts to define what constitutes *controversy, reasonable time,* and *fairly* have caused many networks and independent stations to run afoul of the First Amendment. Some classic court cases have been the result. Consequently broadcasters, with an eye on the specter of litigation, are reluctant about putting controversy on the air.

An equally important reason for the dearth of investigative programming is greed. The television networks get rather cranky when they have to give up highly remunerative paid time in order to provide "reasonable" free time for the "opposing viewpoints" that controversial programs are certain to generate. It also costs a great deal more to produce an investigation on television than it does in a newspaper. And sponsors are not very interested in buying time on such programs because they too abhor controversy. The hot investigative story which sends newspaper sales figures through the roof makes television executives and their sponsors strangely nervous about losing rating points and profits.*

Another aspect of the money problem is the networks' fear of producing controversial programs that will alienate the conglomerates that sponsor their noncontroversial shows. As conglomerates come to control more brand names, the risk of controversy's touching them increases steadily.

Given this picture, the networks will not do more than the absolute minimum required of them in the areas of controversy. And who will define that minimum?

The increase in court rulings limiting the reporting powers of the press, especially in the area of confidentiality of sources. If Woodward and Bernstein had been forced to reveal the identity of Deep Throat, how much would have been revealed about White House involvement with Watergate?

Press bias against the power of the political commercial. Reporters and news editors cannot imagine, let alone admit, that something as seemingly innocuous as a political commercial could be as important or more important to the political process than their own dispatches. In addition, jealousy prevents newspapers from giving more than minimal space to a competitive medium. (When given the chance, however, reporters jump at the opportunity to *appear* on television.)

*CBS's *60 Minutes* is probably the one investigative exception.

The television press's view of political commercials is once again linked to money. Television news departments that take a dim view of the role of the political commercial may nevertheless decide, or be coaxed, to soft-pedal their criticism of them. Political commercials, for all their habitual inclination to deceive, bring revenue to the station. Taking potshots at political commercials may also antagonize product sponsors who have a stake in a particular candidate, may invoke the fairness doctrine, and may provoke the criticized candidate to put pressure on the station if he or she wins the election. And pressure means the threat that the station's license may not be renewed.

The Second Antidote: The Loyal Opposition

In the myth-movies of the forties, the loyal opposition dramatically revealed the incumbent's irregularities in the last reel and crushed the culprit at the polls. Today the real world of electronic politics lacks both the party machinery and the romantic flair, although many people suffering from cinematic cultural lag have not yet caught on.

There are three crucial reasons why the party out of power finds it virtually impossible to counterbalance the president's power and personal privilege.

The power of incumbency. A major goal of every new president is to wrest control of the government machinery and the public consciousness as quickly as possible in the first term in order to be above campaigning for the second term.

Television offers the most expeditious and efficient means for achieving this. For the incumbent president this exorbitantly expensive medium is free and almost always at his call.* An incumbent (and his staff) clever in the television arts can use television to manipulate the public almost at will by:

- Whipping up the public's appetite for war (Kennedy: Bay of Pigs, Cuban missile crisis, Berlin; Johnson: Vietnam when the covert actions were made public; Carter: Persian Gulf).
- Excusing war and intervention (Johnson: Dominican Republic, Vietnam episodes; Nixon: carpet bombing of Hanoi, invasion of Cambodia).
- Calming the public's fears (Eisenhower: Lebanon).
- Calming the public's anger (Ford: before the Nixon pardon).

*Fred Friendly reported that "in Nixon's first eighteen months in office he held center stage on all networks during prime hours [at no cost], more than the combined time of Presidents Eisenhower, Kennedy and Johnson."

- Papering over domestic problems (Kennedy: visits to Berlin and Ireland; Nixon: visits to China, Russia, Egypt).
- Demonstrating diplomatic powers by stroking foreign supplicants (Carter: Israel and Egypt).
- Outright lying (Nixon: Watergate).
- Outright deception (Johnson: Gulf of Tonkin).
- Outright misleading (Nixon: winding down Vietnam).

Getting an edge on a president who knows how to use television, or even one who isn't very good at it, is a little like using your hands to stop a battleship. And there's more than just the president to stop. When he doesn't use television, his surrogates do; when they're off the air, the symbols of presidential power remain, providing an instantly recognizable backdrop for the nightly news: the obligatory report from the White House lawn, Air Force 1, helicopters to Camp David, dignitaries emerging from the White House to report on their meetings with the president.

A president who has used television well in his first term will be able to turn over to his political commercials the bulk of the campaign task when it comes time to run for the second term. He can also choose to implement his advertising in the heat of the campaign by "reporting to the nation" (for free) on "an issue of urgency"—not as a candidate, of course, but as a statesman. The opposition, meanwhile, who are likely to be short of the money needed to make commercials, stalk the empty countryside, shadowboxing with the incumbent's television image.

The power of money. In the aftermath of Watergate it appeared that the Federal Election Campaign Act of 1974 had taken the big money out of politics so that candidates with limited funds, including third parties, could campaign on an equal footing with incumbents and the wealthy (frequently one and the same). The erosion of popular representation seemed to have been stemmed.

The main provision of the act called for presidential campaigns to be financed out of tax money—the \$1 campaign contribution that the taxpayer checks off on the federal income tax form. Candidates for president would then receive matching funds from the U.S. Treasury: one dollar for each dollar they raised privately. Total spending was fixed at \$10 million in the period before the nominating convention and \$20 million during the campaign. Tight limits were placed on the candidate's personal spending. Outside contributions were limited to \$1,000.

Two years later the Supreme Court struck down key provisions of the act, whose loopholes had the effect of benefiting the incumbent and the wealthy:

- Public funding did not have to be accepted by a candidate. If a candidate chose to raise all monies privately, no limit was placed on the amount that could be raised.*
- While the court allowed the $1,000 limit for campaign contributions by an individual to stand, the "limit was removed on contributions by any individual 'in behalf of' a candidate, so long as they are not directly contributed to the campaign fund, and so long as there has been no 'collusion' between the contributor and the candidate." This is vintage gobbledegook; the worst party hack could figure out how to compromise this wording—and no doubt has.
- No limit was placed on how much of their personal wealth candidates can spend on their own campaigns.
- Third-party candidates could not get public funding unless they received a certain percentage of the vote in the election itself.

The effect of these loopholes, the *Wall Street Journal* noted, "may only have made it easier for an incumbent, and especially a rich incumbent, to perpetuate himself in office."† Easier to get the best political media specialists, easier to produce the most "creative" political commercials, easier to buy the most commercial time in the best program periods, the *Journal* might have added.

The power (or fear) of the television station. Although television stations are required by law to operate in the public interest, in fact they devote the lion's share of their attention to the incumbent's views, whether or not those views are in the public interest. Incumbents are the primary news sources; they are not to be offended, if at all possible.

Organizations (out of which legitimate and gifted third-party candidates often emerge) opposed to the incumbent administration's policies attempt to capture free television time for their own views on the nightly news. Demonstrations and singing are the obligatory methods for drawing the attention of the cameras, but such scenes long ago became too familiar to have much impact on either the television audience or the incumbent administration. No one realizes this better than

*John Connally, preparing for the 1980 primaries, announced at the end of 1979 that he would adopt this course.

†In the 1978 elections, the incumbent Senator Jesse Helms of North Carolina spent between $5 million and $7 million on his reelection campaign. Incumbent Governor Hugh Carey of New York spent over $2 million in the 1978 New York primary, and he and his opponent, Perry Duryea, together spent $11 million more in the general election. There are hundreds of similar examples.

the protest groups; they know that the television commercial is now the most powerful and efficient means of making their point.

But television (and radio) stations do not have to accept so-called controversial commercials from "loyal opposition" groups, even for pay; almost without exception they will not; and they have a Supreme Court ruling to back them up.

The genesis of what became known as the paid-time case began during the height of the Vietnam War when the Business Executives' Move for Peace (BEM) attempted to buy one-minute radio commercials on station WTOP in Washington, D.C.* As Fred W. Friendly recounts the history of the case, the station rejected the request on the ground that it had a "long-established policy of refusing to sell spot announcements [dealing with] 'controversial issues.' . . . BEM appealed to the station's top management," who replied that it "considered the announcements insulting to the president and observed that 'subjects of this type deserve more in-depth analysis than can be produced in 10, 20, 30, or 60 second commercials.' " (The station, of course, did not mention the allegedly maligned president's use of commercials of the same lengths, which contained misleading and deceptive statements about his prosecution of the war, or the fact that such commercials were too short for the in-depth analysis that the war demanded.) BEM appealed to the FCC, contending that its First Amendment rights had been violated by the station's refusal to sell it time, and lost; it appealed to the District of Columbia Court of Appeals and won; and ultimately it lost in the Supreme Court. Yet the dissenting opinion of justices Brennan and Marshall is worth quoting here:

> It may unsettle some of us to see an anti-war message or a political party message in the accustomed place of a soap or beer commercial. . . . We must not equate what is habitual with what is right —or what is constitutional. A society so saturated with commercialism can well afford another outlet of speech on public issues. All that we may lose is some of our apathy.

Someday this dissent may be used as a basis for a new test case. But for now the loyal opposition, at least in commercial protest form, is dead. So, it would seem, are the rights of voters to know all sides of an issue.

*When the BEM case reached the Supreme Court, it was joined with a suit brought by CBS against the Democratic National Committee. The Court designated the joint case *CBS et al.* v. *DNC.*

The Third Antidote: The Theory of Accountability at the Ballot Box

Twice in the last sixteen years Americans have clamored to be rid of their presidents for double-crossing them within months of an election. Johnson lied about Vietnam. Nixon continued the lie, in a different direction that led to Cambodia; then he was caught in Watergate. Many people wanted Ford removed when he broke their faith by pardoning Nixon. Many were dismayed by Carter's weak demeanor practically from the start of his term.

Should the press and the loyal opposition fail to counter political deception and lie, the traditional remedy, we have been taught, is to vote the culprit out of office the next time around. But when you know that a hostile missile tipped with multiple nuclear warheads can be targeted over your rooftop from eight thousand miles away in less than half an hour because of—if only indirectly—the conduct of an American president, three years is a long time to wait for a new election. The question is: Can we afford this time-consuming luxury which more and more seems to belong to a slower age?

The answer seems to be obvious: Politicians must be made accountable before they take office. And there are ways in which this can be done.

10

BREAKING THE BACK OF THE POLITICAL COMMERCIAL

Without you there is no deception

I'm mad as hell and I'm not going to take it anymore.

Growing American sentiment in the late 1970s, adapted from the battle cry of a crazed broadcaster in the film *Network*

Consider the American political system as the 1980 elections get under way—and as it will stand for years to come, unless there is what amounts to a popular rebellion against the present political use of the media:

- Politicians are virtually immune from public accountability except in the most extreme circumstances (usually those which involve money).
- Just as the political commercial has become the surrogate for personal campaigning by politicians, the political media specialist is becoming the surrogate for the candidate himself. In many campaigns the influence of the political media specialist is frequently greater than that of the candidate. Thus the specialist's position becomes the candidate's position.
- Once in office, the former candidate continues to rely on the advice and policies of the political media specialist, and the specialist finds a place beside other unelected officials, including spouses, who run the nation without the concurrence of the electorate.
- The public, which should be mad as hell, grows increasingly despondent, cynical, languid, and distant about what should be *their* political process. Consequently voters stay away from both the voting booth and the process, leaving the way

clear for the deceitful politician to steal the office out from under them.

The political commercial did not turn politicians into liars; it only amplified the lie beyond the politicians' fondest dreams and broadcast it simultaneously into every cranny of the nation to the viewer-voter who sat dumbly before a television set, absorbing the lie without knowing what was happening.

The picture is bleak, but the situation is far from being irretrievable. There are ways to fight back. The following guide toward cleaning up the political mess—the politicians' mess and ours—is based on four premises:

1. As dearly as we may wish that television would vanish, it will continue to be the major medium of political campaigning. The question is not whether television should be used but how it should be used.
2. Despite the theories of some political media specialists, the question of truth in the electronic media *is* relevant and vital.
3. It is not necessarily against the natural condition of politicians to tell the truth, though their persistent unwillingness to do so continues to puzzle even the most cynical political commentators.*
4. Ultimately it is up to the public to pressure the politicians to tell the truth, on television and off, during a political campaign and after. Telling the truth, for politicians, includes keeping campaign promises. Getting the truth from politicians will require that the public get off its collective backside and push and push and push.

CLEANING UP THE POLITICAL MESS

I. Making newspapers less provincial

Until newspapers overcome their bias against serious reporting on the dangerous effects of television on elections and realize the power that the political commercial has over the public, politicians will continue to enjoy unrestricted immunity.

Newspapers must also stop glamorizing the way political media specialists prepare candidates for television and begin to examine the

*One commentator has noted that in American politics "there is no great reason to have to do anything other than present your point of view, and what is so peculiar about American politics is that people do everything *but* present their point of view. . . . Why is it the case that Castro virtually always tells the truth in his speeches and the people we elect don't know how?"

content and meaning of what is being broadcast to an unsuspecting public.

But it would not be a great public service if newspapers made political commercials the subject of a page-one hard news story and analysis once or twice during a campaign. Good reporting will be successful only if it is done regularly—daily, if necessary. Any newspaper that can print daily box scores on sports, weather, the Dow Jones, and astrology ought to be able to do the same about politicians whose actions directly affect the lives of each of its readers.

Constant hammering at false and deceptive political commercials will cause the commercials to be revised for truth and intentions. If the next batch appears to have been revised but actually differs little from the first, newspapers must continue to report violations. Crusading is contagious. Candidates soon will have little to run on. The public will begin to see that many politicians have nothing to say or to offer. The careful scenario of the political media specialist will be rendered useless.

If a newspaper will not bear the responsibility for reporting on political commercials, its readers should demand that coverage.

In addition to reporting on political commercials, newspapers, particularly those in small cities and towns, must be relentless in their investigations of political corruption, including political commercials, regardless of how small or local the person and the office. Small-fry politicians involved in petty malfeasance have a disturbing habit of becoming major candidates for high office when not swiftly exposed.

II. Regulating politicians by deregulating television

When the truth is savagely mugged or murdered by false and deceptive political advertising, there is an urge to take the expedient route of censorship as a protective device.

When the public is force-fed a steady diet of politicians who are immoral, afraid to tell the truth, or stupid or cynical enough to mortgage their destinies—and ours—to political media specialists who are frequently power-hungry, malicious, and philosophically bankrupt, it is tempting to think about censoring political commercials when they fail to tell the truth. But censorship, finally, is the wrong route. We cannot have a First Amendment that is convenient only for our personal needs or when it helps us make our point; the First Amendment is bigger than the politician who uses it as a shield for making false statements.

This does not mean that political commercials should enjoy an immunity to defraud the people of their First Amendment rights. Nor does it mean that the rules of conduct established to regulate product commercials cannot serve as legitimate guidelines for exposing the deception of political commercials. It is simply that there is a better and, for democracy, a safer and more exhilarating route: to abolish the fairness doctrine and equal time rule of Section 315. This would finally allow television newspeople to behave as bona fide journalists.

As journalists (instead of talking heads that repeat government handouts) television newspeople would operate in the same unfettered environment as print journalists. Television reporters would be free to criticize political commercials that violate the television code without the worry of editorializing requirements, lawsuits, or the need to give equal time to the candidate being criticized and to other candidates who would also demand time.

A diligent and persevering television press, like its print colleagues, could hold politicians responsible for the promises they have no intention of keeping and for the manner in which they malign their opponents. Unlike print journalists, television journalists would have a vast audience for their reports, and the effect would be all the more powerful because the reports would concern wrongdoing in the same medium.

Letting television newspeople do their jobs, former FCC chairman Richard Wiley has noted, would reduce the effectiveness of the political commercial.

With the equal time rule abolished, Wiley believes, television stations would be free to put on wide-open political programming. If the station chose, it might invite only one candidate to appear on a program. The station could inform the candidate in advance that it would be asking hard questions about his or her advertising claims "without having to worry about bringing in the other twelve candidates . . . the problem right now [is] that everybody gets the same amount of time . . . basically the Equal Time law is a no time law." Television stations "don't put on much of that [wide-open] programming. They put on as little as possible because they're going to have to give everybody else the same opportunity. . . . I think if there were a lot more coverage given . . . and different kinds of coverage . . . it would diminish the importance and the magnitude of a candidate's commercials."

Abolishing the fairness doctrine would provide voters with access to the medium which has so seriously deceived them. Without having to worry about balancing opposing views to the fraction of a minute, a television station could accept for broadcast what might be the unpopular views of organizations that wish to talk back to politicians or buy air time to run their own commercials. (And the station could attack those commercials if they were found to be deceptive!) What harm could come to the country if, for example, the conservative American Enterprise Institute questioned the policies of candidates who claim to be liberal? What harm if Common Cause or Ralph Nader or the NAACP challenged the wisdom of politicians on the right? Why not provide SANE or the National Rifle Association with a television platform if they think they have something to contribute? We have nothing to lose but our myths.

"The American system works," Fred Friendly has written, "because it is able to weigh competing social values whenever two rights collide, and to determine which part of the Constitution shall prevail. The Fairness Doctrine has taxed the system's balancing mechanism to its limits without achieving its goals. Both the regulators and the courts have entered areas from which the Constitution has traditionally excluded them!"

If the concept of free speech is to be something more than a mythical caldron of ideas, Congress and the FCC are going to have to take a chance and retire Section 315. It was never a very good set of rules, and the evolution of television has only made it confuse our understanding of the world in which we attempt to survive.

Some senators, who apparently believe they can be elected without Section 315, have long attempted to legislate its abolition. Senator William Proxmire of Wisconsin is one of them. But his legislation to repeal it has never attracted many supporters, and it has been mired in committee since 1975. Senator Ernest Hollings of South Carolina, chairman of the Senate Communications Subcommittee, which would have to vote out such legislation in order to send it to the Senate floor, does not seem inclined to do so. Hollings contends that it was the equal time rule that got him broadcasting time and led to his victory in the gubernatorial campaign in South Carolina in 1958, and many other senators would join him in protecting the equal time rule for their own selfish purposes.

In the House, Representative Lionel Van Deerlin of California has attempted for several years to write a new Communications Act that purports to reduce government intervention in broadcasting. Some broadcasters think the proposed legislation is not deregulation but more regulation. The language in the section intended to modify the equal time rule is nebulous. The wording of the section modifying the fairness doctrine puzzles many astute broadcasters. A former NBC vice chairman, David Adams, believes it "is intended to give the appearance of a reduction in government requirements and I don't know what it means. It substitutes the word *equity* or *equitable* for *fairness.* If you look in a dictionary, equitable and fairness mean about the same thing. It is very difficult to interpret."

Should Van Deerlin's bill pass—a long shot—it would not help the cause of television journalism.* Modifying the equal time rule and the fairness doctrine will always fall short of the mark. Nothing less than striking both provisions from the law would allow television journalists to maintain a check on politicians and their advertising. But only loud and constant pressure from the public will ever force politicians to deregulate Section 315.

III. Ending presidential incumbency, and limiting service in other offices

A Gallup Poll has found that the majority of Americans endorse the idea of placing sharp limits on the number of years senators and representatives may hold congressional seats—twelve years at the most. Two reasons are traditionally given for limiting congressional tenure: (1) to emphasize talent over years on the job as the most important credential for elected office and key committee assignments and (2) to keep a steady flow of youthful people coming into the governing system who are likely to be more sensitive to changing conditions in the areas they represent.

A third reason to limit congressional tenure should be added: to reduce the temptations of power and money that seem to be the inevitable result of long-term representation for so many in Congress.

The rise of television and advertising to become the chief reelection campaign vehicles has created a fourth and perhaps equally important reason to consider revising the terms of high office.

As we have seen, a president who has "imaginatively" used television and advertising to bully his way into office, and to maintain his standing in a first term, can practically turn over his entire reelection effort to the media while he poses in the role of statesman too busy to campaign. Unless such a president (or senator) turns out to be exceptionally weak or corrupt, this has the effect of making the challenger into a virtual eunuch before the race has begun

*There is little enthusiasm in the House for Van Deerlin's bill. As of July 1979 the bill was still pending in Van Deerlin's subcommittee and no action was planned.

(and thereby in effect lengthening the term of office without constitutional sanction).

Limiting presidents and senators to one term of service (length to be determined) would eliminate the unfair advantages of incumbency and the incumbent's use of television time for purely political purposes. Since each election campaign would then start with new candidates, presidents and senators could actually spend their entire terms in office working for the good of the country instead of for themselves. A novel approach to government!

IV. Ending the electoral college

Many people believe that the electoral college is an unfair and a dangerous way to elect presidents. Under the college's unit rule, a presidential candidate who wins a state by even a handful of votes collects all the state's electoral votes. The machinery of the electoral college can even award the presidency to the candidate who has finished second in the popular vote; this has happened twice since the Civil War.

It is interesting that critics of the electoral college have not used the political commercial as an argument against it. Yet as the commercials feed greedily on the outdated system, they become the chief reinforcers of the system's inequities. Presidential elections frequently are decided primarily on the ability of the candidate's media specialists to hold or to swing votes in a small section of a state or even in a portion of one city.

The political media specialist does this by "firing" campaign messages at the target audience at a rapid clip with virtual pinpoint accuracy. The advisers know that with the "right" commercials they can hit the jackpot even if only a handful of votes in each election district are pulled over to their side.

Thus a candidate may promise a specific audience in one part of a state one thing with one commercial, then promise a second ethnically or occupationally different audience in another part of the state something else with another commercial. Campaign promises can be quickly adjusted if the candidate has the money and a staff clever enough to devise a media plan far enough in advance to secure the best commercial time periods. Nothing has changed conceptually since Rosser Reeves invented the political spot marketing scheme in 1952; twenty years later Nixon's November Group used spot commercials with perfection, running some of them nationwide to give the appearance of not leaving out any one state, while huddling each week to decide which commercials should be poured in heavy doses into specific markets during the following week.

With huge audiences to draw from, even in the dead of night, candidates far weaker than several recent examples can always count on switching some votes. And some votes may be all that the candidate requires to win a state's total electoral votes.

Meanwhile, an ominous new possibility waits in the wings. The technology now exists (and is being used experimentally) to transmit product commercials via satellite from the point where they are produced to markets thousands of miles away. Time of transmission: seven tenths of a second, including traveling 40,000 miles up to a satellite and back down again.

Proponents of the new satellite commercial delivery system expect that it will spawn "a new genre of 'topical' commercials which can be produced quickly for airing in response to the idiosyncratic needs of particular markets" and enable "smaller agencies to launch national spot [commercial] campaigns with the speed and ease of larger firms."

Its proponents have not failed to grasp the satellite system's political campaign potential, though the broader implications appear to have eluded them. "The future is now. The technology is here today and no one can avoid it," one of them has said. "I can project that when we get into the Presidential political campaign in 1980, the candidates will want to get their commercials' messages onto the spot market quickly."

What may be an innovation for product commercials would only accelerate and exacerbate the problem inherent in political commercials. Rapid satellite delivery of false and deceptive political messages into specific markets would make them nearly impossible to keep track of, much less to try to rebut and render ineffective.

Once the satellite delivery system is joined with cable television—a matter of only a few years—and cable television begins to carry commercials (which seems to be an inevitable development), political commercials will be sent not just to specific areas of a state, to pick off electoral votes, but to specific homes on specific blocks!

Since Gallup began surveying how Americans feel about the electoral college more than thirty years ago, it has remained among the most unpopular features of our political system. In 1977 the overwhelming majority of those polled wanted a constitutional amendment nullifying the electoral college in favor of a direct vote for president.

In 1969 the majority of the House voted for such legislation, but the Senate killed it by filibuster. In 1979 Representative Jonathan Bingham of New York introduced a new bill to change the electoral college. Serious discussion of the bill's merits should now include the role of the political commercial. Passage of the bill would greatly dilute the political commercial's effectiveness. Each voter would count; presidential candidates could no longer rely on manipulating a few voters in key states but would have to conduct a truly national campaign.

V. Shortening political campaigns

Most Americans favor a much shorter presidential campaign period, reports George Gallup.* Gallup believes campaigns that "stretch over the better part of a year . . . exhaust the candidates, thoroughly bore the electorate—and end up changing few votes."

Shortening the presidential campaign period would also dilute the effect of the political commercial, but for reasons far different from Gallup's assumptions.

To say that long political campaigns end by changing few votes is to ignore political history since television. Jimmy Carter's rise during the 1976 campaign—to cite one example—was no fluke. His campaign was based on elementary textbook marketing principles: Position your advertising to what consumers think they want, try to keep the central theme and promise in every piece of advertising, and repeat it as frequently as you can in the best locations you can get for as long as the money holds out. This is known in product advertising as "penetrating" the market.

It takes time to penetrate. That is why Gallup's assertion that long political campaigns "thoroughly bore the electorate" is beside the point. Any knowledgeable advertising agent, whether for products or politicians, knows that the job is not to entertain but to sell. Repetition of a commercial may anger viewers, but that does not mean it is ineffective. (Some product commercials run unchanged for *years.*)

If a candidate finds a promise that touches some part of the audience he or she wishes to capture, however false the promise may be when it is made, it doesn't matter very much if the commercial is boring. Jimmy Carter, after all, could hardly be described as being effervescent in his commercials.

It is certainly better not to produce a boring commercial. How-

*In England and France election campaigns are limited to four to six weeks without any appreciable impairment of political debate. The caliber of leadership in those countries does not seem to be noticeably different from ours.

ever, recent evidence suggests that images from a so-called boring commercial probably have the same capacity to "impregnate" themselves in the viewer's brain as the images from a so-called interesting commercial. And the viewer cannot know that this is happening. The only guaranteed immunity from television images lies in not watching television—a superb but unlikely solution to the political advertising problem.

It is obviously in the best interests of a politician, particularly a well-financed unknown, to wage a long campaign by television commercial. The shorter the campaign, the less chance that false and deceptive images will have to penetrate the market.

VI. Lengthening the political commercial

There are three basic arguments for requiring politicians to use longer commercials to advertise their wares than their product counterparts do:

1. It is foolish to believe that anybody can say anything sensible about the serious issues facing society in sixty seconds or less.
2. Distortion is the inherent and inevitable result of compressing political images and information into product commercial lengths, even when the politician sets out to be fair.
3. Commercial lengths used to advertise products are the perfect vehicle for introducing and perpetuating unregulated political lies and deception.

These arguments are what WGN, a Chicago television station powerful in broadcast signal and political influence, appears to have had in mind a few years ago when it decided to sell only units of *no less than five minutes* of commercial time to political candidates.

The FCC overruled WGN. Richard Wiley, then chairman of the commission, voted against the decision to overrule on the ground that it violated the First Amendment rights of the broadcaster. Wiley worried about the "blatant deception" those "quickie little" commercials made possible. "Here's a station that had a policy that was well thought out, that they'd been following and they were trying to promote education in their community . . . should the FCC step in and say, you couldn't do that? No, I disagreed. . . ."

The FCC could reverse itself at any time, and it would be helped in its decision by sufficient public lobbying. But whether even five minutes is time enough to allow serious political discussion is questionable.

The issue should be not how much time should be available for the politician to persuade the viewer but how much time would be required for the viewer to make an informed judgment about the politician. If this were to be the measure of political commercials, one judgment that viewers would quickly make is that most politicians do not have enough to say to fill the time.

VII. Ending political theatrics

It may be coincidence that the two presidents recently driven from office in disgrace rarely appeared in the political commercials that helped to give them their landslide mandates. In any case, it was while Johnson (in 1964) and Nixon (in 1972) remained in the White House that the theatrical images directed by their political media specialists did the real campaigning.

This kind of advertising widens further the already dangerous gulf separating politician from voter. It not only covers up defects in the candidate's behavior, it heightens the political mystique—the last thing that voters need today.

If the FCC were to rule that the candidate must appear in the commercial and that the commercial must consist only of the candidate speaking directly to the viewer (rather than being seen striding through a peanut field, for example), the misleading effects of campaign commercials would be at least modestly reduced.

This step could not, without other checks and controls, assure truth in political advertising. The ability of the political media specialist to edit out a candidate's flaws and infirmities would remain a problem.* So would the arts of costuming and set decoration.

Political media specialists grow sullen when they are given the label of image maker, but that talent is precisely why they are in such high demand. Carter's gingham-shirt-and-jeans commercials were striking examples of the specialist's skill, but that kind of approach was by no means rare. In the 1978 New York City mayoralty primary, political media specialist David Garth draped a trench coat over candidate Edward Koch's shoulder for his commercials, even when the sun was shining, in order to give him a "tough guy" image. For years candidates seeking to portray youth and vigor have been filmed striding

*The unethical lengths to which campaign advisers will go to hide a candidate's health problems from the public is illustrated by a story about the late Clair Engle, a U.S. senator from California. Engle, seriously ill during his last reelection campaign, managed to hold together for a long day of filming. Afterward a campaign commercial of selected takes made him appear healthier than he was.

through the streets with their suitcoats slung jauntily over their shoulders.

The proliferation of theatrical symbols that have nothing to do with the ability to govern will not abate unless the press exposes the techniques, thereby undermining their effect on the voter. Stripped of their props, politicians would be forced to display such skills as they actually possessed. Fewer people might decide that they could run successfully under these conditions.

VIII. Licensing political media specialists

We license those people who treat our physical and mental health as a means of protecting ourselves from charlatans and malfeasance. For the same reason we license those people who enforce our laws and our security. Yet the political media specialist, whose work may eventually affect both our health and our laws, is immune from any licensing control. Uncredentialed beyond the reputation achieved from the last political success, the political media specialist operates at will, foisting on an unsuspecting society falsehood and deception in the name of a candidate whom he may barely know and can hardly have consulted with. Very often the candidate's policies are the pure creation of the media specialist, who simplifies and tailors the alleged policies to fit the time and shock requirements of the television commercial rather than the requirements of a constituency aching for straight talk. No wonder so many victorious candidates have only the foggiest notion of what to do once in office.

If the states required the licensing of political media specialists and set a rigorous standard of ethics for certification, each individual's record being subject to review after each election, it would be a major step toward making the specialists accountable for their actions.

Licensing might be administered by a voluntary panel of nonpartisan political scientists and philosophers from the universities and retired judges from the higher courts. They might be empowered to levy fines for unethical practices—and to order publication of their findings in the media, thereby costing the guilty political media specialist money, public embarrassment, and a probable loss of business. They might also be empowered to lift the license of the offending media specialist, and without it the specialist would be barred from advertising politicians.

IX. Using cable television as a political check

It is estimated that 30 percent of the country will be wired for cable television by the early 1980s. "Superstations" in Atlanta, Chicago, New York, San Francisco, and Boston now use satellite relay to broadcast to millions of homes in remote cable markets thousands of miles away. The only bright prospect about political advertising coming to cable television is cable's capacity for two-way communication: the viewer can be provided with the means of talking back.

This is now happening with product advertising in Columbus, Ohio. Qube, the Warner pay cable system in that city, enables its 30,000 subscribers to respond to questions flashed on the television screen (such as, What do you think of the recent snow removal job?) by pushing a response button on a unit attached to the television set. Answers are fed back to the station and tabulated seconds after being received.

Qube has gathered viewer opinions about program ideas for the Children's Television Workshop. Ralph Nader has asked Qube viewers about their consumer complaints. Qube viewers have debated with authors and taken college courses in which they were able to tell the instructor to slow down or speed up, or to signal that they had a question, simply by pushing a response button in their homes.

Warner is enlarging its Qube subscriber list in Columbus and expanding into Houston, Cincinnati, and other major cities. And other two-way cable television systems are seeking franchises of their own.

Qube's two-way station-viewer relationship could finally give viewers access to the present political process. It could be the beginning of the first political dialogue in the electronic age, a way for voters to voice instantaneous criticism of politicians, a first step toward a new form of community participation and enlightenment.

Subscribers could rate a political commercial shown on Qube, scene by scene, for misleading, deceptive, and unfair writing and pictures. Political scientists, commentators, journalists, and other members of the community could offer points of view conveniently left out of commercials by the candidates. Candidates and their political media specialists could be invited to appear on Qube to explain and defend their advertising claims. (Viewers could draw their own conclusions about candidates who do not appear.) In effect this would put the political commercial on trial (like a real town meeting) as it is being broadcast. The verdict of the viewers would be handed down in seconds, and the results would be picked up by other media. For the first time the television screen would be not a barrier but a useful conduit between politician and viewer. The television advantage that has been held exclusively by the politician for twenty-eight years would be shared equally.

Cable television subscribers have an important weapon in the cable fees they pay each month for controlling what appears on their home screens, including political coverage. Without fees, cable television would go out of business.

The ultimate weapon in the control of political coverage would be the banding together of individual subscribers into neighborhood action groups. There is already a substantial foundation for such action. Across the country, nonpartisan, nonideological neighborhood political action groups, once derided by politicians and their sidekicks, have achieved remarkable successes for their communities by direct action tactics designed to combat what the groups see as "the mindless ravages on residential areas of big government and big business." They have successfully pushed for changes in laws and regulations. They have forced insurance companies and banks to change what they believed were discriminatory policies. They have prevented city hospitals from shutting down. They have lobbied to change laws favoring landlords and obtained funds to start newspapers and crime-control programs. Two hundred neighborhood groups have formed a national lobby called National Peoples Action. Many people see the neighborhood group movement as "a major realignment of urban political forces."

Should neighborhood action groups use their new influence in cable television—as outspoken subscribers with common interests, perhaps even as owners of a cable system—politicians and television would never be the same again, political advertising would be knocked down to size, and political enlightenment could have a rebirth.

X. Offering free television time

Free television time, made available equally to all qualified candidates, is conceived of here as a total substitute for the time presently paid for by candidates. For obvious reasons, television networks and stations would resist this reform; it not only suggests a loss of revenue from political commercials, it involves making available *more* hours than are now consumed by political campaigning.

No one disputes that television is a business. However, there are ways to provide compensation within moderate limits:

1. Let the television station absorb a high percentage of the cost of free time; it can afford this every few years as part of its license responsibilities to the FCC to "serve the public interest as a public trustee."
2. The remaining funds could come from the political contribution checkoff box found on the federal income tax form, currently a source of the matching funds. Why not divide every $1 contribution, half for the candidate's non-television expenses, half for "free" television time? We should not do less for our own political education than we now do for a politician's election.

How would free time be used? There can be many variations, but three units of time that should be outlawed are the present commercial lengths of ten, thirty, and sixty seconds. Fifteen minutes, twenty minutes, half hours and hours are the necessary and natural lengths of time for candidates to describe their qualifications and to offer reasonable discussion of the issues and for the public to absorb intelligently what the candidates say and to form impressions of how they say it.

Free television time will work best if the campaign period is restricted. Four to six weeks is ample time for a discussion of political views, and it is probably the right amount of time for candidates and voters to maintain a focus on each other.

Without basic ground rules, however, free time will end up as an extended commercial. The essence of free speech should be the essence of free time: unfettered, ungimmicked, robust, argumentative. Therefore candidates must sink or swim strictly on their own merits, whether it be done through explanations of who they are, their qualifications, their goals, the people they would bring into government, and their interpretations of issues; debates with other candidates; or give-and-take questioning (but not during a debate) by such third parties as journalists, political scientists, leaders of citizen groups, and citizens selected not by the candidate's political managers but by nonpartisan groups.* No pseudo panelists should be allowed to ask rehearsed parti-

*Real political debate should not be confused with the televised debates of 1960 and 1976, which were not debates at all but merely platforms for the candidates to avoid straight answers (and sometimes platforms for the participating journalists to show off). There was one unexpected benefit from the Carter-Ford "debate": When their microphones went dead and the two men who would lead the nation stared dumbly ahead, speechless, it demonstrated why the edited political commercial is so vital to weak candidates and so dangerous to the public. If there is to be debate, keep the journalists out of it and let the candidates go after each other's hides in the old-fashioned way.

san questions of a candidate, as was the case in Nixon's 1968 campaign. All appearances by candidates should be spontaneous and, whenever possible, live. Candidates should be seen by the viewer as they are, not as the political media specialist would make them. Film and tape should be allowed only when the film or tape is an unedited duplicate of a previous live appearance. *No editing should be allowed in any event.* No manufactured films that claim to represent a candidate's life and times and political accomplishments should be allowed, unless the station is prepared to offer a probing rebuttal.

Using live television to campaign, without political media specialists to help, and without any of the now traditional props of deception, will certainly make candidates nervous, especially during the first free time periods. If the candidate's nervousness continues unabated, that in itself would be a benefit to the voter, for it would indicate that the candidate might not be able to handle decision making of a more intense nature.

What would be the effect of giving candidates free time? In a single stroke, free television time would remove the principal causes of unfair and deceptive campaigning and would create a ripple effect reaching far beyond campaign finance reform:

- Free time would eliminate the misleading effects of unrestricted political commercials.
- Free time would largely eliminate the influence of the political media specialist by depriving him of his main livelihood, the creation of political advertising (and frequently of the candidates themselves).
- Free time would democratize the political and social system by eliminating the unfair campaign advantages presently enjoyed by well-financed candidates.
- Free time could bring outstanding people who are not wealthy to the attention of voters by relieving these candidates of the liability of not being able to buy enough political advertising.
- Free time would smoke out phony and weak candidates who cannot win without substantial political advertising, by denying them the ability to buy heavy television schedules in the best program periods in the most vital markets.
- Free time would nullify the advantages of the incumbent. Without political advertising to serve as a surrogate campaigner, the incumbent would be forced to leave the White House, the Senate, or the state house and go at it toe to toe with the challengers. Gone will be the incumbent's traditional reelection

excuse of being too busy with "affairs of state" to campaign.

- Free time would tend to nullify the potential dangers of the new electronic technology for campaigning.
- Free time would nullify the influence and eliminate the financial power of political action committees for special interest groups who presently can legally outflank campaign finance laws when making their political gifts.
- Free time would make most other campaign finance reform virtually unnecessary.

How would candidates qualify for free time? Perhaps the simplest and most democratic means would be by petition, the same way that candidates get onto many ballots in the first place. There would be a realistic but fair minimum number of petitions required. Such a requirement would eliminate the clutter and chaos of a factionalized field without denying access to the earnest legitimate candidate who, though unable to win, can make a valuable contribution to the political process.

Why isn't free time now in use? A free time law would have to pass Congress. Since free time would tend to take away the advantage that wealthy candidates enjoy, senators and members of the House—many of whom were elected because they could afford the price of political advertising—are not likely to vote for such a bill if it appears that it will make it difficult for them to win reelection. Free time laws for state and local candidates would suffer from the same problem.

It would also appear that free time can be instituted only if Section 315 is abolished or suspended.

Who will "convince" Congress to pass a free time law? The same people who put the senators and representatives into office. The public has more power than it knows. A dozen irate consumer letters can drive corporate public relations departments crazy. Letters written directly to corporation presidents frequently bring results. A spontaneous outpouring of criticism not only bothers politicians, it can force them to do what they were elected to do: that is, represent their constituents.

If constituents decide that they wish to replace paid political advertising with a free time campaign system, they will have to rise up and make their views known and keep demanding. It is a type of lobbying for which the goals seem distant and elusive, but the goals are by no means out of the reach of those with the will to achieve them.

XI. Calling for publicly initiated law

There is now such a profound loss of confidence in politicians and disgust at the way they purport to run the political system that normally law-abiding citizens have begun to wonder why they do not simply take the law into their own hands.

Citizens in twenty-three states need not daydream; there is a perfectly legal, though virtually unknown, way for them to do it when their legislators do not wish to be bothered. These states have granted their citizens the power to initiate their own laws. Those citizens could use this power to circumvent docile or unfair legislators or as a threat to jar them into action; they could use it to enact election reforms, including those discussed here.

Publicly initiated laws have been proposed on a national level. In 1977 James Abourezk, then a senator from South Dakota, and Senator Mark Hatfield of Oregon proposed an amendment to the Constitution that would allow citizens from all states to "initiate Federal laws and enact them through a national election," reserving for Congress exclusively only "the right to declare war, call up troops, and propose Constitutional amendments."

The Senate amendment would allow petitioners for a new law up to eighteen months to obtain signatures (in at least ten states) equal in number to 3 percent of the ballots cast in the preceding presidential election. The Justice Department would have to validate the signatures before the new proposal could be placed on the ballot in the next federal election. Based on the 1976 presidential vote, about two and one half million valid signatures would be required. That is not too many signatures where people are in earnest about controlling their own lives.

Abourezk has called the proposal "an actualization of the citizens' First Amendment rights 'to petition the Government for redress of grievances.' " Although his proposal never made much headway on Capitol Hill—Congress may appear at times to be sluggish and even dense, but it is alert when it comes to giving up power—a Gallup Poll showed that most Americans want the option to institute federal legislation on their own. Gallup reported that if such an option were available, the majority of citizens would vote to pass the Equal Rights Amendment and gun-control legislation and would vote against mandatory busing as a device to balance racial composition among school-age children. It would be surprising if the majority, if "granted" the opportunity, did not also vote to amend its own campaign laws, including those covering political broadcast and advertising regulation.

But that opportunity, as we have seen, will never willingly be given to the country by its legislators; the country will have to raise such hell that Congress will *have* to enact national public law legislation—or face defeat for reelection.

XII. Bringing together a political campaign advertising code with teeth, a Political Fact Bank filled with truth, and some tough Americans to make it work

A new code of ethics for paid political advertising enforced by a tough public interest group very different from the old (1945) Fair Campaign Practices Committee (FCPC) could go a long way toward preventing a repetition of the 1976 presidential campaign and all elections held since the rise of political advertising on television. Such a code and group can be established now, without legislation.

The FCPC has always been seriously flawed. Its role was too narrow; it concentrated on smear charges brought by one candidate against another and overlooked the kind of unilateral campaigning where candidates ignore each other and run on backgrounds and policies filled with fraud and deception. It was reactive; while it kept files of campaign violations, it never made them public until it had received a complaint. Its tax exemption weakened its effectiveness; it could not issue findings of guilt or innocence lest the IRS claim it was intervening on behalf of a candidate. It was too slow; by the time a smear charge was brought to the attention of the press, the political damage was not only done but frequently had been accepted as fact by the public. Its budget ($35,000 a year) was pitifully small and its staff (three people) inadequate. Its code did not cover presidential candidates until 1976 because it was thought unseemly to ask a sitting president to obey a code of ethics. The code was the product of people with a heavy print orientation, and it did not deal with problems created by the electronic media.

In a time when cynicism is an everyday attitude and loss of faith is an article of childhood, codes of conduct—those ponderous documents wrought by well-meaning do-gooders thought to be out of touch with the "real world"—seem old-fashioned and beside the point.

Yet had a political code such as the following proposed one been in force, the lingering causes of our present national and personal despair, beginning but not ending with Vietnam and Watergate, might well have been blunted or even stopped before the system was made to suck in their poisons.

A New Code of Political Campaign Ethics and Citizen Action*

The code that follows would apply to all forms of political advertising but would deal primarily with television. The code would provide a simple yet comprehensive test of the character, background, intent, policies, and promises of those people who would govern the country.

The code, while paying ample attention to what candidates say about each other, would concentrate on the claims and representations they make about themselves.

Politicians would *not* be allowed to sign the code and so attempt to make political capital from the act. The code functions not for the politician's benefit but for the public benefit; the code works whether or not politicians agree with it or like it.

Much of the code is modeled on the present codes of the television networks and the National Association of Broadcasters for product advertising, the codes used here as a standard to measure false and deceptive presidential campaign advertising. The code would apply to political advertising at any level. Although the television networks and stations are legally prohibited from enforcing violations of their codes by political advertising, it would soon become clear to the public from the work of the political code's administrative group what those violations were, who was guilty, how, and why. Political smear, the bulwark of the old code of the Fair Campaign Practices Committee, would constitute but one of many possible violations of the new code.

CODE STANDARDS FOR POLITICAL TELEVISION COMMERCIALS

General Principles

The public accepts political advertising only after securing satisfactory evidence of:

*Most of this code would be applicable if free political television time replaced the paid political commercial.

1. Integrity of advertising and the candidate on whose behalf it has been purchased.
2. Availability of service or programs promised by the candidate.
3. Realistic chances of making good on promises.
4. Existence of support for claims made by candidate and authentication of demonstrations.
5. Acceptable taste of the presentation.

Unacceptable Presentations, Approaches, and Techniques

1. Claims or representations which have the capacity to deceive, mislead, or misrepresent.
2. Claims that unfairly attack opponents, political parties, or institutions.
3. Unqualified references to the safety of a political position, program, or claim if "normal" execution of the position, program, or claim is found to represent a hazard to the public. (Example: a candidate's claim of the safety of nuclear energy.)
4. "Bait and switch" tactics which feature campaign promises not intended to be carried out but are designed to lure the public into voting for the candidate or party making the promise.
5. The use of "subliminal perception" or other techniques attempting to convey information to the viewer by transmitting messages below the threshold of normal awareness.
6. Use of visual devices, effects, or juxtaposition which attempt to deceive.
7. Use of sound effects to deceive.
8. The misuse of distress signals. (Example: a politician's claim that the nation is in poor condition, as in John F. Kennedy's "missile gap" charge.)
9. Use of the flag, national emblems, anthems, and monuments to gain campaign advantage. (Example: an incumbent president using the White House as a setting for a commercial.)
10. Use of the Office of the President of the United States or any governmental body to gain campaign advantage.
11. Interpersonal acts of violence and antisocial behavior or other dramatic devices inconsistent with prevailing standards of taste and propriety. (Example: Nixon's use of Vietnamese civilian and American military suffering for his own benefit in his 1968 commercials.)
12. Damaging stereotyping, including deliberately staged stereotyp-

ing of his or her own image by the candidate. (Example: Carter's "peanut farmer" image.)

13. Unsupported or exaggerated promises to the public of employment or earnings.
14. Preemption of the truth. (Example: a candidate's claiming that a policy is his or hers alone when other candidates also favor it.)
15. Altering of opinion on an issue from market to market to cater to audiences with different views.
16. The use of "guilt by association."
17. Playing on the public's fears. (Example: a candidate's claim of the necessity for what are in fact redundant weapons systems.)
18. Creating fear in voters. (Examples: a candidate describes an alleged flaw in an opponent without showing how he or she is different; a candidate blames an opponent for a condition for which the opponent is not responsible; a candidate alleges that an opponent cannot solve a problem—without telling how he or she would solve it.)
19. Changing facts and conditions. (The facts and/or conditions stated in a candidate's commercial may change as the campaign progresses, thereby rendering a once valid commercial unfair or misleading.)

Comparative Advertising

Opponents identified in the advertising must actually be in competition with one another.

Research and Surveys

1. Reference may be made to the results of bona fide surveys or research relating to the candidate or campaign advertised, provided the results do not create an impression that the research does not support.
2. "Bandwagon" commercials shall be subject to careful scrutiny for misleading effect. (Example: from dozens of "people on the street" interviews a half dozen are edited to appear in rapid order, the individuals speaking in simplistic phrases of the candidate's alleged attributes: "He's honest," "She's truthful." This technique may create the illusion that vast numbers of voters share these beliefs.)

Testimonials

1. Testimonials used, in whole or in part, must honestly reflect, in spirit and content, the sentiments of the individuals represented.
2. All claims and statements, including subjective evaluations of testifiers, must be supportable by facts and free of misleading implications.
3. If presented in the candidate's own words, testimonials shall contain no statement that cannot be supported.

Last-Minute Campaign Charges

No campaign charges against an opponent are acceptable in commercial form, including claims which appear to be valid, unless equal time in the same prime time period is granted to the opponent. If the opponent cannot afford to pay for a last-minute commercial in rebuttal to the charges, then either the station must provide free time or the candidate making the charges must pay for the opponent's commercial.

Heavy Last-Minute Campaign Spending

Excessive advertising expenditures in the closing stages of a campaign provide an unfair advantage to the candidate with the most money. Campaign spending for all major candidates should be as equal as possible in these stages.

POLITICAL FACT BANK AND ITS ADMINISTRATIVE GROUP

1. An administrative group will direct the functions of the code and make reports of violations public.
2. The administrative group will not seek or accept tax-exempt status from the Internal Revenue Service. What the IRS gives in tax savings it more than takes away with impractical restrictions (and the potential threat of political harassment) which would make this organization virtually powerless.
3. The heart of the administrative group is the Political Fact Bank. The bank is divided into two sections.

   The first section will contain the facts of such matters as a politician's formal education; work experience in and out of public life; personal and family wealth; civic affiliations; past and present positions and speeches on public issues such as employment, tax reduction, military spending, nuclear and conventional deterrence, energy development, and environmental protection; definition of the job of the office sought; promises previously broken in past public offices (and why); programs and accomplishments claimed in past and present public office and private life; and other information germane to public enlightenment in an election campaign.

The second section of the bank will contain facts and statistics on a broad range of national and international (and, where applicable, local) issues and problems. These facts and statistics, compiled and cross-checked by prominent nonpartisan authorities from various academic and professional disciplines, would include information concerning nuclear deterrence, environmental pollution, conditions in the ghettos, tax relief, etc. The work of the authorities will eliminate, to the extent that it is humanly possible, the fictions that politicians hand out as fact and reality.

Both sections of the Political Fact Bank might be computerized for instantaneous retrieval.

The first time a political commercial is broadcast (or appears in print form or is sent into homes by direct mail) the Political Fact Bank will be able to cross-check quickly with the truth the facts that the candidate advertises. (Examples: Was the candidate a small peanut farmer, as claimed, or the owner of a big peanut business? Is the candidate a bona fide nuclear physicist, as claimed—if so, where was the physicist's degree earned? —or did the candidate simply take courses in nuclear engineering?) The Political Fact Bank will be able to compare the candidate's definition of the issues with the latest scientific research and facts.

Candidates will be urged to pre-file facts about their backgrounds and policies with the Political Fact Bank. Honest candidates would have nothing to hide. Whether a candidate files or not, he or she will know that the facts about their public lives will be collected as a public service.

Some people may attempt to equate the Political Fact Bank with some dark and covert scheme similar to that of the national information center proposed some years ago, which sought to put every citizen's personal records and financial history on computer tape. That would indeed have been an invasion of privacy. A Political Fact Bank, however, would contain only information relevant to political campaigning and those people who have freely chosen to be public figures. The public has the right to know when a candidate takes a campaign position different from his or her previous actions or statements; however, the public has no right whatever to peep into a candidate's personal life. The Political Fact Bank will neither see nor contain such information.

4. The Political Fact Bank will make the new code an active instrument. The administrative group, which will have been monitoring key campaigns from their inception, will not wait to receive a complaint before taking action. At the first sign of a code violation, the guilty politician will be exposed in the fastest manner possible.
5. The fastest and most effective way to expose guilty politicians is through the news media. Press contacts will be a major function of the code's administrative group. News of code violations will be furnished on a regular basis (daily during the closing weeks of a campaign) by personal contact, telegram, telephone, and news conference. Obviously, the press will have unlimited access to the administrative group and the Political Fact Bank. It would be hoped that the media will see the wisdom of running regular reports of code violations and their meaning not only in a prominent place in newspapers and weekly news magazines but also as part of television news programs in the early morning and at night.

But the administrative group may not always be able to depend on the news media to report all code violations. The group must have the capacity to publish its own findings in the form of *counter-advertisements.* Because of the unfair restrictions of the fairness doctrine, the administrative group's advertising, regardless of the group's credentials and purpose, may not be accepted by television stations (one more reason to abolish Section 315). In this case, counter-advertisements will be placed in newspapers and weekly news magazines. Bulletins describing code violations will be sent to civic groups such as the League of Women Voters and Common Cause; unions, trade and manufacturers' associations; medical, dental, and legal organizations; religious and charitable organizations; and educational organizations—any of which could publish the violations in its publications. Word of mouth, even in an electronic age, is swift and effective.

6. The administrative group, without becoming a tiny bureaucracy, must be larger than the Fair Campaign Practices Committee to be effective. In addition to an executive director and secretarial help, it should be staffed with legislative and administrative assistants of the caliber of good congressional aides (perhaps supported by part-time interns from universities), probably an attorney, perhaps a computer programmer, and a writer, art director, and producer to prepare counter-advertising.

   The administrative group will be supported by a standards and practices board composed of outstanding citizens not previously involved in politics and experts from such fields as economics, political science, disarmament, and urban affairs. Some of these people will be from universities, some from the private sector. They will receive nominal payment for their services.

   In a presidential campaign the administrative group and its standards and practices board must meet as early as the primaries, and in some cases before, to rule on false and deceptive advertising before it is established in the public's mind as fact. In the later stages of a campaign the ruling meetings will probably need to take place daily.

7. A political code is a worthless document unless it is administered by strong people. The staff need not be paid outlandish salaries, but the fatal mistake public service organizations always make is to try to get good people at a piker's price. In addition, there must be an adequate budget for counter-advertising.

How much will it cost to make the political code effective? One to two million dollars annually would be a guess. It seems like a lot—until one realizes that an individual campaign for president now costs fifteen to thirty times that amount. So perhaps the real question is not how much an effective political code will cost but what the price of truth is in political advertising. When the public decides how to answer that question, financing and enforcing a code of political campaign ethics and citizen action will not be difficult.

LAST NOTES ON THE NEXT ELECTION

The lies and deceptions of politicians are not "done" to us willy-nilly. We allow them to happen by sitting passively before television screens, accepting what we are shown and told.

Yet we do not need to be stuck with a system that lies to us and disregards our wishes and our well-being. We are not required by law to vote for images or to live with illusions. We have a constitutional right to demand the truth.

We are in nobody's keep, least of all that of the politicians—unless we wish to be.

People ask, What if we should succeed in putting politicians on notice that they are no longer exempt from telling the truth, that we no longer will tolerate the electronic merchandising of their ambitions and their expedient and cynical policies? What then? Will we have obtained a better brand of politician? A better system? A better way to run it?

Yes; perhaps not right away, but in the long run. Over the long run a code of political ethics—which after all is only a restatement of the qualities by which most human beings are instinctively guided—can provide a public benchmark, a reasonable standard, by which we may measure those who would wish to lead us. Over the long run we may begin to reshape this nation into the democracy it set out to be and which may yet be ours to keep if we choose.

No code, of course, can end corruption, malfeasance, arrogance, and lies when they are inherent in the political body. All a code can do —all it *ought* to do—is to force the offending politician into the light. There he or she will squirm, if only briefly. At that point we will have to decide what to do about the politician—and, consequently, what to do about our own lives.

We can throw up our hands and watch the politician slip away again, in all likelihood to the protection of elected office or another position of public trust. Or we can kick and yell and demand—and if necessary kick and yell and demand again—until the dangerous, the dishonest, and the inept are crushed by the anger of public opinion before a vote is cast, our actions a harsh warning to those who would follow in the same devious footsteps. But make no mistake; the right to make this decision is not granted to us by a higher political authority. It is ours alone. The only question is, How much longer will that right continue to be available to us?

ACKNOWLEDGMENTS

Over the course of my research and writing I met many people who gave me the benefit of their advice and their ideas, then vanished as suddenly as they had appeared. I may have disagreed with much of what they said, but without their views—sometimes as little as a chance remark—the scope of this book would have been lessened and its direction halted short of the mark. Many other people are remembered vividly. I thank them with great affection for their help and most of all for their concern, though their conclusions on the subject may differ from my own.

Murray Polner, my friend and editor at *Present Tense* magazine, encouraged me to attempt a book-length subject for once. Douglas Walker unselfishly opened many doors and was a constant source of polemical material. Both served as gentle sounding boards throughout. Marcus Raskin, as he has done since our boyhood, demonstrated the necessity of probing past conventional wisdom.

Many senior executives in consumer advertising agencies, deeply troubled by the effect of political advertising on the nation and on their own businesses, were generous with their time and help.

I spoke with many people in an effort to make sense of the thicket of broadcast and First Amendment law. I am especially grateful to Alan Campbell of Dow, Lohnes & Albertson, Washington; Richard Dannay of Schwab, Goldberg, Price & Dannay, New York; Herminio Traviesas, former vice president for broadcasting standards policy, National Broadcasting Company; and Richard E. Wiley, former chairman of the Federal Communications Commission. Bruce Felknor, who has labored to rid us of dirty politics for perhaps longer than anyone, was an invaluable source of information.

There is a special place in this book for Joan Raines. I never think of her as an agent, but as a patient friend who willingly shared with me her concern over our deteriorating political process. Our lengthy conversations over the years have been instrumental in shaping the themes of this book.

This was not originally Peg Cameron's project at Lippincott &

Crowell, but she took on its editing with a wise and sensitive hand. She has been as precise and firm with her criticism as she has been generous with her encouragement. However one may view this book, it has left her office with a far more intelligent flow than when it arrived.

My thanks also to Anne McAtee, Dianitia Hutcheson, Diane Saxe, and Susan Bagby at Lippincott & Crowell, who were unstinting with their time and their support. And I am especially grateful to Vernon Nahrgang for his careful reading of the manuscript and for his incisive suggestions.

I am in the debt of the Great Neck Public Library and its superb staff. It is perhaps one of the finest reference facilities in the country, regardless of size. And, in Great Neck, Susan Forman has been not only a fine and tireless typist but a valued friend and critic.

My brother, Richard Spero, helped to keep me on course with his probing questions and a supply of research material. My parents, Lillian and Harvey Spero, were always on hand, even by long distance, to lift my spirits.

Finally, an observation. In a time when the concept of marriage and family seems to have fallen into some disrepute, I have noted how often writers convey to spouses and children their love and appreciation for understanding an often hopeless and distant routine and a behavior pattern which is undoubtedly more quirky than it needs to be. Perhaps this tells us something about the nature of the creative process. In my own case, Jan Spero has understood with great clarity the need for this work, which is better because of her ability to listen and her natural editorial instincts. Our children, Josh, Jeremy, and Jessica Spero, never tired of buoying me up. But their greatest gift has been to allow me to look through their young but perceptive eyes. Without this opportunity, I would have known far less about our times. To my wife and my children I offer my love and appreciation.

Robert Spero

Great Neck, New York
Winter 1979

SELECTED BIBLIOGRAPHY

1. Advertising Law Anthology. National Law Anthology Series. Arlington, Virginia: International Library, 1975. Volume III. Selected Readings.
2. Barnet, Richard J. "Challenging the Myths of National Security." *New York Times Magazine,* April 1, 1979.
3. ______. *The Economy of Death.* New York: Atheneum, 1969.
4. ______. *The Roots of War.* New York: Atheneum, 1972.

   ______. *See also* Stavins et al.
5. Barone, Michael. "Nonlessons of the Campaign." *New York Times Magazine,* November 28, 1976.
6. Bloom, Melvyn H. *Public Relations and Presidential Campaigns.* New York: Crowell, 1973.
7. Boston Study Group. *The Price of Defense.* New York: Times Books, 1979.
8. Brill, Steven. "Jimmy Carter's Pathetic Lies." *Harper's,* March 1976.
9. Carter, Jimmy. *A Government as Good as Its People.* New York: Simon & Schuster, 1977.
10. Congressional Quarterly Almanac, 94th Congress, 1st Session, 1975.
11. Felknor, Bruce L. *Dirty Politics.* New York: Norton, 1966.
12. Fontaine, André. "Saudi Arabia on a Tightrope." *Atlas World Press Review,* July 1979. Originally published in *Le Monde,* Translated and adapted.
13. Friendly, Fred W. *The Good Guys, the Bad Guys and the First Amendment.* New York: Vintage Books, 1975.
14. Gallup, George. "Six Political Reforms Most Americans Want." *Reader's Digest,* August 1978.
15. Gelb, Leslie. "The Secretary of State Sweepstakes." *New York Times Magazine,* May 23, 1976.
16. Goodwyn, Lawrence. "Jimmy Carter and 'Populism.' " *Southern Exposure,* Volume V, Number 1.
17. Graff, Henry. *The Tuesday Cabinet.* Englewood Cliffs, N.J.: Prentice-Hall, 1970.
18. Greene, Bob. *Running—A Nixon-McGovern Journal.* Chicago: Regnery, 1973.
19. Halberstam, David. *The Best and the Brightest.* New York: Random House, 1972.

20. Hall, Bob. "Jimmy Carter: Master Magician." *Southern Exposure,* Volume V, Number 1.
21. ———. "Journey to the White House: The Story of Coca-Cola." *Southern Exposure,* Volume V, Number 1.
22. Hess, Karl. *In a Cause That Will Triumph.* Garden City, N.Y.: Doubleday, 1967.
23. Hiebert, Ray, Robert Jones, Ernest Lotito, and John Lorenz, editors. *The Political Image Merchants: Strategies in the New Politics.* Washington, D.C.: Acropolis Books, 1971.
24. Hyatt, Richard. *The Carters of Plains.* Huntsville, Ala.: Strode, 1977.
25. Ireland, Doug. "The Unraveling of the Carter Presidency." *New York,* October 3, 1977.
26. Johnson, Nicholas. *Test Pattern for Living.* New York: Bantam Books, 1972.
27. Kelley, Stanley. *Professional Public Relations and Political Power.* Baltimore: Johns Hopkins, 1956.
28. Kendrick, Alexander. *Prime Time.* Boston: Little, Brown, 1969.
29. Lippmann, Walter. *The Public Philosophy.* Boston: Little, Brown, 1955.
30. MacDougall, Malcolm D. *We Almost Made It.* New York: Crown, 1977.
31. McGinniss, Joe. *The Selling of the President, 1968.* New York: Trident, 1964.
32. McGovern, George. *Grassroots.* New York: Random House, 1977.
33. McLuhan, Marshall. *Understanding Media: The Extensions of Man.* New York: McGraw-Hill, 1964.
34. MacNeil, Robert. *The People Machine.* New York: Harper & Row, 1968.
35. Mander, Jerry. *Four Arguments for the Elimination of Television.* New York: Morrow, 1978.
36. Mankiewicz, Frank. "A Bull Market in Politicians." *Harper's,* April 1976.
37. Mayer, Martin. *Madison Avenue, U.S.A.* New York: Harper & Brothers, 1958.
38. Melman, Seymour. *Pentagon Capitalism.* New York: McGraw Hill, 1970.
39. ———. *The Permanent War Economy.* New York: Simon & Schuster, 1974.
40. ———. *The War Economy of the United States.* New York: St. Martin's, 1971.
41. Meyer, Peter. *James Earl Carter.* Mission, Kan.: Sheed Andrews and McMeel, 1978.
42. Minow, Newton N. *Equal Time.* New York: Atheneum, 1969.
43. ———, John Bartlow Martin, and Lee M. Mitchell. *Presidential Television.* New York: Basic Books, 1973.

44. Morrison, Philip, and Paul F. Walker. "A New Strategy for Military Spending." *Scientific American,* October 1978.
45. Napolitan, Joe. *The Political Game.* Garden City, N.Y.: Doubleday, 1972.
46. New York Times. *The Kennedy Years.* New York: Viking, 1964.
47. ______. *The Pentagon Papers.* New York: Bantam Books, 1971.
48. ______. *The White House Transcripts.* New York: Bantam Books, 1974.
49. Nimmo, Dan. *The Political Persuaders.* Englewood Cliffs, N.J.: Prentice-Hall, 1970.
50. Ogilvy, David. *Confessions of an Advertising Man.* New York: Atheneum, 1963.
51. Orwell, George. *1984.* Signet Classics edition, New York: New American Library, 1949. Published by arrangement with Harcourt Brace & Co.
52. Radio Laws of the United States. Washington: U.S. Government Printing Office, 1972.
53. Raskin, Marcus. *Being and Doing.* New York: Random House, 1971.
54. ______. *Notes on the Old System: To Transform American Politics.* New York: McKay, 1974.

    ______. *See also* Stavins et al.
55. Reeves, Rosser. *Reality in Advertising.* New York: Knopf, 1961.
56. Roman, Kenneth, and Jane Maas. *How to Advertise.* New York: St. Martin's, 1976.
57. Safire, William. *Before the Fall.* Garden City, N.Y.: Doubleday, 1975.
58. Schlesinger, Arthur M. *A Thousand Days.* Boston: Houghton Mifflin, 1965.
59. Schwartz, Tony. *The Responsive Chord.* Garden City, N.Y.: Anchor Press/Doubleday, 1974.
60. Sorensen, Theodore C. *Kennedy.* New York: Harper & Row, 1965.
61. Stavins, Ralph, Richard J. Barnet, and Marcus G. Raskin. *Washington Plans an Aggressive War.* New York: Vintage Books, 1971.
62. Terkel, Studs. "Reflections on a Course in Ethics." *Harper's,* October 1973.
63. Wheeler, Leslie. *Jimmy Who?* Woodbury, N.Y.: Barron's, 1976.
64. White, F. Clifton (with William J. Gill). *Suite 3505: The Story of the Draft Goldwater Movement.* New Rochelle, N.Y.: Arlington House, 1967.
65. White, Theodore H. *The Making of the President 1960.* New York: Atheneum, 1961.
66. ______. *The Making of the President 1964.* New York: Atheneum, 1965.
67. ______. *The Making of the President 1968.* New York: Atheneum, 1969.
68. ______. *The Making of the President 1972.* New York: Atheneum, 1973.
69. Winn, Marie. *The Plug-In Drug.* New York: Viking, 1977.
70. Witcover, Jules. *Marathon: The Pursuit of the Presidency, 1972–1976.* New York: Viking, 1977.

71. Woodward, Bob, and Carl Bernstein. *All the President's Men.* New York: Warner Books, 1975.
72. Wooten, James. *Dasher.* New York: Summit Books, 1978.
73. World Book Encyclopedia. 1974.
74. World Book Year Book, 1975.
75. Ibid., 1976.
76. Ibid., 1977.

SOURCE NOTES

Bracketed numbers refer to works listed in the Selected Bibliography.

page

Chapter 1: The Arrogance and the Danger of Political Advertising

1 Murrow quoted in Kendrick [28], p. 418.

Lippmann [29], pp. 126, 128.

5 (Herminio Traviesas . . . NBC's "Broadcast Standards for Television"): Author interview.

12 According to the *New York Times* . . . "security issues in the three regions": June 1, 1975, and October 24, 1973.

13 "That seemed to fit perfectly . . ." when the banker invited him to New York for lunch: Meyer [41], pp. 192–93.

14 Carter's admission into the elite club . . . "building support where it counted": Ibid.

"spent time with Carter . . . educated him": Gelb [15], p. 50.

"one of the more outspoken Vietnam war hawks": Meyer [41], p. 83.

"once suggested the bombing . . . rest of the country": Ibid., p. 173.

15 never dreamed "Carter would use . . . presidential race": Wheeler [63], p. viii (Foreword by James W. David).

15–16 "eyes and ears at the national committee . . . nobody would have known Jimmy": Witcover [70], p. 117.

16 to gather "an elaborately detailed portrait . . . symbols they could believe in": Hall [20], p. 43.

18 "projected as the heaviest of the governors . . . Carter—a Presidential candidate": *Newsweek,* May 10, 1976, pp. 28–29.

Back in Atlanta . . . "as befitted a presidential candidate": Witcover [70], p. 115.

page

19 Adopt a "learning posture . . . as a man of integrity": *Newsweek,* May 10, 1976, p. 28.

"For all the frenetic . . . on their TV screens": Witcover [70], p. 14.

20 "Where did Carter get the money . . . at the tail end of 1975?": Ireland [25], p. 11.

"We know that through . . . a big cash 'float' ": *New York Times,* March 19, 1979.

Carter's peanut business . . . 1976 spring primaries: *New York Times,* October 18, 1979. Column by William Safire.

"no evidence whatsoever . . . into the campaign": *New York Times,* October 18, 1979.

21 What Rafshoon did . . . "extended that credit to the campaign": *New York Times,* October 18, 1979. Column by William Safire.

"Message to candidates . . . carry their clients": Ibid.

"I've got a good business . . . I make good money": Carter [9], p. 18.

"I am a farmer . . . almost a professional planner": Ibid., p. 53.

"multi-million-dollar" . . . supplying "peanuts worldwide": Hyatt [24], p. 63.

21–22 "In retail politics . . . with uncommon diligence": Witcover [70], pp. 231–32.

22 "Carter took steps . . . Udall borrowed what he could": Ibid., p. 53.

"I know Jimmy writes . . . We had the first TV set": Cited in Wheeler [63], p. 2.

24 "Nobody heard what Big Brother . . . IGNORANCE IS STRENGTH": Orwell [51], p. 17.

26–31 Note: The facts and figures included in the balance of this chapter are based on information contained in World Book Year Book 1977 [74], Barnet [2, 3], and Melman [38, 39], unless otherwise noted.

27 "$23 billion . . . or were abandoned": Barnet [3], citing figure given by Senate Majority Leader Mike Mansfield.

page

28 Perhaps as many as one out of every ten . . . for the military: Arthur F. Burns, "The Defense Sector and the Economy." Reprinted in Melman, ed. [40], p. 114.

29 "far more killing power . . . for deterrence": Barnet [3], p. 24.

"could expect to emerge . . . or struck first": Ibid., p. 21.

29n "We had given up . . . remarks": MacDougall [30], p. 233.

30 . . . the major concerns of Americans . . . people in government: Potomac Associates Research, Washington, D.C.

Chapter 2: The First Misleading Presidential Campaign Commercial

32 Cleveland quoted in Reeves interview with author.

34 "It was enormous pressure": Author interview.

35 The approach . . . "frankness, honesty and integrity": "Admen Analyze the Campaign Strategy," *Tide,* November 7, 1952. Cited in Bloom [6].

"There [are] no if's, and's, or but's . . . Boy, is that true today": Author interview.

36 "To think that an old soldier should come to this": Mayer [37], p. 297.

38 What Reeves believes he did . . . "Every single one was exactly the same": Author interview.

Chapter 3: The 1960 Campaign

39 *Kennedy realized* . . .: Sorensen [60], p. 195.

. . . nobody could get through to Dick": Cited in White [65], p. 313.

40 "tiny ramshackle shacks . . . as those citing press and periodicals": Sorensen [60], p. 195.

41 "From July 25th . . . his own control of circumstances": White [65], p. 312.

Chapter 4: The Masking of a Quagmire

49 "happy as a dog in a meat market": White, [66], p. 339.

50–51 In an interview . . . "to mean 'advice from the military' ": Graff [17], pp. 49–50.

page

52 "elan and style needed to win": New York Times [47], p. 84.

53 "The battle against Communism . . . a clear-cut and strong program of action": Pentagon papers, Document 21, cited in ibid., pp. 128, 130.

54 "Plans were drawn . . . a 'Phase 4' situation": Stavins et al. [61], p. 41.

Kennedy's policy . . . "preferred a public war": Stavins et al. [61], p. 54.

55–56 Dean Rusk, Secretary of State, urges . . . "perhaps General Taylor": Stavins et al. [61], pp. 90–91.

57 November 24 Johnson meetings with Lodge and the State Department reported in Halberstam [19], pp. 298–99.

58 "makes clear the resolve . . . in South Vietnam": Pentagon papers, Document 62, cited in New York Times [47], p. 274.

McNamara's March 16 report: Pentagon papers, Document 63, cited in ibid., pp. 279, 282, 283.

Johnson directs Doyle Dane "to plan . . . at the White House": Bloom [6], p. 134.

Johnson cable of March 20: Pentagon papers, Document 65, cited in New York Times [47], p. 285.

59 "Attack, jolt Goldwater . . . from the beginning": White [66], p. 339.

in David Halberstam's words . . . "from the journalistic eye": [19], p. 487.

Moyers, "the chief idea channel of the campaign": Bloom [6], p. 155.

"the chief companion of the conscience of the President": White [66], p. 418.

When (according to one report) Doyle Dane: Bloom [6], p. 161.

61 "definitive plan . . . to the public": Ibid.

62 "the absence of a conspiracy . . . to legitimize the war": Stavins et al. [61], pp. 97–98.

65 "kept feeding his personalized conception . . . president to lose a war": Stavins et al. [61], p. 216.

page

65 The Joint Chiefs of Staff tell . . . "against similar targets": Pentagon papers, Document 78, cited in New York Times [47], pp. 354–55.

66 McNaughton memorandum of September 3: Pentagon papers, Document 79, cited in ibid., pp. 356, 357.

"deserve to go . . . political television": White [66], p. 339.

67 "It was the Air Force view . . . to his senior advisers": Stavins et al. [61], pp. 132–33.

72 "a deliberate act . . . operated up to now": cited in New York Times [47], pp. 320–21.

73 McNaughton draws up three military-political options: Pentagon papers, Document 85, cited in ibid., p. 366.

"that over the next . . . first stages of Option C": cited in Stavins et al. [61], p. 147.

"ran the risk . . . embarrassment": Ibid., p. 145.

"targets of opportunity . . . escorting reconnaissance flights": cited in New York Times [47], p. 336.

Chapter 5: The Making of a Straw Man, 1964

78 As Richard Barnet has written . . . presumably to counter the threat: [4], p. 313.

79 F. Clifton White . . . "the nuclear bomb": Author interview.

"This is very interesting . . . in the book": Hess [22], p. 98.

80 "to lob one . . . at the Kremlin": Ibid., p. 85.

Fourteen years later William Bernbach . . . "into the Kremlin": Author interview.

80–81 The NATO Commander Story: As reported in Hess [22], pp. 56, 85, 92–98.

81–82 *The Defoliation Story:* Ibid., pp. 123–25.

84 "Many people . . . reference to Goldwater": Schwartz [59], p. 93.

Another political media specialist, Joseph Napolitan . . . "some crazy thing like that": Author interview.

86–87 "probably had greater penetration . . . Checkers broadcast in 1952": White [66], p. 323.

page

87 "I would like to suggest . . . let him do it": Quoted in White [66], p. 303n.

88 Goldwater explained his position . . . ripping up the card: Hess [22], pp. 86, 98–100.

89 William Bernbach remembers . . . "for Johnson": Author interview.

Chapter 6: The Unselling of the President, 1968

91 "When I wrote . . . or Procter and Gamble": Quoted in Bloom [6], p. 206.

"pretty honest" but not "very charming": Author interview with Napolitan.

92 "was typically Madison Ave. . . . in the whole crowd)": Quoted in Napolitan [45], p. 284.

92–93 The first storyboard . . . "or what to put in a commercial": Scene reconstructed from Napolitan [45], p. 28, and author interview with Bernbach.

93 "My experience working . . . continue unfettered": Napolitan [45], p. 284.

"I watched the film in disbelief": Ibid., p. 41.

"Are you guys out of your fucking minds?": Ibid.

94 "jerrybuilt for the purpose . . . Lennen & Newell [now defunct]": Bloom [6], p. 231.

lacking "warmth and conviction . . . might be too slick": Napolitan [45], p. 284.

94n "They didn't know . . . another nail in [Doyle Dane's] coffin": Author interview.

95 "The people surrounding . . . fourth-rate people": Author interview.

98 "conspicuously, conscientiously . . . to Wallace": White [67], p. 424.

98n "a method for reshaping . . . he wished": Raskin [54], p. 74.

100 "If there's war . . . Democratic prosperity": Quoted in Safire [57], p. 58.

page

100 Johnson "asked . . . from public debate": White [67], p. 451.

101 "Have you noticed . . . what is being said": McGinniss [31], pp. 116–17.

"Without TV, Nixon had it made": Cited in ibid., p. 33.

104 "Humphrey campaign managers . . . candidates previously": White [67], p. 417.

104n "can make the difference . . . into the House of Representatives": Napolitan [45], p. 106.

Chapter 7: Inside the November Group, 1972

106 Woodward and Bernstein [71], p. 139.

107 "leaders are exempt . . . great enough": Cited in Raskin [54], p. 58.

"assigned very specific tasks . . . or the citizenry": Ibid., p. 48.

107–8 Tasks assigned to Nixon's men: Ibid., pp. 48–50.

108 "left hundreds of . . . with CREEP people": Ibid., p. 61.

110 November group official: Statements attributed to this person throughout the chapter were obtained by author interview.

110n "tight control . . . pencils and erasers": Woodward and Bernstein [71], p. 271.

111 "You've got to do . . . why you're here": As quoted in Terkel [62], p. 61.

112 "The most corrupt . . . to respond": Press conference, October 5, 1972.

113n Two examples from Woodward and Bernstein: [71], p. 156.

117 "Certainly I am . . . what it can do to a candidate": Cited in Minow [43], p. 48.

120 "a private company . . . to a consulting firm": Woodward and Bernstein [71], p. 88.

124 "pleased that the case had stopped with Liddy": New York Times [48], p. 829.

128 "five of sixteen . . . with three on active duty": Bloom [6], p. 295.

129 The Boston Study Group are five scientists and students of military affairs who in 1979 published *The Price of Defense,* a compre-

page

hensive analysis of the American military machine and its stupendous cost. Much of the information in this section of the chapter is from that study and from an article by two of its members, Philip Morrison and Paul F. Walker [44].

129 "the Marines have become . . . for beach landings": The Boston Study Group [7], p. 109.

129 "Aircraft especially designed . . . U.S. force structure": Ibid., p. 126.

130 "At $200 [million] to . . . missiles, torpedoes, and bombs": Ibid., p. 129.

1. to provide . . . in that theater: Ibid., p. 130.

131 "the individual soldier . . . or even a ship": Morrison and Walker [44], p. 55.

"1,054 land-based missiles . . . 11,000 targets": Ibid., p. 48.

132 "In the name of national security . . . of national security": Barnet [2], p. 25.

Chapter 8: Honest Jimmy vs. Honest Jerry, 1976

140 political researcher Michael Barone confirmed: [5].

"For several days . . . in television advertising": Barone [5], p. 111.

140–41 "Whichever figures you rely on . . . did not lose ground": Ibid.

142 "world's largest consumer . . . coffee and tea": Hall [21], p. 33.

"In May of 1977 . . . infusion of government money": Meyer [41], pp. 187–88.

143 "Austin legitimized Carter . . . for his foreign trips": Hall [21], p. 42.

"seed money for Carter's . . . the Carter presidential campaign": Meyer [41], p. 187.

144 "You can't do that . . . different ball games": Author interview.

144–45 "Whether it's Coca-Cola . . . of his perspective": Cited in Hall [20], p. 44.

145 "In my mind . . . as 'negative' advertising": *New York Times,* October 25, 1977. Report by Christopher Lydon.

149 "After fifteen months . . . who he is": Meyer [41], p. 150.

page

149 "Jimmy Carter's record . . . by political performance": Quoted in Meyer [41], p. 152.

152 "the Saudis produce . . . their wheat needs": Fontaine [12], p. 19.

155 funded by the state into 30 superagencies: According to Meyer's review of the facts [41], pp. 15–16.

156 "unnecessary hospitalization": [10], p. 616.

160 "the question of truth . . . media content": Schwartz [59], p. 19.

"the best political commercials . . . express these feelings": Ibid., p. 93.

163 "It's quite true . . . not selected in advance": MacDougall [30], p. 173.

"accurately reflected . . . towards Jimmy Carter": Ibid.

"Like most of our . . . all that misleading": Ibid., p. 203.

A private survey: Author's survey.

Chapter 9: Should Political Advertising Be Banned?

168 "Does the state have . . . as the broadcast industry put it?": Friendly [13], p. 103.

"Whatever else it may mean . . . a kind of basic law": Ibid., p. 108 (quoting Bazelon in *John F. Banzhaf III* v. *Federal Communications Commission,* 405 F.2d 1096–97).

169 "did more than . . . clear 'public interest' ": *Bigelow* v. *Virginia,* 421 U.S. 809 (1975). Cited in a speech by Philip Elman before Food and Drug Institute, Conference on Food Advertising and Labeling, Washington, D.C., October 27, 1977.

"a purely economic one . . . has never been protected for its own sake": *Virginia State Board of Pharmacy* v. *Virginia Citizens Consumer Council, Inc.,* 425 U.S. 748 (1976).

172 "decency, veracity . . . to use persuasion": Author interview.

172–73 "We will never turn . . . was the answer": Author interview.

173 "He just never knew . . . want to be sure": Author interview.

174 "We're schizophrenic . . . to be an advantage": Author interview.

178 "Carter's White House . . . good television": Cited in Meyer [41], p. 151.

page

178 Walter Cronkite has been quoted as saying: In a speech by Herbert Schmertz, vice president, public affairs, Mobil Oil Corporation, at the Association of National Advertisers Television Workshop, New York.

180n "in Nixon's first eighteen months . . . Kennedy and Johnson": Friendly [13], p. 123.

182 "limit was removed . . . and the candidate": Mankiewicz [36], p. 18.

"may only have made . . . himself in office": *Wall Street Journal,* November 2, 1978. By James Ring Adams.

183 "long-established policy . . . or 60 second commercials": Friendly [13], pp. 121–22.

Chapter 10: Breaking the Back of the Political Commercial

186n "there is no great reason . . . don't know how?": Author interview with Marcus Raskin.

188 "without having to worry . . . a candidate's commercials": Author interview.

189 "The American system . . . excluded them!": Friendly [13], p. 236.

190 "is intended to give . . . difficult to interpret": Author interview.

192 "a new genre . . . ease of larger firms": *Television/Radio Age,* April 23, 1979, p. 41.

"The future is . . . onto the spot market quickly": Ibid., June 4, 1979, p. 43.

193 "stretch over . . . changing few votes": Gallup [14], p. 61.

194 Wiley worried . . . "I disagreed": Author interview.

198 "The mindless ravages . . . and big business": *New York Times,* June 18, 1979.

"a major realignment of urban political forces": Ibid.

202 Abourezk has called . . . "redress of grievances": Ibid. From remarks Senator Abourezk entered into the *Congressional Record,* July 11, 1977.

INDEX